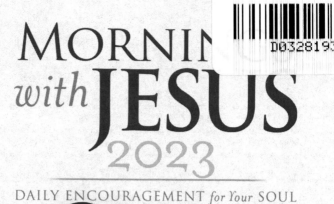

MORNIN

with JESUS

2023

DAILY ENCOURAGEMENT *for Your* SOUL

365 DEVOTIONS

Guideposts

Danbury, Connecticut

Mornings with Jesus 2023

Published by Guideposts Books & Inspirational Media
100 Reserve Road, Suite E200
Danbury, CT 06810
Guideposts.org

Acknowledgments

Every attempt has been made to credit the sources of copyrighted material used in this book. If any such acknowledgment has been inadvertently omitted or miscredited, receipt of such information would be appreciated.

Scripture quotations marked (AMP) are taken from the *Amplified Bible*. Copyright © 2015 by The Lockman Foundation, La Habra, California. All rights reserved.

Scripture quotations marked (AMPC) are taken from the *Amplified Bible (Classic Edition)*. Copyright © by The Lockman Foundation, La Habra, California. All rights reserved.

Scripture quotations marked (CEV) are taken from *Holy Bible: Contemporary English Version*. Copyright © 1995 by American Bible Society.

Scripture quotations marked (CSB) are taken from *The Christian Standard Bible*. Copyright © 2017 by Holman Bible Publishers. Used by permission.

Scripture quotations marked (ESV) are taken from the *Holy Bible, English Standard Version*. Copyright © 2001 by Crossway Bibles, a division of Good News Publishers. Used by permission. All rights reserved.

Scripture quotations marked (GNT) are taken from the *Holy Bible, Good News Translation*. Copyright © 1992 by American Bible Society.

Scripture quotations marked (GW) are taken from *God's Word Translation*. Copyright © 1995 by God's Word to the Nations. Used by permission of Baker Publishing Group.

Scripture quotations marked (KJV) are taken from the *King James Version of the Bible*.

Scripture quotations marked (MSG) are taken from *The Message*. Copyright © 1993, 1994, 1995, 1996, 2000, 2001, 2002 by Eugene H. Peterson.

Scripture quotations marked (NASB and NASB1995) are taken from the *New American Standard Bible*. Copyright © 1960, 1962, 1963, 1968, 1971, 1972, 1973, 1975, 1977, 1995 by The Lockman Foundation, La Habra, California. Used by permission.

Scripture quotations marked (NCV) are taken from the *New Century Version*. Copyright © 2005 by Thomas Nelson.

Scripture quotations marked (NIRV) are taken from *The Holy Bible, New International Reader's Version*. Copyright © 1996 by Biblica, Inc. Used by permission of Zondervan. All rights reserved worldwide. zondervan.com

Scripture quotations marked (NIV and NIV84) are taken from *The Holy Bible, New International Version*. Copyright © 1973, 1978, 1984, 2011 by Biblica, Inc. Used by permission of Zondervan. All rights reserved worldwide. zondervan.com

Scripture quotations marked (NKJV) are taken from *The Holy Bible, New King James Version*. Copyright © 1982 by Thomas Nelson.

Scripture quotations marked (NLT) are taken from the *Holy Bible, New Living Translation*. Copyright © 1996, 2004, 2007 by Tyndale House Foundation. Used by permission of Tyndale House Publishers Inc., Carol Stream, Illinois. All rights reserved.

Scripture quotations marked (NLV) are from the *New Life Bible*, copyright © 1969 by Christian Literature International. Used by permission. All rights reserved.

Scripture quotations marked (NRSV) are taken from the *New Revised Standard Version Bible*. Copyright © 1989 by the Division of Christian Education of the National Council of the Churches of Christ in the United States of America. Used by permission. All rights reserved.

Scripture quotations marked (PHILLIPS) are taken from *J. B. Phillips New Testament*. Copyright © by J. B. P. Society. All rights reserved.

Scripture quotations marked (RSV) are taken from the *Revised Standard Version of the Bible*. Copyright © 1946, 1952, 1971 by the Division of Christian Education of the National Council of the Churches of Christ in the United States of America. Used by permission. All rights reserved.

Scripture quotations marked (TLB) are taken from *The Living Bible*. Copyright © 1971 by Tyndale House Publishers, Inc., Carol Stream, Illinois. All rights reserved.

Scripture quotations marked (TLV) are taken from *Tree of Life Version Bible*. Copyright © Tree of Life Bible Society. All rights reserved.

Scripture quotations marked (TPT) are taken from *The Passion Translation*. Copyright © 2016 by Broadstreet Publishing Group, Savage, Minnesota. All rights reserved.

Scripture quotations marked (VOICE) are taken from *The Voice Bible*. Copyright © 2012 Thomas Nelson, Inc. The Voice™ translation copyright © 2012 Ecclesia Bible Society. All rights reserved.

Cover and interior design by Müllerhaus
Cover photo by Adobe Stock Images
Indexed by Frances Lennie
Typeset by Aptara, Inc.

Printed and bound in the United States of America
10 9 8 7 6 5 4 3 2 1

Dear Friends,

Welcome to *Mornings with Jesus 2023*! In this year's devotional, we have expanded our roster to include twenty writers—up from the fourteen who appeared in *Mornings with Jesus 2022*. With the addition of new and inspiring voices, our sincere hope is that we will be able to share with you the more wondrous ways that Jesus is working in a variety of people's lives.

Our theme this year is "Grace," as found in Hebrews 4:16 (NKJV): "Let us therefore come boldly to the throne of grace, that we may obtain mercy and find grace to help in time of need." In 365 brand-new devotions, twenty women of faith lovingly share how they, and the people they know, have been touched by the grace of the blessed Savior and how their faith has been strengthened because of it.

Many beloved *Mornings with Jesus* writers return in 2023, including Susanna Foth Aughtmon, who generously shares how her experiences as a wife, mother, daughter, sister, and aunt have allowed her to see the abundance of grace in her life. Jeanette Levellie candidly reflects on her shortcomings and how Jesus's grace covers them. Grace Fox contemplates on the loss of her graceful mother, whose faith inspired her own. Isabella Campolattaro meditates on her transition from being a work-at-home mom to a public high school teacher and how the experience has deepened her understanding of the all-encompassing love of Jesus. Dianne Neal Matthews brings us along on her journey as she and her husband approach retirement and discover grace in new places.

Jeannie Blackmer, Pat Butler Dyson, Heidi Gaul, Tricia Goyer, Sharon Hinck, Erin Keeley Marshall, Cynthia Ruchti, Cassandra Tiersma, Suzanne Davenport Tietjen, and Barbranda Lumpkins Walls all return with powerful devotions about how ordinary moments in our everyday lives can give us a glimpse into the extraordinary grace of Jesus. New writers Becky Alexander, Ericka Loynes, Claire McGarry, Emily E. Ryan, and Karen Sargent join the chorus with their own wonderful insight into grace that will undoubtedly touch your heart.

It is our prayer that as you read each writer's first-person reflection and take the "Faith Step" that challenges you to recognize the grace at work in your life, you will be reminded of the beautiful promise of the risen Lord: "My grace is sufficient for you, for My strength is made perfect in weakness" (2 Corinthians 12:9, NKJV). May *Mornings with Jesus 2023* remind you of how desperately we are in need of Jesus's amazing grace and how urgently we are called by Him to freely give it to others.

Faithfully yours,
Editors of Guideposts

Especially for You!

Enjoy the daily encouragement of *Mornings with Jesus 2023* wherever you are! Receive each day's devotion on your computer, tablet, or smartphone. Visit MorningswithJesus.org/MWJ2023 and enter this code: grace. Sign up for the online newsletter *Mornings with Jesus* at Guideposts.org/newsletter-sign-up. Each week, you'll receive an inspiring devotion or personal thoughts from one of the writers about her own devotional time and prayer life and how focusing on Jesus influenced her relationship with Him and others.

NEW YEAR'S DAY, SUNDAY, JANUARY 1

My soul is quiet and waits for God alone.
My hope comes from Him. Psalm 62:5 (NLV)

MY HUSBAND AND I WERE married two days after Christmas and spent our honeymoon in New York City. We couldn't wait to celebrate New Year's Eve in the Big Apple. For years, we'd watched on television as the iconic Times Square Ball dropped. Now we would experience the thrill and excitement for ourselves, ringing in the New Year.

After an evening show on Broadway, we walked out of the theater and into the below-zero temperatures. Immediately, we were swept up into the throng of revelers. Party hats glittered under streetlights. Novelty sunglasses blinked on and off. Confetti hovered in the air like multicolored fog. It was a magical scene—for about five minutes.

We began thinking of our warm, quiet hotel room just a few blocks away, and the festive crowds suddenly seemed congested and claustrophobic. This wasn't how we wanted to begin a new year. We couldn't reflect on what Jesus had done in our lives and invite Him into this next chapter as a married couple when we were surrounded by constant chaos and never-ending noise. We wanted—no, we needed—a more intimate start for the New Year.

It's been almost twenty years since that night, but I still think about it when I'm tempted to kick off New Year's with big dreams, elaborate plans, and audacious goals. The best way for me to celebrate is to open my Bible, calm my soul, and withdraw into Jesus. Quiet time alone with Him is the best party of all. —EMILY E. RYAN

FAITH STEP: *Don't rush through your first moment with Jesus on New Year's Day. Instead, close your eyes, open your heart, and linger in His presence.*

MONDAY, JANUARY 2

*I will sing to the Lord all my life; I will sing praise to
my God as long as I live. Psalm 104:33 (NIV)*

"WHAT DO YOU WISH YOU could do better?" a friend asked me
recently. Without missing a beat, I quickly replied, "Sing." I've long
admired those who have voices that can croon any type of music—
Christian, opera, R&B, pop, jazz, or country. I love to sing and have
done so for as long as I can remember. I've been a member of church
and school choirs and even directed a gospel group in college—but
I don't sing as well as I wish I did.

Sometimes I can't carry a tune at all, and I definitely can't harmonize unless I'm standing next to a strong singer who will help me
stay on key. In other words, no one has ever asked me to be a soloist.
My voice is better suited for blending into the chorus.

I thought about my answer to my friend's question. Yes, I wanted
to be more confident, but my lack of singing talent has never stopped
me from belting out lyrics or singing songs of praise with other
believers and giving glory to Jesus in the process. And that's really
what the Lord asks us to do, isn't it? Just to sing earnestly to Him.

I'll never be a soloist, and I don't have to worry about not having
perfect pitch because I have a strong singer who stands next to me.
Jesus and I harmonize beautifully. My slightly off-key praise is sweet
music to Him. —BARBRANDA LUMPKINS WALLS

FAITH STEP: *What's your favorite hymn or praise song? Take a moment to sing
it to Jesus loud and clear.*

TUESDAY, JANUARY 3

Though you have not seen him, you love him; and even though you do not see him now, you believe in him and are filled with an inexpressible and glorious joy. 1 Peter 1:8 (NIV)

MY GRANDCHILDREN LIVE SEVERAL STATES away, but I think of them every day. Other than FaceTime calls, I can't physically see them. I can look at the photos hanging on the wall. I smile at their favorite books that fill my shelves and often read to them over the phone. I also hum songs we sang together. Until the next visit, I'll miss the tangible ability to hug them, to be with them in person. Yet I love them. I know they are enjoying life, laughing, and playing. Their very existence fills me with joy.

I sometimes complain to Jesus that it's challenging to follow Him when I can't see Him or hear His audible voice. I can't touch Him as the first disciples could. I've learned about Him through Scripture and the truth passed down through generations. I've experienced His spirit in worship and prayer. But I long to be concretely in His presence.

Today, Jesus reminded me of how much joy I feel in my grandchildren, even when I'm not physically present with them.

Like my grandchildren, Jesus doesn't cease to exist just because I can't see Him (John 20:29). He is with me, and that fills me with joy. Just as I eagerly anticipate the next visit with my grandchildren, I'm excited to know that one day I'll stand in the presence of Jesus.

In the end, believing is seeing. —SHARON HINCK

FAITH STEP: *List people who give you joy even when you can't see them. Ask Jesus to increase your belief until you see Him in eternity.*

WEDNESDAY, JANUARY 4

For which of you, desiring to build a tower, does not first sit down and count the cost, whether he has enough to complete it? Luke 14:28 (ESV)

I GAINED A LOT OF weight when I first got married. A lot. From a svelte 130 pounds, I ballooned to a top weight of 207. I was heavier than I'd ever been in my life and was completely miserable.

After my eldest son, Pierce, was born, I decided I was willing to do anything to lose those extra pounds. I started walking on my treadmill and joined Weight Watchers. As a work-at-home new mom, I didn't have time to go to meetings, so I did the online version. The handy app tracked daily points and also provided nutritional value for the foods I considered eating.

With a swipe of my phone screen, I could quickly assess the benefit of having, say, an English muffin at 2 points versus a large blueberry muffin. Although that seemed healthy enough, it could be worth as much as a whopping 24 points—practically a whole day's worth of points! The difference was striking.

Spiritual choices are like that too. I can go with the easier, more appetizing, and self-indulgent choice, or I can weigh the cost, deny my initial impulse, and do that which is healthier, more nutritious, and ultimately more satisfying for my soul.

It took many months, much determination, and constant prayer, but I weigh 140 today. I still pause to count points and not just with my food. Weighing the value of each life decision over the other, I routinely ask Jesus for grace to make the better choice.
—ISABELLA CAMPOLATTARO

FAITH STEP: *Whatever your temptation, ask Jesus for the grace to pause, count the cost, and make the better choice.*

THURSDAY, JANUARY 5

. . . I will utter hidden things, things from of old—things we have heard and known, things our ancestors have told us. We will not hide them from their descendants; we will tell the next generation the praiseworthy deeds of the Lord, his power, and the wonders he has done. Psalm 78:2–4 (NIV)

THE NORTH ALABAMA HALLELUJAH TRAIL weaves through sixteen counties in northern Alabama. Each church on the route is more than a hundred years old, sits on its original site, and still holds services today. I plan to visit all thirty-two—I'm halfway there.

My favorite thus far has been Brilliant Methodist Church, mainly because I love the happy title of the town. The name "Brilliant" came from the glossy appearance of coal and a booming coal industry in the area in the late 1800s. Miners eventually built the house of worship with white-painted wood, stained-glass windows, and a bronze bell to ring before Sunday school.

When I travel from church to church on the trail, I sense a connection with believers who lived before me. They loved Jesus, like I do. They committed their hearts to Him and made sacrifices to build Gospel churches. They passed the Good News to their children and grandchildren.

I want to faithfully carry on the legacy of the North Alabama Hallelujah Trail. By committing to serve Jesus in my home church, and with my life, I'll do my part for future generations to know Him. I'll share the Gospel by writing and talking about His timeless love and grace, just like those faith pioneers who blazed the trail before me. —BECKY ALEXANDER

FAITH STEP: *Stop by an old church in your town. Think about what you can do to share the Good News, then do it.*

FRIDAY, JANUARY 6

... and the master of the banquet tasted the water that had been turned into wine. He did not realize where it had come from, though the servants who had drawn the water knew. Then he called the bridegroom aside and said, "Everyone brings out the choice wine first and then the cheaper wine after the guests have had too much to drink; but you have saved the best till now." John 2:9–10 (NIV)

I STEPPED INTO THE KITCHEN, focused on preparing dinner. I'd neglected grocery shopping for too long, and the pantry was close to empty. Opening the refrigerator, I gazed at a random assortment of condiments, a few eggs, and butter. They seemed to stare back blankly, as if daring me to come up with a recipe. What could I make with what little I had?

As I cooked an omelet, my mind wandered to the way Jesus had chosen me. Just as my empty refrigerator lacked sustenance, I had little, if anything, to offer Him. But He chose me, not for who I was but for who He is. His love transformed my nothing into His something, just like the water Jesus turned to wine—the *best* wine. This was His first public miracle but not His last.

Jesus has done a miracle in me too. I looked inside my soul. Where once there was a hollow shell, I now discovered hope, patience, and love. A mind focused on His truths.

A few random ingredients provided one meal for me, but water became the best wine for many guests in the Master's hand. My eternal Chef is still cooking up miracles, no recipe necessary.
—HEIDI GAUL

FAITH STEP: *What miracle has Jesus performed in your life? List your assets, large and small. Honor Him with your unique gifts.*

SATURDAY, JANUARY 7

And one of them struck the servant of the high priest, cutting off his right ear. But Jesus answered, "No more of this!" And he touched the man's ear and healed him. Luke 22:50–51 (NIV)

BEING IMPULSIVE GETS ME INTO trouble sometimes. More often than not, I act first and think later. When I hit obstacles that interfere with my plans, I tend to immediately do what seems best to remove or go around them. I'm sure life would be much smoother if I remembered to slow down, take a deep breath, think things through, and pray before taking action.

Peter was impulsive too. When the leading priests and the captains of the Temple guard brought their mobs to arrest Jesus, Peter grabbed a sword and cut off the right ear of the high priest's servant. Defending Jesus seemed the logical thing to do, right?

Jesus thought otherwise. He healed the servant's ear and told Peter to put his sword away (Matthew 26:52). Then He said that His Father would send thousands of angels to protect them if He asked for help (Matthew 26:53).

Sometimes, like Peter, I swing and flail my measly sword of human effort in an attempt to solve a problem. Doing so never works well for me. I'd be much wiser to put my sword away and invite Jesus into the circumstance. Because He is full of grace, He repairs the messes I've made. Because He is the host of heavenly armies, He's more than able to overcome any obstacles. —GRACE FOX

FAITH STEP: *Sketch a sword. Label it "my efforts" and draw an X across it. Ask Jesus for His strength to help you overcome a current obstacle.*

SUNDAY, JANUARY 8

How precious are your thoughts about me, O God. They cannot be numbered! Psalm 139:17 (NLT)

I LEAD A WRITERS' WORKSHOP for new novelists. While it's easy for me to teach students dialogue, description, and plotting, their fiction comes to life when I help them understand emotion, exploring their own feelings and applying them to their work.

One common theme from my novels is abandonment. My books often include characters who attempt to earn love and worry that one wrong move will cause others to leave them.

Looking closer at my writing, I discovered why this theme is often found within my novels. I grew up with an emotionally distant stepfather and my birth father wasn't around, so I never experienced unconditional paternal love. My high school boyfriend abandoned me after I became pregnant. I began to believe I was unlovable.

After I married John, I worried if I did something that bothered him, he'd leave me. That distorted feeling transferred to Jesus too. Yet, as I explored my fear of abandonment through fiction, real-life healing happened within me. Helping my characters come to understand Jesus's faithful love toward them, even amidst conflicts and hardships, enabled me to understand that my feelings aren't facts. I don't have to earn love from others. Jesus will never leave me.

By teaching new writers to explore their emotions, I'm helping them write better fiction. I also hope they'll begin to better understand Jesus's feelings toward them so that they know He loves them unconditionally. —TRICIA GOYER

FAITH STEP: *Look at your life as if it were a novel. What events may have caused you to question Jesus's love? Ask Jesus to help you better understand His unconditional love and bring healing to your heart.*

MONDAY, JANUARY 9

". . . the Lord does not see as man sees; for man looks at the outward appearance, but the Lord looks at the heart." 1 Samuel 16:7b (NKJV)

"THIS DIAMOND IS FROM MY grandmother's wedding ring." I handed the heirloom to the jeweler. "My aunt had it reset in this contemporary design, but I'd like a vintage setting reflective of the year my grandparents were married, 1929."

The jeweler peered through a loupe to inspect the stone. "This diamond is over one hundred years old," she said. "Gemcutters stopped cutting like this in 1918." She explained the bottom was flat instead of pointed like modern stones, so it didn't sparkle as brilliantly as it could if it were faceted rather than flat.

Oh no! Was the diamond worthless? The jeweler must have sensed my concern. She assured me the stone was unique, complimenting its color and clarity, even as she spotted inclusions beneath the surface that I couldn't see. Then she recommended a lovely white gold filigree setting, cast from an original 1920s wedding ring. It was perfect.

Unlike the jeweler, Jesus doesn't need a loupe to see the inclusions hidden by my outward sparkle. He knows the history that shaped me, the brokenness that colors me, and the imperfections that cloud my clarity. But Jesus doesn't call me flawed. He calls me redeemed. I have great value to Him.

I'm a gem He is polishing, a light in the darkness. I want to shine brilliantly for Him. —KAREN SARGENT

FAITH STEP: *Ask Jesus to inspect your heart and reveal what He sees. Identify facets that have lost their luster and choose one. What do you need so that facet can shine brighter for Him?*

TUESDAY, JANUARY 10

He must become greater and greater, and I must become less and less.
John 3:30 (NLT)

THE LONGER I LIVE, THE more I appreciate the adage "less is more." Since my husband and I plan to retire soon and move to a different state, I'm evaluating our possessions room by room and filling donation boxes. The less crowded our house is, the more favorable impression it will give potential buyers and the easier our move will be. I recently purged my clothes closet, and getting dressed is now quicker and more enjoyable.

I'm also learning (finally) the benefits of applying this principle to my calendar. If I try to cram too many commitments into one day, I may waste time chasing trivial pursuits while failing to accomplish that which is truly important. I could miss an opportunity that God has placed in front of me or feel too stressed to recognize the blessings He sends my way. Cutting excessive activities from my schedule leaves more time for spiritual endeavors. Less busyness means more attention to what matters most.

As a follower of Jesus, I want to become more like Him. I want my character to be shaped less by my old nature and more by His truth and righteousness, my thoughts to stem less from personal desires and more from His plan for my behavior to be motivated less by natural impulses and more by His mercy, love, and grace. Less of me means more of Him. —DIANNE NEAL MATTHEWS

FAITH STEP: *What does "less is more" mean to you? Evaluate your agenda and your household. What do you need to get rid of to make more room for Jesus in your day?*

WEDNESDAY, JANUARY 11

Not that we are competent in ourselves to claim anything for ourselves, but our competence comes from God. 2 Corinthians 3:5 (NIV)

EVERY JANUARY, WE HOST A fun run at our home in New Hampshire. Thirty to forty people from my husband's running club arrive at 8 a.m. on a Saturday, run five to ten miles, and then come back to our house for a hot breakfast with all the fixings.

My husband, John, is fiercely independent and insists on doing all the cooking and setup himself, no matter how many times I offer to help. Despite his best intentions, there are always several things he overlooks. When I see them, I don't ask anymore—I just jump in and help. Every year, after our guests leave, John tells me how he couldn't have done it without me.

During the pandemic, his need for help went to a whole new level. Having to abide by social distancing, food had to be served from our garage, with club members eating in the driveway, huddled around firepits to stay warm in the nine-degree weather. Hosting from the garage created a slew of complications John never anticipated. Once again, I jumped in and helped. As usual, he thanked me afterward for helping in ways he hadn't even known he needed.

Life can be a lot like our fun run. With fierce independence, we try to go it alone, despite Jesus being at our side, ready and willing to help. It's only when we look back, after the fact, that we see how His grace was at work, helping us in ways we hadn't even known to ask for. —CLAIRE MCGARRY

FAITH STEP: *Reflect back on something you've accomplished and identify where God was the source of your competence.*

THURSDAY, JANUARY 12

Jesus spoke all these things to the crowd in parables; he did not say anything to them without using a parable. Matthew 13:34 (NIV)

I HAD NO IDEA MY carry-on bag would cause such a ruckus. Maybe ruckus is a strong word for the exchange with the TSA employee I'd seen so often at our small regional airport. She usually was a pleasant woman with a bright smile.

That day, she wasn't smiling. She politely but firmly directed me, "Ma'am, I need to go through your bag."

As a frequent traveler, I knew what was and wasn't allowed in my carry-on suitcase. None of my liquids were oversized. No lithium batteries or explosives, although the last time I'd flown, my bottle of cream rinse did a number on the inside of the plastic bag in which I'd nestled it. Nothing about my curling iron looked at all dangerous. But the TSA agent found something and held it in the air.

My miniature toenail clippers. The innocuous item had a tiny file, a feature the agent called a "blade." One inch long. Duller than an overcooked spaghetti noodle.

"You're surrendering this?" she asked. But it sounded more like a command. I watched as she put the tiny clippers in a vault-like container far above its pay grade. Then, with her signature smile back in place, she whispered, "I like what it says."

White letters against a blue enamel insert: *Jesus is the key.*

Of all the ways for Jesus to connect me with another human being! What could I do but be grateful I had something worth surrendering. —CYNTHIA RUCHTI

FAITH STEP: *Think about the last time Jesus used an unusual item to start a conversation about faith. Watch for what He might use today to open a discussion.*

FRIDAY, JANUARY 13

For this world is not our home . . . Hebrews 13:14 (TLB)

I LIVE IN NORTHERN CALIFORNIA, near Mt. Shasta, a destination location. People come from near and far to visit or live here. Consequently, a number of full-time nomadic hikers, aka "travelers," migrate in and out of the area. According to the season, some display cardboard signs with various requests for food, gas, money, or rides. But the sign that makes me laugh every time I remember it was three simple words of exasperation: "Anywhere but Here." The raw honesty of that admission still cracks me up. It's comical to me because, according to local tourism marketing, Mt. Shasta is "Where Heaven Meets Earth." Who'd want to leave *that* place?

I get it, though. Sometimes things don't pan out the way we'd hoped. Or we hit a bump in the road. I don't know the particulars why that traveler was so desperate to get out of our area, but I do understand the sentiment. Sometimes people let us down. When my life doesn't feel like heaven meets earth, it's easy for me to wish I was anywhere but here too.

When the author of the book of Hebrews wrote that this world was not our home, he explained it was because we, as believers, are looking forward to our everlasting home in heaven. No wonder we experience wanderlust in this life here on earth. I might live in a destination location, but it's not my final destination. My home is with Jesus. —CASSANDRA TIERSMA

FAITH STEP: *Are you at home with Jesus? Or are you experiencing spiritual wanderlust, wishing you were "anywhere but here"? Ask Jesus to give you a heightened appreciation for wherever you are in life, regardless of present circumstances.*

SATURDAY, JANUARY 14

Now that I, your Lord and Teacher, have washed your feet, you also should wash one another's feet. John 13:14 (NIV)

ONE WINTER DAY, I WENT to help my friend Amy muck out alpaca stalls. She was helping her elderly neighbor, who owned an alpaca farm and who had broken his leg. She advised me to wear warm clothes, gloves, boots that could get dirty, and glasses, because sometimes alpacas spit.

When I arrived, Amy gave me a rake, a shovel, and a wheelbarrow and showed me how to clean the stalls. Primarily, my job consisted of clearing out the black, bean-shaped droppings. I had no idea alpacas pooped so much.

Amy and I raked mounds of dung, scooped it into the wheelbarrow, and dumped it on a nearby pile while the alpacas followed us around like puppies. The smell was awful, but I actually had fun.

Amy exemplified Jesus-like service as she joyfully dug in doing the thankless job of mucking stalls. Modeling Jesus by humbling herself and getting a bit dirty was a tangible way to show His love to her neighbor. She inspired me to do the same.

Jesus performed an unpleasant task, too, when He washed the disciples' feet. It was a job performed by the lowest-ranking servants of that day. Since people wore sandals everywhere, their feet got filthy. After Jesus finished, He instructed them to do this for each other. I imagine they weren't thrilled with this command because it was a menial, dirty job.

Jesus challenges all of us to humbly serve others, sometimes doing messy, thankless tasks. Once you dig in, as I can attest, it can be quite enjoyable. —JEANNIE BLACKMER

FAITH STEP: *Like Jesus, humbly serve someone today.*

SUNDAY, JANUARY 15

The LORD appeared to us in the past, saying: "I have loved you with an everlasting love; I have drawn you with unfailing kindness. I will build you up again, and you, Virgin Israel, will be rebuilt. Again you will take up your timbrels and go out to dance with the joyful." Jeremiah 31:3–4 (NIV)

MAYBE YOU'VE SEEN THIS FAVORITE meme of mine: The scene is an elementary school gym, where classmates are lined up on risers to perform a music program. The students are dressed in their best and are generally paying attention.

But the group as a whole is not where my attention lands. Up front, one little girl cannot stop the music from taking hold of her. Bouncing to the beat, hands clapping, body swaying, utterly comfortable and uninhibited—she's living her best life.

Because she isn't seeking attention, her innocence is disarming. Unmanufactured, pure joy moves her. She can't keep it to herself, and I can't hold back a smile.

That little girl strikes me as the image of what the Lord desires for us all.

First, He appears to us. Then, He affirms His love—an everlasting love that draws us to Him. And it doesn't just draw us; it draws us with unfailing kindness. This love purifies and rebuilds us and doesn't quit prematurely. Through this process, Jesus prepares us for fresh joy and celebration. When life gets hard and we need Him to rebuild us again, He will do it again. His gracious heart toward us is worthy of our uninhibited joy—a faith that freely dances. —ERIN KEELEY MARSHALL

FAITH STEP: *Listen to a favorite song that brings you joy. Dance as you thank Jesus for His love and grace that builds us up, again and again.*

MARTIN LUTHER KING JR. DAY, MONDAY, JANUARY 16

You, my brothers and sisters, were called to be free. But do not use your freedom to indulge the flesh; rather, serve one another humbly in love. Galatians 5:13 (NIV)

I TAUGHT SIXTH-GRADE SOCIAL studies for one year. My students participated in the schoolwide tradition of writing an essay based on a historical figure of their choosing. Dr. Martin Luther King Jr. was a favorite choice. A dynamic leader and pastor with a passion for people, he championed the injustice of racial inequality.

His inspirational voice resonated with my students. They were drawn in by how Dr. King lived out his beliefs. They admired how he had risked everything to bring light to the darkness. He reminded Americans that people should be judged on the content of their character and not the color of their skin. His dream was for the world to be a place where all were treated equally and where love, hope, and freedom endured.

Like Jesus, Dr. King used his faith and understanding of God to be an activist for change. Both marched to the beat of a different drummer in the societies in which they lived. They both had hearts and hands to serve others, and while many followed their example, many more hated and wished them dead.

It's easy to see why MLK's enduring legacy was a magnet for my students. Like him, I want to serve others, speak out when I see injustice, and speak freely of my belief that Jesus is Lord—not just a Savior for me but for all people. —SUSANNA FOTH AUGHTMON

FAITH STEP: *Watch a documentary or read about Dr. Martin Luther King Jr. today. Choose one way his legacy inspires you to live out your Christian beliefs.*

TUESDAY, JANUARY 17

Set your minds on things above, not on earthly things. Colossians 3:2 (NIV)

EVERY NOVEMBER, WITH HOPE IN my heart, I buy a Christmas cactus, loaded with blooms and alive with promise that it will survive the Christmas season. Every January, with defeat in my soul, I place the latest Christmas cactus, pale, bloomless, and drooping, on my porch, thinking the outdoor air might revive it. That has never happened.

One January, I spotted a small leftover Christmas cactus languishing in the floral department at my grocery store. The price tag read $13.99, but a store clerk said the floral manager would do markdowns the next day. Maybe if I could buy this cactus and nurture it all year, it would survive through the next Christmas season. An exciting prospect!

I arose early the next day and dashed to the grocery store, skipping my devotional reading and my customary time with Jesus. I told myself I'd catch up later. Right now, I had to claim my prize.

At the floral counter, I snatched up the plant, ecstatic to see the pink tag marked $4.99. I fairly danced out of the store with my purchase. *When was the last time I was this joyful?* Driving home, it hit me. Pursuing this bargain, this earthly thing, had interfered with my time with Jesus. If I nurtured my relationship with Jesus the way I'd planned to nurture my discount plant, I could be this joyful every day!

I asked Jesus to forgive me for my preoccupation with an earthly prize rather than Him, my greatest treasure. And now both my time with Jesus and the Christmas cactus are thriving! —PAT BUTLER DYSON

FAITH STEP: *Be honest. Are you putting any earthly things ahead of your time with Jesus?*

WEDNESDAY, JANUARY 18

*And now these three remain: faith, hope and love. But
the greatest of these is love. 1 Corinthians 13:13 (NIV)*

I KNOW TATTOOS ARE POPULAR with many people, but I've never
been a fan. I figured anyone who spent their hard-earned money
permanently marking themselves must be crazy and shortsighted.
What a painful, expensive waste. I hoped neither of my kids ever
got one.

That hope was inked out when our college-age son, Ron, spent
his Christmas money on his first tattoo. Ron was an art student. I
had to admit his robot executive design—with a pen in its pocket
and a striped necktie—was charming. But for $100? *Sheesh.*

Later, I recalled that God mentioned tattoos in the Bible. I found
the reference tucked into a prophecy in Isaiah. The tattoo on His
palm was God's reminder that He loved His children more than the
best mother cherished her baby.

I was overwhelmed to think that God has engraved my name
on the palm of His hand and that each time He sees it, He thinks
of me. And not only me but everyone who's given his or her heart
to Jesus.

Those precious names are the most expensive, painful tattoos in history, paid for by the life and blood of Jesus. Permanently engraved, thank goodness, on God's hand and Jesus's
heart. —JEANETTE LEVELLIE

FAITH STEP: *Look up the words to the song "Jesus Paid It All." Thank Him for
His willingness to buy your place in God's family.*

THURSDAY, JANUARY 19

But you are a chosen generation, a royal priesthood, a holy nation,
His own special people, that you may proclaim the praises of Him who
called you out of darkness into His marvelous light. 1 Peter 2:9 (NKJV)

MY HUSBAND, DAVID, BROUGHT HOME a bouquet of flowers to brighten my mood, "just because." The rainbow assortment included many types of blooms, which I arranged in a vase and placed on the dining table. Their bright colors and fresh scent lifted my spirits during what was shaping up to be a dreary winter.

After a few days, some blossoms dropped their petals, so I removed those stems. One morning, I entered the dimly lit room to find all but one of the flowers wilted and dead. I was tempted to discard the last bud along with the others. The water was murky, and the container was far too large for a single flower. It would be easier to toss them all, but I noticed the one lone carnation still possessed its scent. As I brought it into the kitchen and selected a tiny glass bud vase, my mind flashed on Jesus's work in my life.

When my world seems dark in this season, Jesus plucks me from my hopelessness. He nurtures the spark of faith within me and cradles me safely in His embrace. Like that fragrant carnation I saved from the murky waters of the dying bouquet, Jesus rescued me. My value comes from being one of His children, regardless of my feelings or my circumstances. That everlasting truth brightens my mood even better than a surprise bouquet. —HEIDI GAUL

FAITH STEP: *Consider the circle of loved ones in your life's bouquet. How can you help them—and yourself—to bloom to the fullest beauty for Him?*

FRIDAY, JANUARY 20

. . . He wakens me morning by morning, wakens my ear to listen like one being instructed. Isaiah 50:4 (NIV)

I'VE BEEN PAYING ATTENTION TO the first thoughts of my day. What's on my subconscious mind as I respond to the alarm or become aware that the sun is up?

Most mornings, a song is running in the background of my thoughts. Music is one of the ways I best commune with Jesus. When I wake with a song already playing, it usually remains with me throughout the day.

Sometimes, it's a verse of scripture that has been "playing" while I slept. The Word is deeply embedded in me from years of treasuring it, cherishing it, reading, rereading, pondering, and studying. What if that storehouse were empty? What thoughts would consume me if worship songs and Scripture hadn't collected within me?

Even that is evidence of the grace of Jesus. I am alive during an era when Scripture is more easily accessible than ever before. I was privileged to hear about Jesus from an early age. He softened my heart to believe the Bible, cling to it, and follow Him. He made it clear to me that He loved me. Jesus intervened to keep me from derailing into a life without Him.

I ache for those who wake with worry or fear on their minds. Gratitude explodes at the dawn of each day that I'm privileged to serve Jesus. Each morning, He gives me confidence that together we'll handle whatever comes up as He walks me through it. And that He's been teaching me, even while I sleep. —CYNTHIA RUCHTI

FAITH STEP: *For the next week, take note of the first thought in your mind when you awaken. If it's of Him, let it carry you all day long.*

SATURDAY, JANUARY 21

*Then Samuel took a stone and set it up between Mizpah and Shen.
He named it Ebenezer, saying, "Thus far the Lord has helped us."
1 Samuel 7:12 (NIV)*

AT MY CHURCH'S WOMEN'S RETREAT last fall, we went on a prayer walk around the pine tree–lined grounds of the retreat center and were instructed to find a rock. Back in the meeting room, we created a rock of remembrance using markers and paint. We were told to write a word or phrase on the rock that was symbolic of what the Lord had spoken to us over the course of the weekend.

I turned over a smooth, oblong rock that fit nicely in the palm of my hand. As I thought about what I had learned over the weekend, I picked up a black Sharpie and wrote the word *purpose* in bubble letters. In this season of life, my kids are now teens and young adults. My career in ministry has taken several turns. I felt like my purpose has eluded me.

Or has it? What I realized over the course of the weekend was that my purpose isn't anchored in what I do but in whose I am.

Being loved by Jesus gives me purpose. That purpose is to bring Him glory. Without Jesus, I am purposeless. With Him, I am anchored in the bedrock of hope and grace. Jesus is the Rock of my salvation, stable and unmoving. All I am and ever hope to become is built on Him. My rock of remembrance makes sure I never forget that. —SUSANNA FOTH AUGHTMON

FAITH STEP: *Go for a prayer walk in a park, field, or open space. Find a rock of remembrance and write a word on it that symbolizes how Jesus is working in your life right now.*

SUNDAY, JANUARY 22

For it is by grace you have been saved, through faith—and this is not from yourselves, it is the gift of God—not by works, so that no one can boast. Ephesians 2:8–9 (NIV)

WHEN MY BUSINESS FAILED A few years ago, I was forced to file bankruptcy. The agony of losing my company was amplified by the harm to my formerly great credit rating, the personal stigma, and all the other lasting financial aftereffects. Thankfully, I was able to keep my home, my car, and all my household belongings. I also felt an admitted relief at not having the dark cloud of the giant debt I could never repay hanging over me, as well as the menacing investors looming around me. All told, the bankruptcy, however messy, was full of grace.

A lot like my life.

The Bible tells me that apart from Jesus, I'm spiritually bankrupt (Romans 3:23). Unable to pay the enormous debt of my inherent sin, I'd be doomed to hell. I can never be good enough to pay the sin debt I owe to Jesus.

God the Father is a generous, merciful "creditor." Notwithstanding my giant bill, He provided His own Son as the forever payment on my behalf. I'm saved by grace, and by grace, I enjoy the richness of a heavenly inheritance that I could never earn or buy. Just as the outstanding bills on my failed business were erased, Jesus paid for my failure to be good enough and for my sin with His death on the cross, so I might live debt-free. —ISABELLA CAMPOLATTARO

FAITH STEP: *Take some time to journal and meditate on the blessings you enjoy that you didn't earn or buy yourself. Thank Jesus for them.*

MONDAY, JANUARY 23

The Son is the dazzling radiance of God's splendor, the exact expression of God's true nature—his mirror image! . . . Hebrews 1:3 (TPT)

MY NIECE CHERELLE WAS PREGNANT with twins, and she texted two sonograms to our immediate family. We were all so excited! Messages flew back and forth among us about possible names for the new additions to our boisterous clan. I looked at the first photo and quickly saw the features of Cherelle's unborn son. But as I studied the second image, I had no such luck. Finally, after about a minute or so, the baby girl's scrunched-up face snapped into focus for me. She looked just like her mom!

It took me a little while, and I had to look hard to see my great-niece's face in the image, but it was there all the time. Just as I had trouble seeing the baby in that sonogram, I often don't see Jesus in every person I encounter. I may focus on someone's not-so-likable characteristics, like selfishness, narcissism, or rudeness. Quite honestly, I sometimes don't look like Jesus myself.

The immortal and invisible God made us all in His image. And His only son, Jesus, is His mirror image too. Regardless of what I see, we each carry Jesus's image in us because we are His creation. Just like that sonogram, I may have to look a little harder to see Jesus in each person, but He's there. —BARBRANDA LUMPKINS WALLS

FAITH STEP: *How does the thought of Jesus in each person help you to see him or her in a different light?*

TUESDAY, JANUARY 24

*The boundary lines have fallen for me in pleasant places;
surely I have a delightful inheritance. Psalm 16:6 (NIV)*

SOMETIMES I STRUGGLE WITH THE gap between my expectations and my reality. I don't know exactly what I imagined my forties would look like, but I often find myself thinking, *I sure didn't think they'd look like this!* If I'm not careful, I can spiral into a perpetual state of discontentment.

My attitude began to change, however, when I came across the words of David in Psalm 16. For the first time, I thought about our house that often feels too small for our four growing children and thought, *The boundary lines have fallen for me in pleasant places.* I considered my career that has taken twists and turns I tried desperately to avoid and repeated the poetic prayer in my heart: *The boundary lines have fallen for me in pleasant places.* I pictured our bank accounts (too small), my waistline (too big), my kitchen (too messy), and my hair (too straight). Everything that didn't measure up to my expectations was finally viewed under the words of Psalm 16, and I realized that the boundary lines *have* fallen for me in pleasant places! The boundary lines that Jesus has drawn for me.

Now, when I feel those old familiar thoughts of negativity creeping into my mind, I remember to thank Jesus for all the pleasant places He has put in my life. By letting go of my expectations, embracing the reality of my circumstances, and trusting Jesus, I know each boundary is just right. —EMILY E. RYAN

FAITH STEP: *List the areas of your life you feel are too "something." Then cross each one out and write, "Just right!" beside it.*

WEDNESDAY, JANUARY 25

Either way, Christ's love controls us. Since we believe that Christ died for all, we also believe that we have all died to our old life. 2 Corinthians 5:14 (NLT)

A BOOK I READ SEVERAL years ago addressed the issue of busyness. It suggested that if we feel overworked from trying to balance too many roles, we should look at our motives for assuming them. For instance, are we participating in these activities because we have an inherent need to prove our worth? Do we agree to take part in every opportunity because we're afraid of missing out? Are we saying yes to each person who asks us to do a task because we're people-pleasers?

I felt as though the author wrote the book specifically for me. Deeply convicted, I asked Jesus to forgive me for making decisions based on a desire to gain man's approval or establish my reputation. I asked Him to help me identify my motives before saying yes to a request or pursuing a new project. If the motive was selfish in any way, then I wanted no part of it. But if it was a directive authorized by the Lord, then the answer would be a resounding yes.

Jesus came to earth for unselfish motives. He didn't seek to develop a following or establish a name for Himself in human terms. He was born as a man to do His Father's will because love for His Father controlled Him. Like Jesus, I want my motives to be unselfish in everything I do. —GRACE FOX

FAITH STEP: *Write out some activities in which you're involved. Pray for His eyes to see your motives behind them. Ask Jesus to show you how to change your motives so you're doing His work.*

THURSDAY, JANUARY 26

Brothers and sisters, we do not want you to be uninformed about those who sleep in death, so that you do not grieve like the rest of mankind, who have no hope. For we believe that Jesus died and rose again, and so we believe that God will bring with Jesus those who have fallen asleep in him.
1 Thessalonians 4:13–14 (NIV)

I RUMMAGED THROUGH MY BOX of handmade greeting cards. A friend's parent had died, and I wanted to send a note of sympathy. I still had plenty of birthday, get-well, and thank-you cards but had used up all my condolence cards.

Too many funerals had filled my calendar in the past year—a stark reminder that all of us have a limited time on this earth. That reality stares me in the face more frequently the older I get. I wanted to comfort my friend, and I wished I had more to offer than a card, hug, or casserole.

Jesus invites me to view death in a new way. When I'm hurting, Jesus *does* provide more. Instead of sending a sympathy card or a bouquet of flowers, He renews my hope through Scripture. Because of Him, I don't have to grieve in emptiness. He holds me when I weep, but He also whispers His promise that death is not the end.

When I come across a photo of a friend who is no longer with us in body, the pang of loss transforms into gratitude for the time we spent together on earth. Because of Jesus, I look forward to seeing my loved ones again for a joyful reunion in eternity. —SHARON HINCK

FAITH STEP: *Think of loved ones who have died. As Jesus consoles you, ask Him to fill you with joyful anticipation of your reunion with them one day.*

FRIDAY, JANUARY 27

Everything on earth has its own time and its own season.
Ecclesiastes 3:1 (CEV)

ORDINARILY, I'M SOCIABLE AND ACTIVE in a number of organizations and commitments. But following the death of our beloved kitty, Tom Thumb, I hadn't felt like socializing. We'd had little Tommy less than a year. He loved to play fetch, then curl up on my lap like a baby.

Compassionate, understanding friends are allowing me the space I need in which to grieve. It's strange, going through a season of life different from that of everyone around me. These transitions, particularly when unexpected, affect each of us differently, including our connections and interactions with others.

One gentleman in my church sent a comforting note saying he was sorry for my loss, expressing, from his own experience, the dear place pets hold in the hearts of their owners. My friends extend grace by patiently waiting for me to get through my grief, which I'm doing by spending time alone with Jesus, before resuming my usual commitments. In my sadness, I know I'm fully accepted by Jesus, regardless of whether I'm able to perform my usual duties. His comfort covers me.

Like my thoughtful brothers and sisters in Christ, I want to be sensitive to the seasons of life among the people around me. Just as others accept the time it has taken me to move through my loss, I want to extend that same grace to others, wherever they're at in their own lives. I know Jesus will guide me in doing that, just as He always understands and accepts me in all seasons. —CASSANDRA TIERSMA

FAITH STEP: *If you know someone going through a challenging time, extend the love and grace of Jesus by sending a card or note to show your support.*

SATURDAY, JANUARY 28

May the God of hope fill you with all joy and peace as you trust in him,
so that you may overflow with hope by the power of the Holy Spirit.
Romans 15:13 (NIV)

IT WAS GETTING DOWNRIGHT EMBARRASSING. When the exterminator, the heating repairman, and the UPS driver all asked why we still had our Christmas decorations up, it was probably time to take them down. My husband, Jeff, had removed all the outside decorations, but inside of our house, Christmas cheer reigned. The calendar showed January 28, which is not the latest I've left my Christmas decorations on display. One year, we were well into February when I justified, "Valentines are red..."

It all started when my son, Scott, was three. His birthday is January 6, and he asked if we could leave the Christmas decorations up until his birthday. Of course! January 6 marks the Epiphany, the Twelfth Day of Christmas. So every year since, even though Scott is no longer under our roof, I've kept the Christmas decorations up for his birthday. And sometimes way beyond.

An Elvis song posed the thought, "If Every Day Was Like Christmas." I like that sentiment! It's not just the twinkling lights, the fragrant smell of evergreen, and the baby Jesus in the manger that I can't bear to part with. It's the whole feeling of Christmas—the joy, hope, peace, kindness.

With Jesus in my life, it can feel like Christmas all year through.

I'm going to read the Christmas story in Luke. And then, maybe, I'll take down the tree. —PAT BUTLER DYSON

FAITH STEP: *Do you yearn for Christmas after the season has passed? Read Luke 2:1–21 and recapture the feeling of Christmas whenever you want to relive the joy.*

Sunday, January 29

If we confess our sins, he is faithful and just and will forgive us our sins and purify us from all unrighteousness. 1 John 1:9 *(NIV)*

For many years, I had a wall around my heart. I built it as a means of protecting myself. Keeping others at arm's length was painful, but it was better than risking being hurt when I let someone see my true self, mistakes and all.

This worked for me until one day, at Bible study, I dared to confess a dark, secret sin. Instead of looks of condemnation, compassion filled the women's faces. One by one, they each confessed hidden sins. None of us were perfect.

The understanding and grace those ladies extended to me allowed me to believe in Jesus's forgiveness and grace. My burden lifted, and I felt the wall around my heart begin to crumble.

My confession was news to my Bible study group but not to Jesus. He knew my dark sin and the other women's as well. He watched me build the unnecessary wall around my heart, waiting for the moment when I would feel strong and confident enough to break it down and let Him and others come in.

Sharing my true self, sins and all, with my group and seeing their compassion helped me realize that Jesus had that same compassion waiting for me. No sin was too big or dark for Him. Jesus would eagerly forgive me too. I need only ask.

Funny thing about that wall around my heart—I thought it blocked rejection by keeping others out. But by keeping others out, it also blocked what I craved most—love and acceptance. —Tricia Goyer

Faith Step: *Has unconfessed sin built a wall around your heart? Take a moment to confess it to Jesus.*

MONDAY, JANUARY 30

And He said, "My Presence will go with you, and I will give you rest."
Exodus 33:14 (NKJV)

I FELL INTO BED EXHAUSTED after an especially long day. My mind focused on an approaching deadline for a project I'd only half-finished. *I won't think about that tonight.* I remembered a couple of medical-related decisions that I'd been dreading. *Can't put that off much longer…*My mind switched to a difficult conversation I needed to initiate the next day. Suddenly, I sensed a still, small voice saying, "Just rest in Me." It took a moment for the message to sink in, but then I smiled and settled down, concentrating on the One who is truly in charge of my life as I drifted to sleep.

Every day we're bombarded by commercials, articles, and blog posts promoting something to help us relax and rest: supplements, prescription medicines, diffusers, bath products, special beds and mattresses, sound machines, and apps that promise to induce relaxation through music or spoken messages. Yet as a society, we seem to grow more restless and stressed.

Maybe our souls crave a deep rest that can only come from a relationship with Jesus. He loves us more than we can comprehend (John 3:16). Jesus wants to help when we feel stressed out or burned out (1 Peter 5:7). Once we learn to depend on His power, we can turn anything that weighs on our mind over to Him—and settle down in the restorative rest of His presence. —DIANNE NEAL MATTHEWS

FAITH STEP: *Do worries or trials keep you awake? Write out 1 Peter 5:7 to keep by your bedside. When you can't sleep, read the verse and ask Jesus to take your burdens. Imagine Him telling you to rest in Him all night.*

TUESDAY, JANUARY 31

Until now you've not been bold enough to ask the Father for a single thing in my name, but now you can ask, and keep on asking him! And you can be sure that you'll receive what you ask for, and your joy will have no limits! John 16:24 (TPT)

WHENEVER MY KITTEN, PRINCESS, SEES me head down the hall to the bedroom, she races past me and jumps onto my desk. Standing on her hind legs, she plants her front paws on the windowsill above the desk.

Princess doesn't utter a sound. She simply looks over her shoulder and gazes at me with sparkling amber eyes. I can almost read her thoughts. "Mom! I want to sit in this window and bird-watch, but I'm not strong enough to lift it open. You, oh powerful one, have the strength to help me."

On my way to the window, I wonder, *How would my life be different—no, better—if I had that same attitude toward Jesus?*

I tend to wait until I've exhausted all my human resources before I turn to and ask Jesus for help. That's as silly as my four-pound kitten trying to open a window. At least she acknowledges where her help comes from.

In His Word, Jesus encourages me to ask Him for help. I not only need to cry, "Help me, Jesus!" with huge problems that overwhelm me but also with those that seem minor. Like Princess, I'm not strong enough to open all of life's windows on my own. —JEANETTE LEVELLIE

FAITH STEP: *Are you relying on your own strength or Jesus's power to deal with situations? Make a list of the issues you face and pray Jesus will use His strong arms today to help you.*

WEDNESDAY, FEBRUARY 1

When my life was slipping away, I remembered you—and in your holy temple you heard my prayer. Jonah 2:7 (CEV)

A FEW OF MY JUNIOR high students were talking to me before class one day and caught a glimpse of my computer screen. "Whoa! Mrs. Ryan! How many tabs do you have open?" one student exclaimed with wide eyes. "Don't you think that's a little much?"

"Don't judge me," I said with a playful laugh and was about to close my laptop when I saw what he was talking about. Sure enough, at the top of my internet browser, more than three dozen tabs were open at once. I thought about how stressed I'd felt lately. My calendar, filled to the brim with activities and tasks, came to mind, making me cringe. My heart felt heavy in my chest, and my shoulders and neck instantly tightened up into a knot.

That student was right. My computer had become a reflection of my overstuffed schedule. It was no wonder I felt overworked, stressed out, and squeezed tight. I also realized that in all my planning and doing, my time with Jesus had been reduced to just another open tab on my computer screen.

As soon as the bell rang and my lunch break began, I shut my classroom door and covered my window so I wouldn't be disturbed. Then I closed each tab on my computer, one by one, until only my Bible website remained open. For the next thirty minutes, I ignored my to-do list and focused only on Jesus. When my next class began, my heart already felt lighter. —EMILY E. RYAN

FAITH STEP: *Spend ten minutes reading your Bible. Open your heart and mind by focusing on Jesus and asking Him to lighten your load.*

THURSDAY, FEBRUARY 2

Be strong in the Lord and in his mighty power. Put on the full armor of God, so that you can take your stand against the devil's schemes.
Ephesians 6:10–11 (NIV)

I HAVE ALWAYS BEEN SELF-CONSCIOUS about my looks. As a child, I was embarrassed because I had an overbite and a notably sized gap between my two front teeth. After getting braces in my early twenties, my teeth became perfect, but I wasn't fully confident. I couldn't completely shake the emotional toll the perceived flaw had on how I had seen myself for the past two decades.

Paul opened up about his imperfection to the Corinthians. Despite Paul begging for that "thorn in his flesh" to be removed, it wasn't. Paul's disability, whatever it was, never healed. Scripture indicates it stayed to keep him from thinking too highly about his own abilities and, instead, to keep him grounded in the fact that his power was tied to Jesus. Jesus was the source of Paul's strength, reminding Paul that he was still capable and effective in spite of his weakness.

No one wants to look frail or flawed. Despite my insecurities about the way I look, Jesus loves and accepts me just as I am—braces or no braces. My identity is in Him, as His child, and that gives me more confidence than perfect teeth. —ERICKA LOYNES

FAITH STEP: *When you start to feel weak or notice imperfections, take a deep breath and celebrate how you show up strong in Christ in spite of your insecurities.*

FRIDAY, FEBRUARY 3

"Have I not commanded you? Be strong and courageous. Do not be afraid; do not be discouraged, for the Lord your God will be with you wherever you go." Joshua 1:9 (NIV)

I LEANED AGAINST THE BALCONY railing, staring down into the sunlit atrium of the cruise ship. We had docked in Tortola, and passengers wearing sun hats scurried in all directions to disembark. My thoughts weren't on the tiny Caribbean island, though; they were two thousand miles away with my dad in Alabama.

My new friend Derek touched my arm. We'd met a few days earlier and discovered we both served as ministers in churches. "I didn't mean to startle you," he said. "This is going to sound strange, but I saw you while I was eating breakfast in that restaurant." He pointed toward some open-air seating. "Jesus nudged me in my spirit to come talk to you."

"Thank you for following His lead," I said, my voice quivering as I blinked back tears. "I received a call this morning. My dad had a massive stroke. He's dying."

Derek put his arm around my shoulder. Right in the middle of the busy cruise ship, he lifted up a prayer for me and my dad.

I had no family aboard, yet Jesus made sure I wasn't alone in my sadness. Dad and I were miles apart, but Jesus connected me to another believer—comfort in the Caribbean from heaven above. —BECKY ALEXANDER

FAITH STEP: *Invite Jesus to use you to comfort others. Ask for sensitivity to His nudges.*

SATURDAY, FEBRUARY 4

My sheep listen to my voice; I know them, and they follow me. John 10:27 (NIV)

LEADING WEEKLY ZOOM BIBLE STUDIES has become part of my ministry. Midway through each, I begin asking Jesus to show me the topic of His choice for the next study. On one occasion, I felt impressed to write a curriculum about the names of God. I researched and wrote about five names, including Yahweh Shalom, which means God of peace. I delved into the New Testament to show how Jesus—the Prince of Peace—modeled peace and promised it as a gift to believers.

Immediately following the week we studied Yahweh Shalom, one participant's husband lost his job. Another's daughter-in-law died unexpectedly and left five children motherless. A third experienced intense stress at work. It was obvious to all that Jesus orchestrated the timing of this lesson to help these women in their particular seasons. They shared that His personal care made them feel loved and brought hope into their pain and uncertainty.

I'm amazed at Jesus's perfect timing. I also marvel at how He communicated so clearly through a simple impression in my spirit. I'll confess that I've sometimes made finding His will more complicated than need be. There's no secret or magic formula. It's a matter of listening for and recognizing His voice. He might speak to me through a sermon, podcast, song, or poem. He always speaks to me through His Word and often through an impression in my thoughts. Because of His grace toward us, He communicates to me in a way that I can hear and understand. I needn't second-guess. I just need to follow. —GRACE FOX

FAITH STEP: *Spend five minutes in silence with no agenda other than to listen for Jesus's voice. Write down what He says.*

SUNDAY, FEBRUARY 5

---

*And let us consider one another . . . not forsaking the assembling of
ourselves together, as is the manner of some, but exhorting
one another . . . Hebrews 10:24–25 (NKJV)*

MY DAUGHTER RANDI'S ARTISTIC EYE analyzes the empty spaces of the
1,000-piece jigsaw puzzle we've nearly completed. She spots the missing piece in a pile that looks all the same to me. Across the table, my
husband, Russ, has no method, only madness. He crams similar shapes
into holes and insists they fit, which elicits a sharp, "Dad!" from Randi.

What a pleasant Sunday afternoon, except something is missing.

Due to my husband's ongoing health concerns, we haven't been
able to attend church for several months. Instead, we watch services
online in our living room. I'm grateful technology allows us to worship at home, but my soul feels like something is missing.

I brushed my fingers over our unfinished project. An unassem-
bled puzzle is a useless pile of pieces, but once each piece finds its
place, an intricate image emerges. The same is true for believers. We
need to be connected together as the body of Christ.

Jesus modeled the importance of connecting with others. He
assembled the disciples to "follow Me"—two words He stated
twenty times in the Gospels. Jesus fellowshipped with friends and
tax collectors (Mark 2:15). Jesus brought the disciples together
for the Last Supper (Matthew 26:20).

Like our puzzle, I feel unfinished being disconnected from the body
of Christ. *So that's why I feel so out of place with church online.* I need to
assemble, to interlock with a body of believers to feel complete.

Puzzle solved! —KAREN SARGENT

FAITH STEP: *Connect with another believer for fellowship today. Host lunch,
schedule coffee, walk in the park, or maybe work a puzzle together.*

MONDAY, FEBRUARY 6

And he said: "Truly I tell you, unless you change and become like little children, you will never enter the kingdom of heaven." Matthew 18:3 (NIV)

THIS MORNING I CAUGHT A snowflake on my tongue. My husband and I walked around the block, savoring the fluffy snowfall. Sounds became muted. Grubby streets shimmered with a coating of brightness. It stirred memories of being a child and waking up the day of a blizzard. A snow day—school was closed. Instead of the expected routine, we had a surprising day of freedom and fun. Snow angels, sledding, and cocoa!

When I ponder what Jesus means in His call to become like a child, that sense of excitement and joy comes to mind. Children have the capacity to embrace a gift and revel in it. Jesus offers a surprise far more exhilarating than a snow day. Instead of trudging along trying to draw close to God by my own efforts, Jesus steps in to whisper, "The work is done. You're free" (John 19:30).

Strange as it seems, that's not always easy for me to embrace. I often slip into striving for God's approval, when Jesus reassures that His love is already unconditional. I feel a need to remind everyone of the rules, instead of celebrating undeserved grace. I worry about temporary problems on every side, even though Jesus has said He has gone ahead to prepare a place for me (John 14:3) and that eternity will be free of pain and tears (Revelation 21:4).

So today, I'll respond like a little child to a blessed snow day. —SHARON HINCK

FAITH STEP: *What brought you delight as a child? Enjoy an activity that reminds you how to have childlike faith and exuberance for all Jesus has done.*

TUESDAY, FEBRUARY 7

When I consider your heavens, the work of your fingers, the moon and the stars, which you have set in place, what is mankind that you are mindful of them, human beings that you care for them? Psalm 8:3–4 (NIV)

ON A RECENT SATURDAY NIGHT, I jumped into the car to pick up some food at a neighborhood Chinese restaurant. After I went in and got my order, I drove off and was startled by a bright light in the dark, cloudless sky. For a few seconds, I wondered if it was a searchlight of some sort. Then I realized it was the moon! It was so full, brilliant, and low it seemed that I could reach out and touch it. Simply breathtaking and a little mysterious. *Wow! Look at God*, I said to myself.

I was dazzled by the Lord's handiwork, just as the psalmist David was. I'm also moved by a starry sky on a clear night, and I smile at a perfectly sunny day or a glorious sunset. I remember a time when I stopped in my tracks while taking a walk. Or when I spotted the huge, perfect dome of a white mushroom growing in the middle of a neighbor's yard. It was so stunning I had to take a picture of it.

It's also amazing that the God who created the heavens and earth could care so much about me that He sent His son Jesus to die for my sins and the sins of the world. I wonder, too, sometimes how Jesus could care and put up with me. But He does—because of His grace. —BARBRANDA LUMPKINS WALLS

FAITH STEP: *Look around today. Where do you see the glory of Jesus?*

WEDNESDAY, FEBRUARY 8

"The LORD your God in your midst, the Mighty One, will save; He will rejoice over you with gladness, He will quiet you with His love, He will rejoice over you with singing." Zephaniah 3:17 (NKJV)

"IF YOU STEP ON IT, we can slip into church during the first hymn," I told my husband, Jeff. He rolled his eyes and didn't speed up. "Why are we always late?" I moaned. Jeff wisely didn't respond. Who was I kidding? I was the one who made us late.

I've heard people arrive late because they like to make an entrance. Not me! I strive NOT to be noticed. But I have an idea why I'm often running behind. It's because I try to do *one more thing* before I leave the house—empty the dishwasher, put a load of clothes in the washer, or answer an email. Then the toilet overflows or the cat has a hairball and I'm doomed.

Luckily for me, Jesus is never late. When I call out to Him, He is there, just when I need Him to help me. If I'm sad, He's there to comfort me. If I have reason to rejoice, He's joyful with me. If I'm down on my knees, begging for mercy, He's right beside me.

There are times, especially when I grieve over unanswered prayers, He feels distant. But in my heart, I know He's present, waiting and watching with me. He's not distracted by other things that need doing; His focus is on me, alone.

No matter what time it is, Jesus's timing is always perfect.
—PAT BUTLER DYSON

FAITH STEP: *Make a list of the times Jesus was there for you, right on time, in the past week.*

THURSDAY, FEBRUARY 9

The name of the LORD is a strong tower; the righteous run to it and are safe. Proverbs 18:10 (NKJV)

As I LAY IN BED, I listened to the skittering overhead and shuddered.

Ew. My husband was out of town, and the idea of an animal in the attic was unsettling.

Common sense told me it couldn't come through the ceiling into the bedroom. But when the sounds seemed to move down into one of the walls, I got up and crept near to listen. I tapped here and there on the wall to prompt movement, hoping the noise had been my imagination.

After a few minutes, I crawled back into bed, yearning for quiet. I knew there was nothing to fear, but I didn't want to hear creepy sounds in the dark.

"Jesus," I whispered into the stillness.

This year I've developed a habit of speaking His name out loud. I've spoken it more times than I can count.

"Jesus." The one word that is *the* Word. It's a call, a claim, a surrender.

Even on a typical critter-free night, when I'm in bed listening to the house's hush, speaking the name of Jesus secures me to rest. If I awaken during the night, I speak His name and immediately feel assured His Spirit is near.

That night, as I drifted off, I realized the attic was not over the master bedroom. The vaulted ceiling meant the animal had to be outside, on top of the roof.

Grinning at my silly fears—and thanking Jesus—I fell asleep.
—ERIN KEELEY MARSHALL

FAITH STEP: *Invite Jesus into your life 24/7. Develop the habit of speaking His name to help remind you that He is always near and ready to listen.*

FRIDAY, FEBRUARY 10

But be sure to fear the LORD and serve him faithfully with all your heart; consider what great things he has done for you. 1 Samuel 12:24 (NIV)

AT THIS WRITING, I'M ABOUT midway through a spiritual retreat focused on discerning my vocational calling. Finally returning to work full time after fifteen years as a work-at-home mom, I'm reconstructing a career that reflects who I am today. The retreat was prompted by some failed experiences on new career paths I thought I wanted to follow. I completely trust that nothing in God's economy is wasted, and I've mined all sorts of insights from my seeming mistakes.

The retreat has been powerful. Lingering over the assigned themed scriptures with clear intention helps me better see who Jesus designed me to be and what type of service He has for me to do.

One of the framing prayers for week two is "Lord, give me the grace to grow in freedom to answer my calling." How I treasure that prayer, in which Christ-won freedom from sin figures prominently. Freedom to think outside the box. Freedom to be who I am. Freedom to honor what I don't like. Freedom to be led by the Spirit. Freedom to not be motivated by money, title, or what people will think.

I'm still waiting to discover exactly where Jesus is calling me to best serve Him, but grounded in freedom, Jesus's gentle leading so far is richer and more imaginative than my bound-up mind could fathom. —ISABELLA CAMPOLATTARO

FAITH STEP: *Join me in praying, "Lord, give me the grace to grow in freedom to answer my calling," then journal the gentle and loud prompts Jesus sends to guide your path.*

SATURDAY, FEBRUARY 11

Delight yourself in the LORD, and he will give you the desires of your heart.
Psalm 37:4 (ESV)

ONCE, WHEN VALENTINE'S DAY FELL on a Sunday, the ladies in our women's ministry prepared beautiful Victorian valentines inscribed with Psalm 37:4 as a way to bless members of our congregation who'd most likely not receive a valentine from anyone else. Recipients of these expressions of the love of Jesus included bachelors, unmarried women, widows, and widowers. Everyone who received an unexpected valentine was truly grateful.

After hand-delivering the valentines, I had one left over and slipped it into my purse. Midway through the service, I noticed someone we'd missed. An elderly gentleman sat alone. I didn't know his name, but I felt Jesus prompting me to give him the last valentine.

I rose from my seat, handed it to him, and wished him a happy Valentine's Day. He accepted it with a smile. After the service ended, he approached me. "Thank you. I felt like I'd received a valentine from Jesus."

Each of us in the women's ministry had truly enjoyed serving Jesus in this way. In return, Jesus gave us the same thing we wanted to share—His love.

I'd like to live every day as if it were Valentine's Day Sunday—*serving Jesus,* whether I'm serving in my home, neighborhood, or church. Like a valentine from above, His Word promises, if I do so, He'll give me what I desire most—to please Him. That's something to celebrate all year long! —CASSANDRA TIERSMA

FAITH STEP: *Make a list of the ways you serve Jesus and note what you enjoy about each one. Ask Jesus to show you someone you could surprise with a valentine or the gift of service.*

SUNDAY, FEBRUARY 12

"So the last will be first, and the first will be last." Matthew 20:16 (NIV)

I'M INTRIGUED BY OPPOSITES AND appreciate when opposing words are combined to make oxymorons: jumbo shrimp, deafening silence, clearly confused. When I recently heard someone say that the world's gravity pulls us down, but Jesus's gravity lifts us up, I was enthralled. The more I reflected on that statement, the truer it rang.

Nothing drags me down more than focusing on worldly trappings. When I'm world-focused, I dwell on my problems, giving them permission to weigh me down. When I'm Jesus-focused, He turns everything upside down, causing my burdens to fall away and my perspective to flip right side up.

Suddenly, I'm filled with a new lightness that helps me see beauty in the mess, potential in the hardships, and grace in the chaos. As He lifts me higher, I embrace how the last shall be first, the exalted will be humbled (Matthew 23:12), and those who die to themselves will live (Romans 8:13). My heart takes flight when I meditate on how Jesus's life exemplified opposites. He was the Son of the Most High born in a lowly stable. He was the noblest of kings who served others with humility. He triumphed over life by dying on a cross. The more I view things through His lens, the louder the call becomes to quietly implement the Beatitudes in Matthew 5. If I succeed, I'll live contrary to the world but compatible with Christ. —CLAIRE MCGARRY

FAITH STEP: *Spend time with the Beatitudes in Matthew 5:1–12. Write the one that resonates most on an index card, using it to inspire you to live it out.*

MONDAY, FEBRUARY 13

God knew what he was doing from the very beginning. He decided from the outset to shape the lives of those who love him along the same lines as the life of his Son. Romans 8:29 (MSG)

I'M A TAPESTRY ARTIST. ALTHOUGH tapestry is fabric, it isn't worn or used. It's art—meant to be seen. To elicit emotion or to tell a story.

I start by placing a warp of strong cord or yarn on the loom. The vertical warp provides structure for the weaving and is the hidden core of the finished work. I draw a pattern on the warp threads with permanent marker before I weave the first weft pass. The sideways weft threads stack up tightly to fill each section of the pattern.

While weaving, I must focus on the pattern in front of me. If my gaze drifts away, the image I hoped to create will be lost or unclear. So it is with life. When I look at the world and try to fit in with what I see there, I'm in danger of following the wrong pattern.

Jesus is called our pattern more than once in the Bible. He is the image of the invisible God (Colossians 1:15). Jesus commands us to follow Him (Matthew 4:19).

When I follow His pattern, Jesus's image can be woven into me by the power of the Holy Spirit. I don't do the work any more than the yarn does the weaving. And only by following Jesus's pattern can my life become the beautiful tapestry the Artist and Creator intended it to be. —SUZANNE DAVENPORT TIETJEN

FAITH STEP: *Try looking to Jesus today in every choice and situation. Picture His face, yield, and respond as He leads you. Let His image be formed in you.*

Valentine's Day, Tuesday, February 14

Let all that you do be done with love. 1 Corinthians 16:14 (NKJV)

Two of my closest friends write incredible romance novels. When the main character finds herself in a terrible situation, along comes the hero. Somehow, against dismal odds, they solve the problem and fall in love in the process. These stories are entertaining, and the characters are memorable. But aside from these colleagues' works, I rarely read books in that genre. Why? Because I'm already living a romance. Nothing beats reality.

My first years together with my husband, David, were like a winding road with a washboard surface. We struggled to understand the mystery of wedded bliss, clunking along until we found the answer in Luke 6:31 (NIV): *Do to others as you would have them do to you.* If I want romantic moments, I need to offer them. If I need forgiveness, I first must give it. And to be appreciated, I must possess a thankful heart.

Like a novel, David and I perpetually find ourselves in the midst of one fix or another. Now married for forty-two years, our current challenge is the bathroom. At this point, it has a toilet. That's it. And it's been years getting it this far. Will our love survive this test or will our relationship fall by the wayside, yet another victim of household repair? I've peeked at the conclusion of this story and know it ends happily.

Today is Valentine's Day. There will be kisses and secret smiles and maybe a flower or two. But the gift I'm most thankful for is my husband's devotion. Jesus's love permeates our union, whether we have a bathroom sink or not. —Heidi Gaul

Faith Step: *Be fully present for your dear ones today, offering all you do in love.*

WEDNESDAY, FEBRUARY 15

But he said to me, "My grace is sufficient for you, for my power is made perfect in weakness." Therefore I will boast all the more gladly about my weaknesses, so that Christ's power may rest on me. That is why, for Christ's sake, I delight in weaknesses, in insults, in hardships, in persecutions, in difficulties. For when I am weak, then I am strong.
2 Corinthians 12:9–10 (NIV)

MY FIFTEEN-YEAR-OLD SON, ADDISON, is growing like a weed. At six-foot-one-inch tall, he's also getting stronger. He likes to prove this by tackling me on the couch. Or by hugging me in a tight squeeze and dragging me through the kitchen.

I've started using his strength to my advantage. Whenever anything requires a strong back and a firm grip, I call on Addison. Boxes of books? Bins full of files? Heavy air-conditioning units that need to be carried up the stairs to a friend's apartment? He's my guy. Addison does the heavy lifting for me now.

In much the same way, Jesus does the heavy lifting where my spiritual weaknesses are concerned. His grace is all-encompassing. I want to be courageous, patient, and loving. I want to be kind, forgiving, and faithful. I fall short in so many ways. But His grace enables me to be and do more than I could ever hope or imagine. His power is made perfect in my weakness. When I am weak, He is strong. Jesus? He's my guy! —SUSANNA FOTH AUGHTMON

FAITH STEP: *Recognizing your weakness is the first step to allowing Jesus's strength to flood your life. Find your strength in Jesus by doubling the amount of time you spend feeding your soul with His word.*

THURSDAY, FEBRUARY 16

For God so loved the world that he gave his one and only Son, that whoever believes in him shall not perish but have eternal life. John 3:16 (NIV)

THE FIVE LOVE LANGUAGES DEVELOPED by Gary Chapman explain how we give and receive love. For instance, my primary love language is acts of service. I often express love by doing practical things for people. I'll bake brownies or muffins, for instance, and give them to our marina friends. Similarly, I feel most valued when someone does an act of service for me.

My husband's love languages are quality time and physical touch. For years, I thought I was showing him love by baking his favorite cookies, cooking healthy meals, and packing his lunches. In reality, he wished I would spend less time in the kitchen and, instead, join him on the couch to snuggle together and watch a movie. We laughed when we finally figured out the disconnect, and I've since learned to speak his love languages more effectively.

Jesus understands our unique bents. He also knows the universal need for people to feel loved, so He assumed human form to communicate with us in a language understandable to all. He taught the message of unselfishness, forgiveness, and eternal life through the spoken word, and then He demonstrated it through His life, death, and resurrection. He did the hardest thing ever when He gave up His rights as God, humbled Himself to become a servant, and died a shameful death for our sake. Jesus's love language supersedes all others, wouldn't you agree? —GRACE FOX

FAITH STEP: *The five love languages are acts of service, gifts, quality time, physical touch, and words of affirmation. Identify yours and those that apply to the people closest to you.*

FRIDAY, FEBRUARY 17

*For the law was given through Moses, but grace and truth
came through Jesus Christ. John 1:17 (NKJV)*

IF JESUS WERE A SUPERHERO—*Oh, wait. He is!*—His nickname might be Opposite Man. He was always upending traditional patterns and erasing preconceived notions. He loved to engage those who considered themselves religious and point out how their diligent, humanly devised plans were in direct opposition to the teachings of God.

He confronted a Pharisee who boasted about tithing down to a tenth of his last mint leaf (Matthew 23:23). Jesus responded, in essence, "You call that tithing? Have you called your mother lately?"

Jesus called the dead "not dead." Lazarus, for instance (John 11:1–44). Jesus said life after death was true living (John 11:25). He made His point with dust motes rather than daggers. Who does that? Opposite Man.

When one of His hotheaded companions sliced off a soldier's ear in defense of Him, Jesus bent down, picked up the ear, and reattached it (Luke 22:49–51). Classic Opposite Man.

What could be more opposite than that?

Jesus did the unexpected, the opposite, the unheard of, and is still operating that way today. He forgives me even though I don't deserve to be forgiven. He loves me despite my unlovable behaviors. He offers me eternal life after I die, just because I believe in Him. Even if I give up on myself, He doesn't give up on me.

I pray I never take for granted the wonder of Opposite Man's power and wisdom. Since I'm not a superhero, I find myself in need of it every single day. —CYNTHIA RUCHTI

FAITH STEP: *Make a list of recent behaviors that were in direct opposition to the teachings of Jesus. Then pray for wisdom and strength to next time offer actions of love in the face of conflict and strife.*

SATURDAY, FEBRUARY 18

Let all that I am praise the LORD; may I never forget the good things he does for me. Psalm 103:2 (NLT)

THE ALL-TOO-FAMILIAR BROWN CARDBOARD BOX bearing the Amazon smile logo rested near my front door, greeting me with that grin. *Hmm, I wonder what that is?* I thought as I picked it up and carried it inside. When I opened it, I found a cookbook I had ordered. I had utterly forgotten about it. Sadly, I had a case of primenesia. According to the online Urban Dictionary, it's defined as, "Amnesia caused from over-ordering from Amazon. Forgetfulness regarding what one ordered." Apparently, many others are suffering from primenesia too.

This occurrence of forgetfulness in our culture is not surprising. The human tendency to forget is emphasized throughout the Bible. Many stories are told about God's people forgetting what He had done for them. The Israelites repeatedly failed to remember how God rescued them from slavery under the Egyptians. At one point, they even wished they could go back to the misery (Numbers 14: 1–4). Jesus, too, reminded His disciples not to forget Him. The evening before He died, during the Passover meal, He told them to eat bread that was His body and drink wine that was His blood. And then Jesus gave the famous command, "Do this in remembrance of me" (Luke 22:14–20).

Jesus gave us the cure for forgetfulness. Remembrance. Remember the promises in God's Word. Remember Jesus's sacrifice. Remember to praise Him for all He's done. *Lord, help me to never forget all the good things You do for me.* —JEANNIE BLACKMER

FAITH STEP: *List three specific memories of things Jesus has done for you, such as answering a prayer, guiding you in an important decision, or experiencing His grace in a situation.*

SUNDAY, FEBRUARY 19

Preach the word of God. Be prepared, whether the time is favorable or not. Patiently correct, rebuke, and encourage your people with good teaching. 2 Timothy 4:2 (NLT)

RECENTLY, MY FRIEND CHRISTINE POSTED on social media, "Check out my photos from Rome!" I followed the link and saw Christine had not traveled to Rome in person but was going on virtual tours. Through an online venue, out-of-work tour guides gave free virtual tours to "travelers." In addition to tour guides offering tips, hodophiles (people who love to travel) were enjoying unique places worldwide while meeting those from other countries—all in the comfort of their own home.

I joined some tours, and my heart was drawn to people from across the globe. *Lord, each virtual tour is a window to the world. How can I reach the numerous "guides" and "travelers" for You?*

Jesus prompted me with an idea. Knowing that some people in the world don't know even one Christian, I decided to become a virtual tour guide myself. I signed up and shared not only the beauty of Arkansas, the state in which I lived, but also my life and faith. Showing others downtown Little Rock and Riverside Park provided a chance to talk about the wonders of Jesus in creation and my faith. Strangers from around the world became friends and hopefully would one day become my brothers and sisters in Christ.

By hosting virtual tours of Arkansas, I joined Jesus's real mission to spread the Good News about Him. Even though we toured the Ozarks virtually, I let travelers know that Jesus was never virtual—He is the real, rock-solid foundation. —TRICIA GOYER

FAITH STEP: *Pray and ask Jesus to show you opportunities to share the Good News about Him, whether online or in person.*

Presidents' Day, Monday, February 20

But store up for yourselves treasures in heaven, where moths and vermin do not destroy, and where thieves do not break in and steal. For where your treasure is, there your heart will be also. Matthew 6:20–21 (NIV)

I WATCHED THE PRICE OF my latest novel plummet at a major online bookstore. A $25 hardcover book that had taken years of work and a major investment from my publisher was priced at less than $4 only months after its release. I felt the stabbing sensation of society telling me I had no value. Ego deflated, I resigned myself to knowing what I had to offer had been shoved to the back of the store's sale rack like outdated merchandise. Last season's styles or damaged goods. All my effort and hard work was bargain basement, at best.

Yet in His mercy that same week, a writer messaged me to say that one of the scenes on the page made her cry grateful tears. Someone else confided the impact of the book's faith theme on his walk with God. Another thanked me for writing a morally clean story she could share with younger relatives.

In His quietly profound way, Jesus let me know sales numbers or book prices were not what He valued. Jesus whispered to my heart that He measured treasures in a different way than popular culture.

Have you ever felt like you fall short by the world's standards? Take heart! The kingdom that Jesus invites us into values the weak, the broken, the insignificant. He blesses others out of simple, humble offerings, even when they are bargain-basement priced. —SHARON HINCK

FAITH STEP: *Reach out to someone who needs encouragement, even if your effort seems small by human standards. Rejoice that Jesus uses a different measuring stick to determine what's important.*

TUESDAY, FEBRUARY 21

"But what about you?" he asked. "Who do you say I am?"
Matthew 16:15 (NIV)

MY DAUGHTER HAS HER OWN apartment now, and she often texts to ask questions. *How often should I water my houseplant? Should I set the Crock-Pot on high or low?* Her queries remind me of her preschool years, another season when she was full of questions. *Why is the moon so bright? Where is heaven?* One answer produced another question and so the cycle began.

I've been caught in the asking cycle myself. *Why is this happening, Jesus? When are You going to take care of this problem? Where are You?* I fret and pray and doubt my faith as I force one trusting foot in front of the other.

Can't you see Jesus shaking His head? "O ye of little faith," He must be saying to me. I'm like the hungry disciples who once again found themselves without anything to eat. They worried they'd forgotten bread, but Jesus had them remember something greater. They'd watched Him multiply a few loaves and feed thousands—twice! After reminding them of the miracles they not only witnessed but participated in, Jesus posed a question of His own, quite possibly the most important question in the history of mankind: "Who do you say I am?"

Peter knew the right answer: "You are the Messiah, the Son of the living God" (Matthew 16:16).

Within Jesus's single question lies the answers to all of mine: Jesus. Jesus is all-knowing when I don't know, all-powerful when I am powerless, and ever present even when I don't feel Him. How could I have forgotten? —KAREN SARGENT

FAITH STEP: *Are you waiting for answers? Write down your questions and pray. Look at each of them and whisper your answer: Jesus.*

ASH WEDNESDAY, FEBRUARY 22

These things I have spoken to you, that in Me you may have peace.
In the world you will have tribulation; but be of good cheer, I have
overcome the world." John 16:33 (NKJV)

WITH THE BABY SPOON, I scooped another bite of mashed carrots and offered it to my ten-month-old granddaughter. I knew Chloe Grace was getting full, but like a baby bird, she opened her tiny mouth to accept it anyway. She smiled, put her lips together, and happily blew orange specks in my face, on my shirt, and across my pants. I giggled, wiped off the mess, and tickled her chubby chin.

The little girl with strawberry-blond hair and deep blue eyes holds the first spot on my "Be of Good Cheer" list. I started the list after her birth to help me focus on the positives in my life rather than on the negatives swirling in the world around me. "Be of good cheer," of course, is not an original phrase—Jesus said it first.

Jesus spoke the phrase to a man with paralysis and then healed him (Matthew 9:2). He gave the same encouragement to a woman who had been sick for twelve years, just before He restored her health (Matthew 9:22). And in John 16, He used the four words to comfort the disciples who felt afraid and confused. I treasure everything Jesus said, but "be of good cheer" uplifts me most of all.

Adding items to my "Be of Good Cheer" list redirects my thoughts from the worries of the day to the peace of Jesus. As I reread the past entries, I celebrate each one anew, beginning with the carrot bath from sweet Chloe Grace. —BECKY ALEXANDER

FAITH STEP: *Create your own "Be of Good Cheer" list. Thank Jesus for every blessing.*

THURSDAY, FEBRUARY 23

The faithful love of the Lord never ends! His mercies never cease.
Great is his faithfulness; his mercies begin afresh each morning.
Lamentations 3:22–23 (NLT)

I WATCHED MY HUSBAND, KEVIN, crawl around the dining room picking up pieces of the jigsaw puzzle we'd been working on. No doubt they'd landed on the floor because of one, or all, of our four cats.

I dropped to my knees to join him. We'd worked the puzzle on a card table and were nearly finished. Now, patches of brown tabletop stared up at us through a dozen huge holes. I suggested we catproof our project. We moved the card table and puzzle to the back bedroom, and then we closed the door.

Like my fur babies did with our puzzle, I sometimes undo the work Jesus has accomplished in my life. After years of disciplining my tongue to speak gracious words, I catch myself gossiping. Jesus guides me to save money instead of spending it foolishly, but an impulse purchase of books, clothes, or cat toys becomes a *must-have*.

Does Jesus condemn me when the puzzle of my life has dozens of holes in it? Or when He needs to reassemble entire sections? No. He simply picks up the pieces I've scattered and begins His work anew, creating the beautiful picture He has envisioned for my life. I still may mess up and, like my cats, not understand the damage I'm doing. That's okay. Jesus is ready to help. His patience, faithfulness, love, and mercies are no puzzle to me. —JEANETTE LEVELLIE

FAITH STEP: *Cut a piece of paper into several pieces and scatter them on the floor. As you pick them up, thank Jesus for His mercy and patience.*

FRIDAY, FEBRUARY 24

See how very much our Father loves us, for he calls us his children, and that is what we are! 1 John 3:1 (NLT)

As A MOM OF SEVEN adopted children, what surprises me the most is how often my love is pushed away. Recently one of our daughters turned eighteen and left our safe environment to return to the unhealthy one she'd been removed from as a child. While her decision hurt me, I understood it. All of us want to be loved and appreciated. Sometimes, our longing to be loved leads us to people who will hurt us, even to the detriment of those who genuinely care for us.

This is true for me too. Sometimes, in the longing to feel the love of another person, I've shut out the person who loves me most, Jesus, and pushed Him away. To return to Jesus and embrace the love He offered, I needed to trust that I was wanted and worthy just as I was. I had to let the love of Jesus fill the empty place in my soul. I also had to believe that Jesus's love will never fail me.

Our daughter is still with her biological mother, yet she has begun to reach out to me. Today, she called to tell me about her school. Although I don't hear from her often, I pray she feels the love of Jesus, that our relationship will be restored, and that one day she'll be more open to accept the love I have for her. —TRICIA GOYER

FAITH STEP: *Think about when you've strived for love in an unhealthy relationship. Instead of focusing there, turn your attention to Jesus. See the love in His eyes and ask Him to help you feel love deep down.*

SATURDAY, FEBRUARY 25

Imitate God, therefore, in everything you do, because you are his dear children. Live a life filled with love, following the example of Christ.
Ephesians 5:1–2a (NLT)

SIX MONTHS AFTER I MET my neighbor Susan, her husband, Terry, passed away unexpectedly one night. I never had the chance to meet him. As I read his obituary and followed comments posted about him on social media, two things jumped out at me: This man lived his life loving others, and he was prepared to meet His Savior.

Susan shared about their last evening together: "We had Bible study and prayer, then he was singing 'In the Presence of Jehovah' as we were getting ready for bed. He woke up in the presence of Jehovah! Although this was unexpected and such a shock, there is one thing I know for sure...He HAD prepared to be ready to meet Almighty God."

A few months later, Susan received the Valentine's Day card her husband had bought for her. Her son-in-law had found it while cleaning out Terry's truck. Family members signed it and saved it for Susan to receive at the right time.

The New Testament is sprinkled with advice about being prepared for the end of our earthly life. In Matthew 25:1–13, Jesus urged us to have this attitude in His parable about bridesmaids waiting for the bridegroom to appear. Susan's husband helped me understand the best way to put this into practice. To be prepared to meet Jesus, I need to do my best to imitate Him every day, especially the way He loved everyone who crossed His path. —DIANNE NEAL MATTHEWS

FAITH STEP: *Think of one habit or practice to add to your daily routine to help you love others or be prepared when Jesus calls you home.*

SUNDAY, FEBRUARY 26

"No weapon forged against you will prevail, and you will refute every tongue that accuses you. This is the heritage of the servants of the Lord, and this is their vindication from me," declares the Lord. Isaiah 54:17 (NIV)

I LEFT THE RESTAURANT THINKING over my colleague's words, amazed how her experience struck a chord with me.

Over lunch, we'd talked about spiritual warfare, which prompted a flow of new insights—along with relief and hope. I was coming off a period of intense warfare and was still recovering from some emotional wounds. Satan's lies had battered me, and I was leaning on people close to me and lots of scripture to stand on truth and prevail.

She had shared about her challenges in deep warfare and then commented that, through it all, she learned that intense attacks from the enemy often preceded Jesus's launch of something new in her. With her revelation, I realized that He had begun something new in me too.

Thank You, Jesus. Gratitude overwhelmed me. Gratitude for the freedom Jesus offers. Gratitude for His presence in the details. Gratitude for His growing opportunities and His victory. Gratitude for how, as believers, we shared battle strategies over lunch.

Jesus is launching a new thing. It's still forming. But His Word will serve as armor as I grow stronger. I know that Jesus remains my Warrior in warfare. —ERIN KEELEY MARSHALL

FAITH STEP: *On a sheet of paper, list any physical, emotional, mental, spiritual, financial, or relationship battles you may be fighting. Pray over them daily and when they are won, mark them out and write the word VICTORY on top of them with a marker.*

MONDAY, FEBRUARY 27

Charm is deceitful, and beauty is vain, but a woman who fears the Lord is to be praised. Proverbs 31:30 (ESV)

I COMBED THROUGH THE STACK of mail on the kitchen counter. A squishy, flat package piqued my interest. It was addressed to me, but I couldn't imagine what was inside. I ripped it open and roared with laughter. *My wig!* Five months earlier, in the throes of debating whether to keep coloring my hair or let it go natural, I had (what seemed to me) the brilliant idea to order a wig. I reasoned that if I disliked how my white locks looked growing out, I could still pretend to have red hair. But the custom color had to be special ordered. Now that the fake hair arrived, I'd come to terms with my natural look.

I pulled it onto my head and gazed into the bathroom mirror. I laughed so loudly that my husband came running to make sure I was okay. I looked like Little Orphan Annie's grandmother.

"What was I thinking?" I said, as I caught my breath and put it back in the bag.

My white-headed reflection stared back at me as I fixed my hair. My laughter melted. Why had I ordered it? Was I afraid to grow older?

No matter what my age or my hair color, Jesus accepts and loves me. I don't need to conceal my true self or pretend to be someone I am not. Whether I wear my natural hair or Little Orphan Annie's grandma's wig, Jesus sees my heart. —JEANETTE LEVELLIE

FAITH STEP: *Are you accepting and loving your authentic self at this life stage? Look at your reflection in the mirror and clear your mind. Listen for Jesus to tell you how He sees you.*

TUESDAY, FEBRUARY 28

Be kind and compassionate to one another, forgiving each other, just as in Christ God forgave you. Ephesians 4:32 (NIV)

THE PHONE CONVERSATION LEFT ME shaken and confused. It had broken through my defenses, forcing me to look hard at the way I'd shaped my world. I walked around the living room, touching one keepsake and then another, holding them close, as if their very tangibility could set things right.

Had I put being right ahead of our friendship? Had I allowed my position to shift from defendant to prosecutor—maybe even to judge? Hidden within the words my loved one spoke, I heard a message from God. It was time I listened. Shoulders slumped, I found my mind running in circles until the next day. After a fitful night, I understood. I needed another long conversation but with Someone greater. Jesus.

Tears welled in my eyes as I bent my head to pray. I repented and begged for His wisdom. Words from James 3:17 (NIV) sprang into my thoughts: *But the wisdom that comes from heaven is first of all pure; then peace-loving, considerate, submissive, full of mercy and good fruit, impartial and sincere.*

My focus moved from hurt and indignation to forgiveness and hope for reconciliation. With a final prayer request for courage, I walked to the phone and gripped the receiver. The moment had arrived for me to make the call. And He'd be listening. —HEIDI GAUL

FAITH STEP: *Has the Holy Spirit been niggling at your heart to make a difficult—and perhaps overdue—call? As you reach out in peace, ask Jesus for help. He'll be there.*

WEDNESDAY, MARCH 1

All things were made by him, and nothing was made without him.
John 1:3 (NCV)

I'M CURRENTLY JUGGLING AN ARRAY of projects in process. That's because I'm converting a forty-foot school bus into a rolling home. This entails a multitude of do-it-yourself projects: planning and designing the layout; installing electrical, heating, cooling, plumbing, flooring, and window coverings; and choosing paint colors, fixtures, appliances, and more. If I wasn't having so much fun with this challenge, I'd feel overwhelmed by this big project. Especially since follow-through isn't my strength.

Realizing the magnitude of this undertaking, I'm inspired by the characteristic follow-through of Jesus. He successfully completed every single thing He set out to do. From the creation of the world to the salvation of humankind, Jesus is a finisher.

I'm relying on Him to give me the help and fortitude to follow through with this project. The Good News Translation states John 1:3 this way: "not one thing in all creation was made without him." Which means, whether converting a bus into a tiny rolling home, publishing a book, or organizing a VBS program, nothing was created except through Him. That takes the pressure off me.

While I'm building my own little world out of repurposed materials in a used school bus, Jesus created the entire universe out of nothing. From start to finish. With that in mind, my big rolling-home bus project seems small. With Jesus by my side, I know I will finish well! —CASSANDRA TIERSMA

FAITH STEP: *Are you facing a big project? Ask Jesus to give you the follow-through needed to bring it to a successful completion.*

THURSDAY, MARCH 2

"Be still, and know that I am God! ..." Psalm 46:10 *(NLT)*

I'M A TEACHER AT A small private school where elementary, junior high, and high school kids and staff meet in separate buildings on one campus. Every morning, after I put my belongings in my classroom, I grab my coffee cup and make the long walk across campus to the main building where the industrial coffee machine is located. No matter how early I arrive, I'm always in a rush to get back to my classroom so I can tie up loose ends before the first bell rings.

I often cross paths with other teachers, and over time I noticed a significant difference between another teacher and me. When Jenny walks her daughter to class each morning, she never seems to be in a rush. While my walk seems underscored by trumpets and cymbals from a fast-tempo, action-adventure soundtrack, hers seems better suited to the calm, soothing sounds of a cello. Her arms don't flail about. Her heels don't click like the keys of a 1950s typewriter. She simply *strolls*.

Her peaceful, unhurried demeanor inspired me. I decided to intentionally slow down and use my morning coffee runs as time alone with Jesus. Now as I walk, I ask Him to prepare my heart for the day ahead and to help me love my students well. I have found that the slower I walk as I pray, the more peaceful and settled my heart feels. —EMILY E. RYAN

FAITH STEP: *Take a walk today without counting your steps, listening to music, or trying to be home by a certain time. As you stroll, talk to Jesus about the small details of your day. Don't rush while you pray.*

FRIDAY, MARCH 3

But grow in the grace and knowledge of our Lord and
Savior Jesus Christ.... 2 Peter 3:18 (NIV)

IT WAS A HARD BUT necessary lesson. Refusing to ignore it any longer, I took a look at all the automatic renewals on my credit card. I didn't even recognize some of the companies to which I'd been paying a monthly or annual fee. It happens. I'm probably not the only person who forgot to cancel a trial subscription, or who decided on the paid version of software I experimented with, then realized it was more cumbersome than what I was already using.

It was time to clean up those oversights. The sums weren't huge, but I was paying without reaping the promised benefits. Stagnant, inactive, unnecessary.

As I finished unsubscribing and deleting, it occurred to me that sometimes I treat my faith in Jesus as an automatic renewal. It's there but hovering in the background where I pay it little to no attention. But I want Jesus to be in the forefront of my thoughts, the songs in my head, what drives me forward, what and who I live for, work for, adore.

I pray no one ever has to ask me, "Do you realize what you signed up for? Aren't you aware of what Jesus makes available to you?" I have a vast storehouse of mercy and grace at my disposal. And the thing is, it's paid for in full by my Savior.

Jesus and me? Not a trial subscription but an on-purpose decision I wanted to sign up for with no annual fee. —CYNTHIA RUCHTI

FAITH STEP: *Are you treating Jesus like an automatic renewal or taking advantage of all He has to offer? List ways you can make the most of your relationship with Him.*

SATURDAY, MARCH 4

"The LORD your God, who is going before you, will fight for you . . . your God carried you, as a father carries his son, all the way you went until you reached this place." Deuteronomy 1:30–31 (NIV)

MY HUSBAND, STEVE, AND I have moved a lot over two decades of marriage. First, we moved into our starter home, then remodeled and flipped a few houses along the way; we even downsized at one point. But with all the upheaval, I wondered if Jesus was moving our family forward. He'd moved us again and again and again, in and out of jobs and homes. I felt like we kept circling, instead of landing.

Last year, we sensed God was preparing us to relocate, again. *Really, Jesus?* I wanted to ask. We went through the familiar motions. Our home sold in two days with multiple offers. It took us three tries to buy our current home (sight unseen, God bless our realtor). We were down to the wire before our kids started in their new schools, but the sellers' own relocation timeline coordinated with ours and we closed in two weeks.

Turns out, this has been the perfect move in many ways. The layout served ideally for off-and-on virtual learning during the pandemic. It also provided space for my parents to live with us—a situation that allowed them time to look for their own home and blessed my family while Steve was away transitioning our business. Jesus provided church, school, and work connections—and lessons in faith. Where He leads, He does make a way. I'm experiencing the security of trusting Him whether I'm moving forward, circling, or landing. —ERIN KEELEY MARSHALL

FAITH STEP: *In what circumstance have you questioned the move of Jesus? Write it down and ask Him to show you the way.*

SUNDAY, MARCH 5

Are not two sparrows sold for a penny? Yet not one of them will fall to the ground outside your Father's care. So don't be afraid; you are worth more than many sparrows. Matthew 10:29, 31 (NIV)

THIS MORNING, I DRANK MY tea from a ceramic mug with painted images of birds sitting on a wire. The cup used to be my mom's. Now a week after her funeral, I cherished the memories of how much she loved her morning coffee and how often she watched and identified birds outside her window. The picture on the mug also brought to mind one of her favorite hymns—"His Eye Is on the Sparrow."

At a time when I'm grappling with exhaustion and grief, I thought about sparrows. They are small, common, everyday birds that Jesus says are cherished by God.

I'm not like a majestic eagle or a brilliantly plumed macaw. And that's all right. In my ordinary ways, my Savior sees me, knows me, and loves me. His grace isn't based on my value but on His abundance of love and compassion.

That's not to say I'll never "fall to the ground." Life has painful moments. Caring for Mom in her final weeks proved that to me. But the tender hands of Christ are always there to catch, to cradle, to carry me.

Jesus also says, "So don't be afraid." My little sparrow heart doesn't always feel particularly brave. But when I remember that Jesus is always with me and how much He cares for me, my fear takes flight. I know His eyes are on me. Whatever I will face today, I can face it with Him. —SHARON HINCK

FAITH STEP: *Watch birds today. Thank Jesus that you have tremendous value to Him and that He never looks away.*

Monday, March 6

Dear friends, now we are children of God, and what we will be has not yet been made known. But we know that when Christ appears, we shall be like him, for we shall see him as he is. 1 John 3:2 (NIV)

RECENTLY, MY SISTER ERICA TEXTED me a baby picture of herself sandwiched between her two granddaughters' pictures. The three of them could have been triplets. Erica's daughter is glad her girls inherited their grandma's looks. I called Erica as soon as I saw the picture. "Girl, you've got some strong genes!"

My own boys don't look much like me, or Scott, or each other. They are uniquely their own people. But one thing we all have in common is our sense of humor. Our "funny gene" has been passed down to the next generation. Our sons may not physically look like us, but the humorous way they look at life is an inherited family trait.

Jesus's family traits are written on the hearts and in the behavior of everyone who follows Him. Loving kindness. Generous mercy. Outrageous generosity. Inexplicable power. Steady faithfulness. Extravagant grace. When Jesus adopted me into His family, forgiving my sins and showering me with His grace, His traits began to rub off on me. His love has changed my outlook on life. More than anything, I yearn for His strong genes to be evident in me.

I want to be His look-alike. —SUSANNA FOTH AUGHTMON

FAITH STEP: *Which of Jesus's family traits have started to rub off on you? Make a list and thank Him for the ways you resemble Him.*

TUESDAY, MARCH 7

*Be completely humble and gentle; be patient, bearing with
one another in love. Ephesians 4:2 (NIV)*

I OPENED THE EMAIL AND quickly became irritated. I'd helped orga-
nize a program and the sender wasn't pleased about the way something had been handled. I agreed that all hadn't gone as smoothly
as I had planned. What ruffled my feathers was the cranky, snarky
tone of the message.

My first reaction was to fire off an equally rude response. But after
taking a few minutes to calm down, I decided against it. *Lord Jesus,
what should I do? How should I respond?* I thought. *Extend grace* was
what I heard in my spirit. *No! I can't do that,* I said to myself. But
then I sought guidance from a trusted friend. "Apologize," she said.
I pushed back. She repeated, "Apologize." I told her I would, but I
was still fuming. I decided to sleep on it.

The next day during my morning devotions, I came across
Ephesians 4:2. *Okay, Jesus, I get it!* The Lord confirmed what He
had already told me. This time I obeyed and wrote a gracious email,
apologizing to the sender for the inconvenience and promised to do
better next time.

I was thankful that Jesus spoke to me again loud and clear. He
let me know that it's all about Him and I'm to represent Jesus
well every day. Sometimes that means being humble and kind—
and extending a little grace, like He has done for me countless
times. —BARBRANDA LUMPKINS WALLS

FAITH STEP: *Who or what has gotten under your skin lately? What would
extending grace in that situation look like to you?*

WEDNESDAY, MARCH 8

Then Jesus told his disciples a parable to show them that they should always pray and not give up. Luke 18:1 (NIV)

OUR CAT, EARL, WAS NOT at the door one morning, demanding to be fed, as usual. I wasn't particularly concerned, but as the day wore on and Earl didn't appear, I worried. I beseeched Jesus to send the feisty stray, whom we'd adopted a few years earlier, home.

Night fell and still no Earl. I put a picture of him on a lost pet Facebook page. I walked around the neighborhood calling his name. I put flyers in nearby mailboxes.

I barely slept as I begged Jesus to send Earl home. The next morning, I hurried to the door, but Earl wasn't there. All day long, I searched, called, and prayed.

By the third morning, Earl had still not appeared. With a heavy heart, I gave up and stopped praying. Earl was gone for good.

My daily devotion that morning addressed Jesus's parable about the persistent widow who pleaded with the unfair judge to grant justice against her adversary. She kept praying, never gave up, and finally, the judge granted her request (Luke 18:1–8).

This *Jesus nudge* was a message to me. I couldn't give up, either. I called the area animal shelters and resumed my prayers for Earl's return.

Early the next morning, my husband hollered, "He's back!"

Earl had been trapped in a neighbor's garage. They'd been out of town, and when they'd returned, Earl quickly escaped. I hurriedly shook kibble into his bowl, as I thanked Jesus for bringing Earl home and for teaching me to never give up in prayer. —PAT BUTLER DYSON

FAITH STEP: *What have you given up praying about? Make a new resolve and petition Jesus like the persistent widow.*

THURSDAY, MARCH 9

But God shows his love for us in that while we were still sinners,
Christ died for us. Romans 5:8 (ESV)

MY STINT AS A PUBLIC high school teacher was positive in some respects but deeply disillusioning overall. As a longtime work-at-home mom who lived in something of a spiritual bubble, being knee-deep in a broad cross section of humanity was eye-opening.

Many days, I'd leave school in tears or enraged over the impact of my students' dysfunctional homes and lack of moral training. It troubled me to see exhausted, underappreciated teachers and to be one myself. I struggled with the futility of my efforts to make a difference. How could me being in the classroom make things better?

I lamented my plight to a friend. She listened with empathy. "Now you know how God felt," she whispered. "That's why He sent Jesus."

Our perfect God, full of mercy, loving kindness, and righteousness, must look on us with outrage and sadness, seeing how we humans harm each other and ourselves. He sees we are but dust and provides a remedy, Jesus, to save us from ourselves and to love us as we are.

Early in my high school teaching adventure, I decided to be an ambassador for love on behalf of the One who especially loved ruffians and wretches like me. Though I couldn't say His name in school, I could pray to see with Jesus's eyes and graciously share His redemptive love. Through Jesus, I have no doubt that me being in the classroom made a difference. —ISABELLA CAMPOLATTARO

FAITH STEP: *Are you outraged or hurt by something you've witnessed? Ask Jesus for the grace to see with His eyes and share His love. Make it a point to pray for all teachers and students in the classroom this school year.*

FRIDAY, MARCH 10

Show hospitality to one another without grumbling. 1 Peter 4:9 (ESV)

ONE SUNDAY, MY HUSBAND, ZANE, invited a young couple over for dinner without asking me. That afternoon, we were already hosting our small group, so I felt overwhelmed. When we got home, I scurried around cleaning the house. I found myself grumbling about entertaining so many people. *Couldn't he have invited the couple over a different night?* I thought as I threw dog toys into a basket. I was in a crummy mood, definitely not an attitude of hospitality, at least not the type of hospitality Jesus modeled.

Jesus, of course, didn't grumble when He made a meal for thousands of hungry people out of fish and bread without a kitchen (Luke 9:16). He created an intimate moment of connection by cooking breakfast over a fire on the beach for some of His disciples after His resurrection (John 21:9). In fact, Jesus graciously offers what we need most. He nourishes us without food and satisfies our thirst without water (John 6:35). He restores our souls (Psalm 23:3) and gives us rest (Matthew 11:28).

Grumbling when preparing for guests is an indication my heart was not right. I had subtly slipped into wanting others to admire our lifestyle, a tidy home, and fancy food, rather than offering them the gift of friendship, acceptance, understanding, and love. People can enjoy themselves in a messy house, but an unclean heart is never hospitable. True hospitality is not about the house; it's about the Host. —JEANNIE BLACKMER

FAITH STEP: *Think of a time you focused more on how your home looked than how your guests felt. Ask Jesus to help you focus on what really matters the next time you have the opportunity to host others.*

SATURDAY, MARCH 11

Praise the Lord, all you nations. Praise him, all you people of the earth. Psalm 117:1 (NLT)

A FEW MONTHS AGO, I received a message from my friend Gabi, who lives in the Czech Republic. "My new granddaughter is here, in your part of the world," she said.

"And my grandson will be joining our family soon, in your part of the world," I replied.

Gabi and I met fifteen years ago on a mission trip. In the years since, my daughter moved there and married a Czech man. And Gabi's daughter moved to the United States and married an American. Our friendship is built on our love for Jesus, and Jesus has connected us across the nations.

I used to think Jesus's love was for Christians like me. However, the longer I followed Him, the more I understood Jesus's love was also for those unlike me—others worldwide from all walks of life.

Many Psalms called Israel to give praise to God, but the shortest one, Psalm 117, encourages *all* the people of the world to praise Him. This is one of the six Psalms sung as part of the Passover service, which means Jesus would have sung these words with His disciples the night before His death.

After Jesus's death, "all you nations" was brought to fruition forty days after His resurrection when three thousand believers from many nations were baptized and added to the church.

It's beautiful to see Jesus connecting people from all nations in friendship today and sharing in their faith in Him across the globe. —TRICIA GOYER

FAITH STEP: *Do you know someone in your church or neighborhood who is from a different country? Reach out in friendship, even in small ways.*

SUNDAY, MARCH 12

Make a joyful noise unto the Lord, all ye lands. Serve the Lord with gladness: come before his presence with singing. Psalm 100:1–2 (KJV)

MY CHURCH DECIDED TO CREATE a library of video recorded hymns to use in online services. The music director asked for soloists and duets to come in and record a few songs. With more enthusiasm than sense, I signed up for a duet with my husband. The night we were scheduled to record, I was fighting laryngitis.

When we began the first hymn, the music director stopped us. "Sharon, you're straining on the high notes." He coached me, and the organist lowered the key. I felt embarrassed, wishing I was a stronger singer.

Then we started "Beautiful Savior." When we reached verse two, I confidently belted out verse three by mistake. We had to stop and start over. When we sang "Abide with Me," I cheerfully sang a choral arrangement I'd once learned instead of the melody I was supposed to be singing.

I had to laugh. The experience was similar to the many times I've sought to serve Jesus with more enthusiasm than skill. I say yes to a speaking engagement but worry that I'm not funny or profound enough. I agree to a writing project but believe my words are stiff and flat. I call a friend who is in crisis but struggle to find encouragement to share.

I take great comfort in knowing Jesus welcomes my clumsy service. I'll keep trying my best, but when I fall short, I know He will graciously welcome my joyful noise. —SHARON HINCK

FAITH STEP: *Sing a hymn to Jesus today. Focus on the song in your heart more than what comes from your lips.*

MONDAY, MARCH 13

The plans of the diligent lead to profit as surely as haste leads to poverty. Proverbs 21:5 (NIV)

MY OLDEST SON, ZACK, SIGNED up for boxing last year. We bought all the gear, but one essential item he used drove me nuts—his wraps. Wraps are two-inch wide, fifteen-foot-long strips of fabric with Velcro on the end. Wound around the knuckles and wrists, they provide protection. Because Zack's hands sweat, I had to wash his wraps between classes.

Those long, sticky wraps always came out of the washer tangled. As I fought to unsnarl the endless length of wet fabric to line-dry them, my irritation level rose, especially when the Velcro kept grabbing on, complicating the process.

I was thrilled when I found a wrapless version that slipped on like fingerless gloves. It would make the hassle of my sparring with Zack's extra laundry items so much easier. But when I asked his coach, he blocked the idea. Although the new wraps might be easier to wash, they didn't provide sufficient wrist support. Not wanting Zack to break a bone, I had no choice but to keep fighting with those darned wet wraps.

The world may try to sell different shortcuts: self-help books, the latest time-saving merchandise, technological advances that are supposed to make life easier, or wrapless wraps. Each has its own merit, but sometimes the results don't live up to the hype.

I'm thankful that Jesus didn't take shortcuts. He went to the cross and did the hard work for me. Because of His sacrifice, I'm a winner in any fight that comes my way. —CLAIRE MCGARRY

FAITH STEP: *Write down a situation you're struggling with. Wrap it up in a rubber band or towel. Imagine Jesus is wrapping His arms around you and whatever you're fighting against.*

TUESDAY, MARCH 14

So you are no longer a slave, but God's child; and since you are his child, God has made you also an heir. Galatians 4:7 (NIV)

OUR TWO-YEAR-OLD CHOCOLATE LABRADOR, ODY, loves the outdoors. The other day I found him outside the front door. "How did you get out?" I said as I let him in. Then, he escaped again. I was puzzled until one day I saw him jump up and hit the downstairs door handle, which is a lever. He pulled it down with his paws and opened the door. He had figured out the key to his freedom—the door handle.

I wondered what my life would be like if I escaped the confines of my world and lived freer. Every day I have a long to-do list. I've even started getting up at 5:30 a.m. to get it all done. Because I work at home and have taken on all sorts of obligations, I rarely go outside. Perhaps I'm enslaved to achievement, security, and productivity. I've created my own housebound life.

But I know the door handle that sets me free. It's Jesus. Jesus died to set me spiritually free once and for all. By trusting Him, I'm also free from things holding me hostage in life, such as overcommitting, self-imposed workloads, and getting my to-do list done. My own obsessions have kept me from living carefree.

Ody's talent as an escape artist reminded me that Jesus came to set me free. Jesus's sacrifice broke the chains I had placed on myself and opened the door to living freer. Today, I'll take Ody, and myself, for a good romp outside. —JEANNIE BLACKMER

FAITH STEP: *What's keeping you from living the carefree life Jesus offers? Today, take a walk and ponder ways to live freer.*

WEDNESDAY, MARCH 15

So we fix our eyes not on what is seen, but on what is unseen, since what is seen is temporary, but what is unseen is eternal. 2 Corinthians 4:18 (NIV)

I'M STANDING OUTSIDE ON MY deck in early spring, surveying the patio below where a bunch of ceramic and plastic pots are filled with dead plants. It's a somewhat depressing sight, and I wonder if the perennials will come back to life. I know they won't with any help from me—I'm a serial plant killer. My husband, Hal, is the one with the green thumb. He's out there, early in the season, tidying up the space and preparing for the new growth.

I know in my heart that when spring really kicks in, many of those sad-looking plants will begin to sprout and later flourish. What I see now is only temporary. Change is happening in the garden; I just can't discern it with my eyes. In my mind, I remember the blooms of last season and imagine the flowers that will bring me joy in the coming months.

That was the message the apostle Paul delivered to the Corinthian church. Although it appeared they were taking a beating and facing hardships because they were following Jesus, like my dead plants, they were actually being renewed each day because of their belief in Jesus. Eternal joy was on the horizon, not only in heaven with the Lord but also coming to them on earth.

Despite this season of seemingly lifeless surroundings, I use my eternal vision and look forward to better days and the glory of spring that's ahead. —BARBRANDA LUMPKINS WALLS

FAITH STEP: *In what situation do you need eternal vision? Journal about what seems to be happening and pray for Jesus to show you what's really happening.*

THURSDAY, MARCH 16

"Look! I stand at the door and knock. If you hear my voice and open the door, I will come in, and we will share a meal together as friends."
Revelation 3:20 (NLT)

I'VE DISCOVERED THAT AT A certain age, one's junk mail takes on new themes. Several years ago, my husband and I began receiving cards and letters that, on the surface, look like desirable invitations—often to a nice dinner free of charge. In reality, these mailings are attempts to lure us into attending sales pitches for different Medicare plans, investment services, and even hearing aids. We RSVP by tossing them in the trash.

My favorite invitations are the ones from Jesus, printed in the Bible. First, He invites us to accept forgiveness for our sins and receive eternal life (John 3:16). Then, He bids us to follow Him and help build His kingdom (Matthew 4:19); live abundantly (John 10:10); and come to Him when we feel weary, burdened, and need rest (Matthew 11:28). Jesus offers living water to quench our spiritual thirst and the Bread of Life to satisfy our soul (John 6:35).

Just like any invitation, biblical invitations call for an RSVP. Jesus pictured Himself standing at the door, waiting to be invited in so He could fellowship with us. I choose whether to open the door to receive all Jesus has to offer. Every day I'm flooded with loving invitations from Jesus. He's just waiting for me to respond. No sales pitches, but joy and satisfaction guaranteed. —DIANNE NEAL MATTHEWS

FAITH STEP: *Focus on the condition of your heart at this moment. Which divine invitation do you need to respond to today? Thank Jesus for His promises and tell Him you gladly accept His offer.*

FRIDAY, MARCH 17

*He rescued me from my powerful enemy, from my foes,
who were too strong for me. Psalm 18:17 (NIV)*

MY CAT, IVY, ADOPTED FROM a farm, proves that although you can take a cat out of the country, you can't take the country out of the cat. She loves to hunt and is an excellent mouser.

One bright spring morning, she stood before me in the living room, her stance proud. And then she dropped a surprise offering at my feet. She'd brought in a bird—an unhurt but terrified bird. It immediately flapped its wings and flitted to a windowsill. My husband and I formulated a plan on how to catch it. Minutes later, we carried the frightened creature to our front yard, careful to lock Ivy indoors. As we set the tiny bird on our porch railing, she stood stock-still, then seemed to shake the situation off. A moment later, she flew to our maple tree, where she perched and stared at us as if to say thank you. As we watched, she took flight and was gone.

Years ago, Jesus rescued me from the dangerous and damaging life choices I'd made. While I was frightened and confused, He picked me up and held me in the palm of His hand. He carried me away from the hurt and the pain and led me to a place of safety. I no longer need to hide my face in shame or act in fear.

Today I rest in the security of His grace and fly unrestrained, covered in the limitless grace He provides. I am free, indeed. Free as a bird. —HEIDI GAUL

FAITH STEP: *Take a few minutes to watch birds as they swoop and soar. Consider the ways your faith in Jesus has provided you with genuine freedom and give thanks.*

SATURDAY, MARCH 18

And so it is in the body of Christ. For though we are many, we've all been mingled into one body in Christ. This means that we are all vitally joined to one another, with each contributing to the others. Romans 12:5 (TPT)

MY COAUTHOR AND FRIEND, BETH, often tells me she'd like to have a more outgoing personality. "I have to think about everything I say and always second-guess myself. I wish I were more spontaneous, like you."

But I disagree. I may act and speak quickly, but that impetuousness gets me into trouble more often than I care to admit. I pray—a lot—to control my words and impulses. Actually, when I think about it, I should be more like her.

Beth is the perfect balance for my gregarious, bold nature. Just having her in the same room with me is calming and helps me focus. Her insights and wisdom, spoken in a soothing tone, often keep me from making foolish mistakes.

Jesus knew what He was doing when He made each of us unique and then gave us friends with opposite personalities. Even Jesus's own close friends were a wild mix: impetuous Peter, sensitive John, left-brained Thomas. Jesus, alone, is the perfect blend of qualities.

Aha. Rather than Beth and I aspiring to act more like each other, our best bet is to be more like Jesus. —JEANETTE LEVELLIE

FAITH STEP: *Read a story about Jesus's life from one of the gospels: Matthew, Mark, Luke, or John. Afterward, tell the Lord a quality of His character you'd like to develop.*

SUNDAY, MARCH 19

And so, dear brothers and sisters, we can boldly enter heaven's Most Holy Place because of the blood of Jesus. Hebrews 10:19 (NLT)

I'M NOT TYPICALLY A FEARFUL person, but approaching border security guards unnerves me. One time, a uniformed, gun-packing guard did a random check of my belongings and found a sandwich bag filled with sugar snap peas in my backpack. It had been there for a week, and I'd completely forgotten about it. He accused me of smuggling and interrogated me to see if he could catch me in a lie. Thankfully, he believed my explanation and waived a three-hundred-dollar fine for failing to declare an agricultural product. Ever since, I've wondered if the stress of forgetting something critical makes me look like a nervous, suspicious traveler.

There's a stark contrast between how I feel about approaching border guards and how I feel about approaching God in prayer. In Old Testament times, the high priest entered the holy place in fear and trembling. He faced immediate death if he didn't perfectly perform every item of the law as he shed animals' blood to atone for the sins of the people (Leviticus 10:1–2).

But Jesus changed everything. Because of His death on the cross, we live under grace. We have direct and bold access to God. We can talk with Him at any time and on any topic with assurance that He welcomes us to do so.

I'll probably never feel bold around border guards, but I'll never feel afraid to approach God in prayer. Jesus did the work. Because of His sacrifice, the border between heaven and earth is open. —GRACE FOX

FAITH STEP: *Pour your favorite hot drink, relax, and talk with Jesus about something that's unknown to anyone else.*

MONDAY, MARCH 20

'For in him we live and move and have our being.' As some of your own poets have said, 'We are his offspring.' Acts 17:28 (NIV)

I FIND MYSELF SITTING FOR hours while working from home. I become so absorbed in what I'm doing that I forget to get up and move around. It didn't take long for my aging body, especially my knees, to signal that I had to make some changes.

Since I can't always break away for an outdoor walk or a treadmill workout, I decided that I would do something quick and easy that I enjoy: dance. I played a couple of my favorite R&B or funk tunes and shimmied in my kitchen when no one was watching. I loved the heart-pumping music and ability to freely move.

After a few days, it occurred to me that I could turn my midday dance party into a midday praise break. I remembered that King David danced before the Lord with all his might (2 Samuel 6:14), so why not me? Instead of secular music, I chose contemporary gospel and Christian praise songs on my Alexa app. I waved my arms, jumped with joy, and sang loudly as I thanked Jesus for His goodness and mercy. The words of the songs and praise phrases energized my body and soul and revived my midday slump.

What started out as a desire to move away from my desk has turned into a daily praise party to exercise my body, mind, and soul. —BARBRANDA LUMPKINS WALLS

FAITH STEP: *What new way can you praise Jesus today?*

TUESDAY, MARCH 21

But he said to me, "My grace is sufficient for you, for my power is made perfect in weakness." Therefore I will boast all the more gladly about my weaknesses, so that Christ's power may rest on me. 2 Corinthians 12:9 (NIV)

I WAS A TIMID KID, insecure and often picked on. I also faced many family issues I simply could not fix, no matter how hard I tried. Weakness, I thought, was definitely bad. Very bad. This notion persisted well into adulthood and even after meeting Jesus. I was conditioned to develop and muster strength to tackle any obstacle, task, or problem with all my might. If it didn't work? Well, that just meant I needed to redouble my efforts and try harder.

Mostly, this approach not only didn't work, but it also exhausted me. Often, this fatigue would lead to my getting sick. True to form, I'd power through, artificially energized by DayQuil and too much coffee. I'd get so sick that, eventually, I could do nothing but lie in bed.

The task or problem would just have to wait. I'd fret about it, but there was nothing I could do. I discovered that often, despite my inactivity, the urgency would subside, the problem would solve itself, or some solution would present itself out of nowhere.

I finally realized, reluctantly at first, how the words in 2 Corinthians 12:9 were positively and very practically true. Jesus's power flows freely when I'm not exerting my own. By tapping into His unlimited, sufficient grace, His power is made perfect in my weakness. I don't need to try harder. I can finally rest. —ISABELLA CAMPOLATTARO

FAITH STEP: *Are you tired of struggling to fix something or someone to no avail? Make a list of those challenges. Give up and give it to Jesus.*

WEDNESDAY, MARCH 22

Each of you should use whatever gift you have received to serve others, as faithful stewards of God's grace in its various forms. 1 Peter 4:10 (NIV)

MY EIGHTY-SOMETHING-YEAR-OLD COFFEE BUDDY, PAT, walks two miles every morning, texts a prayer to nearly one hundred people each day, and spends many afternoons mentoring me in my new season of life as an empty nester.

Recently, I began to notice changes in her complexion and exhaustion in her eyes. Pat confessed she'd been skipping her walks and taking more naps. We both agreed she should see a doctor.

First, the doctor scheduled an EKG, then an echocardiogram, and finally a stress test. Nothing peculiar surfaced, so he adjusted her medication. "The doctor says I have a good heart," she reported.

A good heart indeed! No medical testing is required to reveal Pat's goodness. She organizes Bible studies and prayer groups, recruits for a global mission project, and raises money to purchase Bibles for a local orphanage. She slips a book about grief into the hands of a recent widower, encourages new foster parents through a difficult challenge, and provides a temporary home for a sister in need.

Pat has the gifts of teaching, compassion, and listening. She's generous with her time and money. Her heart belongs to Jesus, but she also has given Him her hands to do His work, her feet to follow His path, and her lips to speak His truth.

Pat may be mentoring me as I become an empty nester, but what I most need to learn is how to have a heart like hers. —KAREN SARGENT

FAITH STEP: *Do you have a friend with a good heart? How does she use her gifts to serve? Find ways you can mirror her service and bless others.*

THURSDAY, MARCH 23

. . . And let us run with perseverance the race marked out for us, fixing our eyes on Jesus, the pioneer and perfecter of faith. . . . Hebrews 12:1–2 (NIV)

I'M ALWAYS TRYING A NEW fitness gadget or changing my exercise routine to lose weight and rebuild my muscles. My latest workout plan includes a hula hoop. Before that, I bought a pair of professionally fitted running shoes. The first few weeks of exercising are always exhilarating, but, before long, I run out of steam to keep it up. I quickly forget about what motivated me in the first place. I take my eyes off the prize, my goal, and lose focus.

It's natural to want to give up when I'm tired, bored with my gadgets, not seeing results from routines, or just a little too comfortable carrying around that extra weight. When I get discouraged, I picture Jesus facing me, running backward, taking two fingers to point to His eyes and then back to mine, signaling me to keep my eyes on Him while I run. He knows where the terrain gets tougher. He knows when I'll need an extra boost of energy to go uphill. He knows when I need to catch my breath, take a sip of water, or slow down the pace. He's running the race with me and gives me grace to run at my own pace.

With Him, I don't lose my focus. Jesus helps me exercise my motivation by keeping my eyes on the ultimate prize—Him. —ERICKA LOYNES

FAITH STEP: *Whatever race you're trying to finish, whether you're running a marathon, writing a book, raising children, performing optimally on the job, or just getting out of bed each day, imagine Jesus is right there with you, cheering you on to the finish line.*

FRIDAY, MARCH 24

Carry each other's burdens, and in this way you will fulfill the law of Christ. Galatians 6:2 (NIV)

WHEN MY HUSBAND, DAVID, SUFFERED a life-threatening accident, I reeled beneath the weight of it. His injuries left him physically debilitated and mentally fragile. The hours slipped past as I juggled his medicines, prepared meals, and helped with his personal hygiene. During his naps, I converted our home to be handicapped accessible. I plotted my time like an emergency room doctor, making the most of every second, each moment a testimony of both my love and my self-perceived capability under duress. By the time night fell, I'd collapse into bed, overtired and unable to sleep. I was overwhelmed.

Then reality crept in. I couldn't do everything all the time. I dearly loved my husband, but I broke under the burden of caring for him.

Enter my loved ones. Each of them reached out to help in their unique way, with cards, calls, gifts, or meals. My favorite blessings were those special friends and family members who sat with Dave so I could have a few hours of "me" time.

Jesus carried His cross without complaint, until he couldn't take another step. At that point, Simon of Cyrene picked it up and carried it for Him (Matthew 27:32). All of us have crosses to bear during our faith journeys. Those challenges teach us about ourselves—our needs, our strengths, and our weaknesses.

With the help of Jesus and my loved ones who helped carry my burden, I stretched my understanding of love in the form of helping. I'm grateful to friends, family, and Jesus, who lightened my load. —HEIDI GAUL

FAITH STEP: *Consider the burdens your dear ones carry. How can you lighten their load today?*

SATURDAY, MARCH 25

At that moment Jesus himself was inspired with joy, and exclaimed,
"O Father, Lord of Heaven and earth, I thank you for hiding these things
from the clever and the intelligent and for showing them to mere children!
Yes, I thank you, Father, that this was your will." Luke 10:21 (PHILLIPS)

YESTERDAY I READ AN ARTICLE about commitment to Jesus. Afterward, I brooded. *What's wrong with me? I spend time worshipping and talking with God every morning. But most days I feel no excitement or zeal. Am I a lukewarm Christian?*

Near the end of the day, I took my feelings to the One who knows everything. Before I even finished, He sweetly reminded me of the scene in Luke 10. A group of Jesus's followers returned from a mission trip. When they reported their success to Him, Jesus praised God with joyful abandon.

I also recalled how Jesus grieved over Jerusalem (Luke 19:41), sighed over religious leaders who wanted a sign instead of relying on faith (Mark 8:12), and tossed thieves out of the temple in righteous anger (John 2:14–16). Jesus showed an array of emotions.

But my feelings are fickle. They soar on angels' wings when the sun shines and plummet when dark clouds fill the sky. I realized that my moods and emotions are unreliable barometers for my commitment to Him.

Thank goodness Jesus doesn't measure my loyalty to Him by my emotions. He sees my heart and knows how deeply I love and adore Him, despite my fickle feelings. —JEANETTE LEVELLIE

FAITH STEP: *Sing a praise song to Jesus, regardless of your current emotions.*

SUNDAY, MARCH 26

Do not be anxious about anything, but in every situation, by prayer and petition, with thanksgiving, present your requests to God. And the peace of God, which transcends all understanding, will guard your hearts and your minds in Christ Jesus. Philippians 4:6–7 (NIV)

I HAD AN INSIGHTFUL DREAM where I was riding a bike through our town of Boulder, Colorado, carrying all three of my adult sons. One was on the handlebars, and the other two were in a cart I was pulling. I was struggling to ride up a hill. I glanced at my feet, exerting all of my strength, but I was unable to pedal because of the heavy load. This dream gracefully awakened me to grasp that I still worry about my children, even though they are capable adults.

I know the boys don't want me to worry about them. And Jesus doesn't want us to be anxious about anything either. He says, "Let not your heart be troubled; you believe in God, believe also in Me" (John 14:1, NKJV). Learning to trust Jesus and actually letting go is an ongoing mom struggle for me. But awareness of my worry, such as a stressful dream, is a beginning to overcoming it.

Reading scriptures, like the one above, and practicing what it says help too. I saturate my day with prayers, overflowing with gratitude. I tell Jesus every detail of my life. I ask for His unexplainable peace and to guard my heart and mind. Basically, I get off my bike and let Jesus pedal up the hill. —JEANNIE BLACKMER

FAITH STEP: *Keep a notebook by your bed, and if you remember a dream, write it down. Then contemplate it to see what message Jesus has for you.*

MONDAY, MARCH 27

I have considered my ways and have turned my steps to your statutes. I will hasten and not delay to obey your commands. Psalm 119:59–60 (NIV)

I'VE ALWAYS LOVED VOLUNTEERING. OVER the years, I've served in a wide variety of roles at church, ranging from chairing committees to staining baseboards during a remodel and everything in between. While my kids were in school, I helped with classroom parties, listened to students read so they could earn prizes, and sat on the P.T.O. board. Looking back, I realize that whether I was lining up a cleanup crew or planning a Christmas dinner, there always seemed to be one or two certain people I could count on. Those dependable folks were always ready, willing, and able to jump in and serve wherever needed.

Matthew 26:17–19 tells about someone who jumped at a chance to serve Jesus when needed. Looking ahead to Passover, Jesus instructed Peter and John to go to "a certain man" in Jerusalem and say, "I will keep the Passover at your house with my disciples." This man received a great honor from Jesus; he played a key role in the Savior's last days. Yet he remained anonymous in Scripture. All we know is that this man owned a house with an upper room large enough to hold Jesus and His twelve disciples. And that Jesus knew the man would say "yes."

I want to be like that anonymous man. I can't think of a worthier goal than to be that "certain person" whom Jesus knows is ready, willing, and able to serve Him with my resources, time, and energy.
—DIANNE NEAL MATTHEWS

FAITH STEP: *Tell Jesus that your answer is "yes" to whatever job He has for you. Then watch for His instructions.*

TUESDAY, MARCH 28

Let your eyes look straight ahead; fix your gaze directly before you.
Proverbs 4:25 (NIV)

I HUSTLED FROM THE GREETING card shop to my car, preoccupied with the next errand I needed to run. I pressed my clicker key and heard the reassuring *beep beep,* then hopped into the front seat of my car. And onto the lap of a strange man!

Panicked, I asked, *Lord, why is this man in my car?* And I heard the Lord whisper, *Pat, this is* not *your car.*

Mortified and scared, I jumped up, apologized, and scrambled out of the car. The man could have been a murderer, a kidnapper, or at the very least, a purse snatcher, but Jesus protected me.

"I'm so sorry," I babbled. "I have a silver car, see, there it is right across from you, and all silver cars look the same to me. I'm so embarrassed. Oh, my goodness. Please forgive me, sir. This is terrible!"

As I skulked away, I stole a glance at the man who was shaking with laughter.

In 1895, American composer Clara H. Scott wrote the beloved anthem, "Open My Eyes, That I May See." Mrs. Scott, the first woman to publish a volume of anthems, based the hymn on Psalm 119:18 (NIV): "Open my eyes that I may see wonderful things in your law."

How many things have I missed because I didn't open my eyes? This world invites distractions, but I must remember to keep my eyes on Jesus.

And my car. —PAT BUTLER DYSON

FAITH STEP: *Look up the lyrics to "Open My Eyes, That I May See." Sing those words or find a recording of the song. Then practice doing it!*

WEDNESDAY, MARCH 29

When they had sung a hymn, they went out to the Mount of Olives.
Mark 14:26 (NIV)

A POPULAR TELEVISION SHOW'S ENDING segment often featured broadcaster Andy Rooney asking, "Did you ever wonder…?"

Did you ever wonder why Jesus frequently quoted Psalms? He had such a good command of God's Word that He could pull out an appropriate scripture verse for any situation. After forty days in the wilderness, Jesus then exchanged volleys of sacred texts with Satan, who misused, misapplied, and lied about what Jesus knew like the back of His soon-to-be-scarred hands (Matthew 4:1–11).

Judging from His frequent quotes from the writings of David and the other psalmists, the Book of Psalms provided comfort and wisdom for Jesus on His earth journey. He applied Psalms to His followers and the crowds listening as if they were a balm and worship with which He was well familiar.

Since they were written primarily as song lyrics, I wonder if the words resonated as music in Jesus's heart. Did He hear ancient melodies accompanying the text? Did He quote them or sing them during His earth ministry?

Partial answer. The scene in Mark 14—right between the Last Supper and Mount of Olives, which was on the way to the night of torment for Jesus in the Garden of Gethsemane—shows Jesus and His followers singing. I can't imagine He stayed silent. For all we know, Jesus might have chosen the hymn.

I don't have to wonder about the benefits the Psalms provide; I simply can read them myself. —CYNTHIA RUCHTI

FAITH STEP: *Turn to a passage from Psalms and read it as if Jesus were reading it to you. Where do you imagine He would put the emphasis?*

THURSDAY, MARCH 30

When Jesus spoke again to the people, he said, "I am the light of the world. Whoever follows me will never walk in darkness, but will have the light of life." John 8:12 (NIV)

FOR MONTHS, I PUT OFF washing the windows across the back of my house. Centered behind a flower bed in our backyard, they were hard to reach. It was much easier to ignore the layers of grime that had built up on the window screens than fight the overgrown tree limbs and bushes that blocked them. But when rumors of quarantining first echoed through the world in 2020, my windows came to mind. I couldn't be stuck at home for an extended amount of time with those dirty windows blocking the sunlight.

After an afternoon scrubbing the screens and polishing the windows with a special glass cleaner, I went inside to survey the results. I was amazed by how much brighter it was now that the light could pour in unhindered. My living room looked like a joyful, peaceful place of refuge.

The change made me realize how I needed to take the same approach in my relationship with Jesus. When I fail to clean my slate with Him, ugliness and sin build up, making it difficult for me to see how He is answering my prayers. I need to allow the light of the world to shine brightly into my life every day through prayer and Scripture. Only then will I be able to see clearly. —EMILY E. RYAN

FAITH STEP: *Give the windows in your home a good scrubbing. As the light pours in, ask Jesus to reveal His plans and provisions for you.*

FRIDAY, MARCH 31

Each one must give as he has decided in his heart, not reluctantly or under compulsion, for God loves a cheerful giver. 2 Corinthians 9:7 *(ESV)*

AT FORTY-EIGHT, I NEVER EXPECTED to be one of the youngest women in our small Bible study group, which included homeschool families. Most members were senior citizens, some in their nineties. I was also the only one in my group who brought children to the concurrent program. After taking my six kids to their classes, I usually arrived frazzled, had little to offer compared to others' insights, and hurried out afterward.

When it was announced that everyone would go to lunch the following week, I quickly declined. Taking my whole crew to a sit-down restaurant wasn't in our budget. But the elderly ladies in my group insisted. They said they wanted to meet my children so much that six of them had come up with the idea to pay for each of my kids.

I couldn't believe their generous offer! Eagerness and excitement filled their faces. Although I knew most of them were on fixed incomes, they made it seem like I was doing them a favor by allowing them to treat us.

When the day of the outing arrived, each woman beamed as she picked out a child to buy lunch for. My children and I were deeply touched. "Thank you!" my five daughters and son said. Young and old smiles lit up the room.

Some people say there are no free lunches, but I saw each of us receive a gift that day—both the happy receivers and the joyful givers. —TRICIA GOYER

FAITH STEP: *Consider one small way you can be a cheerful giver or receiver. The next time someone offers a gift, accept it with gladness.*

SATURDAY, APRIL 1

Your word is a lamp to my feet and a light to my path. Psalm 119:105 (NRSV)

THE CURVY COUNTY ROAD NARROWED as the fields of bluebonnets encroached on the blacktop, reducing it to one lane. If a car approached from the opposite direction, it couldn't possibly pass without hitting mine. Not that I'd seen another vehicle on this desolate road pitted with neglected potholes. *How in the world did I end up here? Did I take a wrong turn?*

With no cell service, I couldn't ask Siri to navigate. I considered turning back, but there was no place to turn around safely. I had no other choice but to slow down, keep driving, and enjoy the view.

Beyond acres of purple wildflowers stood grand hills covered in green foliage, topped by a bright blue sky. I saw a doe and her spotted fawn drinking from a creek as I drove across a low water bridge. The dogwoods and redbuds along the bank saluted in full splendor. A few miles farther, the road opened up. The highway I sought was ahead. I sighed with relief. I'd ended up right where I needed to be.

Finding unexpected beauty during my road trip was not unlike some spiritual journeys I've taken. Problems, misunderstandings, or neglecting my prayer life have landed me in a few desolate places, leading me to ask Jesus, "How did I get here?"

Like the surprising splendor I found along the roadway when I thought I was lost, Jesus shows me the beauty that can come when I trust Him with the twists and turns of life. —KAREN SARGENT

FAITH STEP: *Recall a time you thought you were on a road to nowhere. What beauty or blessings came out of that journey?*

PALM SUNDAY, APRIL 2

Rejoice greatly, Daughter Zion! Shout, Daughter Jerusalem! See, your king comes to you, righteous and victorious, lowly and riding on a donkey, on a colt, the foal of a donkey. Zechariah 9:9 (NIV)

KEN AND REBECCA LOVED TO surprise their friends with unexpected gifts—a pot of cheerful flowers on the front porch, a gift card to a restaurant in the mail, a basket of fresh peaches on the church pew. Just before Palm Sunday one year, they loaded blessings into their truck and began their route from house to house.

When my parents answered the knock at their door, Ken presented them with a three-foot cross made from treated pine. "Happy Easter!" he said. "Hammer this into the ground at the end of your driveway."

Rebecca handed them three sashes: one purple, one black, and one white. "Drape the purple one on the cross on Palm Sunday," she said. "Purple stands for royalty and for King Jesus riding into Jerusalem on a donkey. On Good Friday, change it to the black sash to represent Jesus's death. Then on Easter Sunday, drape the white cloth on the cross to celebrate the resurrection."

Though years have passed and Ken is now in heaven, my family continues the touching tradition of the draped cross. Easter after Easter, the special gift portrays the story of King Jesus to passersby. It also provides a creative tool for us to teach our children and grandchildren about the resurrection. Ken and Rebecca's example of giving challenges me to surprise others with kindness, especially in ways that proclaim Jesus to the world. —BECKY ALEXANDER

FAITH STEP: *Give a friend an unexpected goodie basket. Include simple items that are purple, black, and white. Add a card that explains the significance of the colors.*

MONDAY, APRIL 3

After this I looked, and behold, a great multitude that no one could number, from every nation, from all tribes and peoples and languages, standing before the throne and before the Lamb... Revelation 7:9 (ESV)

AFTER LIVING IN A RATHER tiny bubble as a work-at-home mom for many years, my stint as a public high school teacher dramatically broadened my appreciation of diversity. I've always considered myself a cosmopolitan people person, but the variety of individuals I met while teaching humbled me.

My classes had students of multiple nationalities, including those who didn't speak English at all. Many had family backgrounds, life experiences, economics, and spiritual traditions that were dramatically different from mine. Personalities, skills, talents, and academic orientation covered the gamut. Highly motivated to help them, I sought to understand the teens in order to connect with them as individuals and to teach each one as best I could.

It was very difficult work for many reasons, and I leaned heavily on Jesus, praying a lot through the day. Jesus whispered for me to love and value each student as a unique creation made in His image. He challenged some stereotypes I didn't even know I had, and He enabled me to outgrow some limiting beliefs by teaching me that all people were uniquely gifted and different by design.

Jesus used my teaching job to school me to see all people as He sees them, as God created them: equal and equally loved, no matter what color, nationality, gender, or behavior. The more I opened my mind and heart and relied on Jesus, the bigger my bubble became. —ISABELLA CAMPOLATTARO

FAITH STEP: *Ask God to help you see the diversity of His kingdom with an open mind and heart. Try connecting with a person outside your normal social sphere.*

TUESDAY, APRIL 4

Then he said, "Jesus, remember me when you come into your kingdom."
Jesus answered him, "Truly I tell you, today you will be with me in paradise."
Luke 23:42–43 (NIV)

I FOLDED THE PAPER THIS way and that as I taught the Easter lesson. "The thief on one side of Jesus yelled at Him. The thief on the other side believed in Jesus and asked for His help." The kids stared while I folded the paper two more times. "Jesus showed kindness to the man who asked and said he would go to heaven that very day!" I slowly tore the folded paper from bottom to top. With unusual focus, the kids watched me unfold the pieces to reveal a paper cross.

An ordinary paper and a simple Bible story introduced the kids to the grace of Jesus. The surprise on their faces duplicated my own the first time I saw the paper cross.

Try it yourself with a sheet of paper and four folds. Fold the top left corner to the right edge of the paper, about three-fourths of the way down. Fold the top right corner to the left edge the same way. It will look like a house with a pointed roof. Fold the "house" in half, right to left, and then fold it in half again, left to right. Tear or cut the paper up the middle from bottom to top. Unfold the pieces to find your cross.

Just as the torn paper cross surprised the children, Jesus, no doubt, surprised the dying thief on the cross beside Him by offering His unmerited grace. Likewise, Jesus's grace toward all of us never ceases to surprise me. —BECKY ALEXANDER

FAITH STEP: *Talk about Jesus's grace while teaching someone how to fold and tear a paper cross.*

WEDNESDAY, APRIL 5

Praise be to the God and Father of our Lord Jesus Christ, the Father of compassion and the God of all comfort. . . . For just as we share abundantly in the sufferings of Christ, so also our comfort abounds through Christ.
2 Corinthians 1:3, 5 (NIV)

"MR. SELBY, YOU CAN'T TAKE that into the operating room. You'll have to leave it with your wife," the nurse said.

My dad tightened his grip around the tiny metal cross in his right hand. "Then I won't have surgery," he stated. The cross was a gift from my daughter to her papaw, engraved with the words "God loves you." He had found great comfort by carrying it into multiple surgeries.

"But you know you really need this heart stent," the nurse pleaded.

"Nope. Not without my cross." Eventually, the nurse gave in, and the staff wheeled him down the hall, cross in hand. Dad had endured so many procedures that I'd lost count. Each time, in the pre-surgery room, he joked and laughed and acted confident. But I realized he had to be afraid. Outcomes were always uncertain, and recoveries were often painful. I think holding the metal cross reassured him that he wouldn't be alone during the operation. The Father of compassion and the God of all comfort (2 Corinthians 1:3) would stay by his side, guiding the doctors and protecting my dad's life.

Clutching the cross brings me comfort and courage in moments of dread and fear, whether it is a physical cross or the knowledge of the cross of Jesus. It reassures me that God is everywhere, at all times, and through all scary experiences. —BECKY ALEXANDER

FAITH STEP: *Make or purchase a cross of any material (2 inches tall by 1 inch wide). Squeeze it tightly, as needed.*

MAUNDY THURSDAY, APRIL 6

And behold, there was a great earthquake; for an angel of the Lord descended from heaven, and came and rolled back the stone from the door, and sat on it. Matthew 28:2 (NKJV)

I HANDED MY FIVE-YEAR-OLD GRANDDAUGHTER, Sadie, a pretty cross, crocheted from threads of yellow, blue, green, and pink.

"My friend Kathie made Bible bookmarks for us," I explained. Picking up her children's Bible, I located the picture of Jesus on the cross and began: "Jesus died on the cross. Everyone who loved Him felt sad. But they forgot something important. Jesus had said He would see them again soon." I placed Sadie's crocheted cross between the pages and closed the book.

"Wait, wait, wait!" she exclaimed. "Read more."

I smiled, found the bookmark, and continued. "Jesus's friends sealed His tomb shut with a big round stone. Three days later, an angel of the Lord came down from heaven and pushed that stone away."

Sadie used to beg me to read tales of a talking pig family or a princess with long hair, locked away in a tower. I told her we should always read the Bible first. Now, she loves the stories inside its cover.

Sadie's excitement for the Easter story challenges me. I don't enjoy stories of talking animals or princesses, but I want to make sure I read the Bible first too. My crocheted cross bookmark keeps me on the right page in my Bible and places a reminder in my soul too. —BECKY ALEXANDER

FAITH STEP: *For a fresh and simple view, read the crucifixion and resurrection accounts in a Bible story book or a children's Bible (Matthew 26–28, Mark 14–16, Luke 22–24, John 18–20).*

GOOD FRIDAY, APRIL 7

Let your eyes look straight ahead; fix your gaze directly before you.
Give careful thought to the paths for your feet and be steadfast in all
your ways. Do not turn to the right or the left; keep your foot from evil.
Proverbs 4:25–27 (NIV)

I WALKED ALONG A PAVED nature trail under towering trees. Suddenly, the ground seemed to rush upward, and I fell. I'd recently had some moments of weird dizziness, but that fall from an unexpected flash of vertigo sent me to vestibular training for balance. I learned a few techniques to use when I have a sense of being unbalanced. The two most helpful are to plant the soles of my feet firmly down as I walk and to keep my eyes on a focal point straight ahead.

Those tips work in a spiritual sense too. Jesus calls me to walk on a narrow path, keeping my feet planted firmly and my eyes fixed on Him. John 1:14 describes Jesus as being full of grace and truth. He spoke hard truths to those who needed to hear, but He also never hesitated to offer grace and mercy. After refusing to condemn the woman caught in adultery, He instructed her to stop sinning (John 8:3–11).

If I focus solely on the doctrine and instructions in the scriptures, I'll probably lean toward legalism and rule following. If I emphasize mercy and compassion while ignoring biblical standards, I can fall into behavior that's destructive and displeasing to Christ. The best way to keep my equilibrium in life is to imitate Jesus, by balancing truth and grace together. —DIANNE NEAL MATTHEWS

FAITH STEP: *Search the Gospels for other examples of how Jesus displayed a balance of truth and grace. Ask Him to help you do the same.*

SATURDAY, APRIL 8

As Jesus was walking beside the Sea of Galilee, he saw two brothers, Simon called Peter and his brother Andrew. They were casting a net into the lake, for they were fishermen. "Come, follow me," Jesus said, "and I will send you out to fish for people." At once they left their nets and followed him.
Matthew 4:18–20 (NIV)

"WHICH FLAG BELONGS TO YOUR state, Becky?" a guest on my Kennedy Center tour asked.

"The least creative one in the entire Hall of States," I said, pointing at the Alabama flag hanging from the ceiling. The plain red *X* on a solid white background seemed dull to me. I preferred the yellow and red sunset rays on the Arizona flag or the white magnolia blossom above "In God We Trust" on the Mississippi flag, or the farmer, covered wagons, and riverboat on the Kansas flag.

A bit of research into the meaning of my state flag, however, changed my opinion. The *X* represented a Christian symbol known as the "Cross of Saint Andrew." Andrew was one of the first disciples called by Jesus. He heard Jesus teach in person, participated in His miracles, and witnessed His crucifixion and resurrection. Historians believe Andrew remained a committed follower and was himself crucified, in a manner resembling an *X*.

Now, when I look at the Alabama flag, I don't see it as dull at all. I see a plain cross that testifies of my Savior to the nation. And Andrew's story challenges me to live out my days, serving Jesus, faithful to the end. —BECKY ALEXANDER

FAITH STEP: *Andrew played a special role in one of Jesus's miracles. Read about it in John 6:1–13. Write how he might have felt at the end of Verse 13.*

EASTER SUNDAY, APRIL 9

. . . But where sin increased, grace increased all the more, so that, just as sin reigned in death, so also grace might reign through righteousness to bring eternal life through Jesus Christ our Lord. Romans 5:20–21 (NIV)

OUR EASTER SHOPPING LIST INCLUDED a ten-foot-long board, nails, a roll of chicken-wire fencing, a staple gun, and several baskets of cut flowers. My husband sawed and hammered to create a simple wooden cross and then stapled fencing over each part. Not a pretty sight but exactly what we needed for our church service.

Families arrived on Sunday morning wearing yellows and blues, bonnets and ties, sandals and shiny shoes. As they entered the worship center, the ugly cross at the front caught their attention. With wide eyes, kids pointed and asked, "What's that?" Adults did their best to explain, though they weren't sure themselves.

The pastor began, "The cross once symbolized sin and death. But because of Jesus's resurrection, the cross now symbolizes grace and eternal life. Join me as we change this ugly cross into something beautiful. Today, we celebrate our risen Savior!"

Family by family, we chose blooms from the baskets at the foot of the cross and tucked them through the openings in the wire. After the last child added his flower, not an inch of wood could be seen, only daisies, roses, orchids, and lilies.

Often, I think about my bad choices and past mistakes, and I feel more like staples and nails than daisies and lilies. That's when I have to remember the great price Jesus paid on the cross for our sins. We are forgiven, and we are beautiful because of His grace.
—BECKY ALEXANDER

FAITH STEP: *Sketch a cross with a flower on it. Place it somewhere as a reminder of Jesus's grace.*

MONDAY, APRIL 10

. . . If you enter your place of worship and, about to make an offering, you suddenly remember a grudge a friend has against you, abandon your offering, leave immediately, go to this friend and make things right. Then and only then, come back and work things out with God. Matthew 5:23–24 (MSG)

LAST NIGHT, I MADE A mistake while knitting a silk and wool hat in a complicated pattern. The directions had a multicolor symbol chart with arrows to show the direction of each row, which I desperately needed.

When I stopped for the night, I counted my stitches and came up with 23 instead of 24. Somewhere along the way, I'd dropped a stitch. I couldn't find the error and threw my work down in frustration.

My scheduled Bible reading resonated with my knitting situation. Jesus gave his Jewish listeners unexpected advice when He told them to go back and make things right with anyone they'd offended before presenting their offering at the temple. Some of these people would have been holding a lamb or leading livestock. Their baked offerings would be ruined after having to retrace their steps, but it was still necessary.

I knew I needed to rip out many stitches on the hat and start again from the place where I messed up. I didn't want to rip out my work, but I realized that if it was ever going to be made right, I had to go back.

In the end, going back to fix the hat allowed it to become something beautiful, rather than something forever flawed.
—SUZANNE DAVENPORT TIETJEN

FAITH STEP: *Ask Jesus to show you a situation you need to go back to and make right. Be willing to make amends to another, if necessary.*

TUESDAY, APRIL 11

"One thing I do know. I was blind but now I see!" John 9:25b (NIV)

JUDSON STUDIED EACH WORD BEFORE slowly pronouncing it out loud. "Should I sip a fizzy soda through a curvy, crazy straw?"

"Good, Judson," I said. "Keep going." I tutored the blond-haired second-grader on Tuesdays after school. He tried hard, and his family helped him, but he still struggled to read.

"Or munch a sour pickle sure to pucker up my jaw?" He rubbed his eyes and sat back in his chair, frustrated and exhausted.

Judson's poor grades in all subjects puzzled his teacher. He was bright and articulate in conversation. Might he have a vision problem? The teacher contacted his parents, and a visit to the optometrist confirmed it—Judson needed glasses. Immediately, he flourished in his schoolwork and, after a short period of time, no longer required my assistance. To show his gratitude, Judson gave me a colorful cross painted with inspiring words: hope, believe, love, faith, trust; the word grace adorned the foot of it. Today, the painted cross sits on my fireplace mantel.

The man in John 9 couldn't see either…until he met Jesus. Jesus spat on the ground, mixed some mud, and spread it over the blind man's eyes. As the man washed the mud away, a view of the world appeared for the first time ever! When we accept Jesus's offer of grace and salvation, our vision changes too. What once seemed blurry and dark becomes clear and vivid. We can truly say, "I was blind but now I see!" —BECKY ALEXANDER

FAITH STEP: *In your journal, draw the outline of a cross. Color or paint words on it that inspire you.*

WEDNESDAY, APRIL 12

Teach them his decrees and instructions, and show them the way they are to live and how they are to behave. Exodus 18:20 (NIV)

MY HUSBAND RECENTLY BOUGHT THE truck of his dreams. It has all the bells and whistles—heated seats (with a massage feature), satellite radio, sensors that assist with parking, a premium sound system, and rain-sensing windshield wipers. There are so many fancy features that even now, months later, Hal still doesn't know how more than half of them work.

"Yeah, I gotta read the manual to figure that out," Hal often says while we're driving, after I ask why an icon on the digital dashboard lights up. I frequently remind him that he's missing out on enjoying a lot of the great benefits the truck has to offer.

I have to say that I'm guilty of the same. Sometimes I miss taking advantage of all the benefits in the most important manual of them all—the Bible. If I read the Word quickly and fail to meditate upon it, I can easily overlook a key message or instructions that Jesus has just for me. But when I take the time not only to read but also to ponder and listen for Jesus's voice, I ride through my day much smoother.

Just like the fancy features of Hal's truck make his driving experience better, my life experience is better when I allow Jesus and His Holy Manual to drive me. —BARBRANDA LUMPKINS WALLS

FAITH STEP: *Pick a passage of Scripture to read today. Pause and ponder. What is Jesus revealing to you through it?*

THURSDAY, APRIL 13

"Truly, I say to you, whoever does not receive the kingdom of God like a child shall not enter it." And he took them in his arms and blessed them, laying his hands on them. Mark 10:15–16 (ESV)

MY YOUNGEST DAUGHTER ASKED HER dad and me to consider living with her family to lend a helping hand when she developed complications with her second pregnancy. We were happy to say yes, especially because this gave us an opportunity to be more involved with our two-year-old granddaughter's care for three months.

Building a stronger relationship with little Lexi brought immeasurable joy. During our stay, we saw her motor skills develop and independence grow. She learned to express her desires and dislikes. She began talking in eight-word sentences. At the same time, she remained dependent for pretty much everything. She needed us to bathe and dress her, provide her meals and snacks, take her outdoors, oversee her safety, and tuck her in bed. We read stories to her, kissed her "owies," and comforted her when she cried.

People in Jesus's day considered children a nuisance. Jesus taught otherwise. When others shooed little ones away, He invited them into His arms and blessed them. Small, weak, and empty-handed they came, and He embraced them.

Jesus does the same for us, no matter what our age. He invites us into a relationship even though we bring nothing to offer but ourselves and our neediness. We come small, weak, and empty-handed, but He never shoos us away. Like my husband and I were happy to spend time helping with Lexi, Jesus delights in us. —GRACE FOX

FAITH STEP: *Read Ephesians 1:5 and meditate on the truth that adopting you into His family brings Jesus great pleasure.*

FRIDAY, APRIL 14

"Today, if you hear his voice, do not harden your hearts..."
Hebrews 3:15a (NIV)

PAM, ONE OF MY BEST friends, is a personal trainer. When I pulled a muscle in my back recently, I asked her to teach me some stretches that could help strengthen the area. As she showed me different moves, she emphasized the need to lean into each stretch for at least thirty seconds.

Apparently, muscles have a defensive reflex for protection. When engaged, they automatically tighten as a way to avoid being stretched too far. Pam told me I needed to remain in each position, waiting for the reflex to let go. After that is when the change occurs and the muscle extends.

I have a defensive reflex when I read my Bible. I automatically think of someone else who could benefit from that day's message. It's my way of avoiding any self-introspection and the possibility I'll discover a change I need to make. In my deflecting, I can even go as far as snapping a photo of the scripture and texting it to whomever I feel needs to be inspired. If I end my prayer time there, however, I'll never really stretch my own spiritual muscles.

It takes a lot of discipline, but when I lean into the passage, beyond my reflex to let it go, I stretch my own spiritual muscles to better hear what Jesus has to say. There are times His instruction extends me further than my comfort, but like a personal trainer, my Spiritual Trainer provides the exercises I need to get stronger. —CLAIRE MCGARRY

FAITH STEP: *Challenge yourself to remain in a Scripture passage for as long as possible. When you're inclined to walk away, stay and lean into the lesson, listening for Jesus's personal training instructions for you.*

SATURDAY, APRIL 15

To this end I labor, struggling with all his energy, which so powerfully works in me. Colossians 1:29 (NIV84)

I GROANED AS I LOOKED at my watch and saw that the hands had not moved. Having a solar-powered timepiece had been great—for two years. No need to ever change the battery and nothing special to do to ensure that the watch absorbed enough light. Then, suddenly, it became unreliable. After a couple of weeks, I left it in a sunny window all afternoon and reset it. Success! I put it back in my jewelry box, but the next morning it wasn't working again.

The warranty had expired and repairs would likely be too expensive, so I got ready to throw the watch away. As a last resort, I retrieved the little booklet that still sat in the box. Then I read this warning: *The watch will be adversely affected by strong magnetism. Keep it away from close contact with magnetic objects.* I'd recently stored magnetic scarf clips in the jewelry tray—in the same section where I kept the watch. I removed the magnets, and my wristwatch kept perfect time again.

Naturally, I was thrilled to discover what had caused my watch to malfunction, but I began to sense a deeper lesson. Some days I don't function so well as a Christ follower. I let the magnetic pull of the world's pleasures and pains weaken my devotion and obedience. Or I seek help from sources other than the power the Son has made available. Now, whenever I check the time, I remind myself to live every minute *for* Him and *through* His power. —DIANNE NEAL MATTHEWS

FAITH STEP: *Ask Jesus to reveal anything in your life that's drawing you away from living fully in the power of His indwelling presence.*

SUNDAY, APRIL 16

Humble yourselves, therefore, under God's mighty hand,
that he may lift you up in due time. 1 Peter 5:6 (NIV)

MANY YEARS AGO, A GAME show treated women as "Queen for a Day." The winner was lauded with a royal robe, a bouquet of roses, and many prizes.

While the fantasy of sitting on a throne with treasures at my feet might be fun, Jesus challenges me to chase a very different path. He is the King of Kings. Yet He set aside His throne and crown to become fully human, to ride into Jerusalem on a lowly donkey, to suffer and die for my sake.

The righteous and victorious Son of God could have ridden on a fiery horse surrounded by thousands of glowing angels. Yet He chose humility—from His birth in tiny Bethlehem to His ministry among the poor and outcast to His entry into Jerusalem.

I confess that I'd rather be "Queen for a Day" than a humble servant. When someone slides ahead of me when I'm in line at the store, my impulse is to assert my rights. When a friend shares a story, my mind races to barge in with my even more interesting tale. I'd rather let someone else clean the dish drain, replace a roll of toilet paper, or peel the potatoes for dinner. But since I long to become more like Christ, I'm learning that if I practice a path of humility and service in small ways, His grace can change my heart. —SHARON HINCK

FAITH STEP: *Think of humble tasks you can do for others. As you do them, thank Jesus for being a King who shows us how to embrace being a servant.*

MONDAY, APRIL 17

Who can find a truly excellent woman? One who is superior in all that she is and all that she does? Her worth far exceeds that of rubies and expensive jewelry. Proverbs 31:10 (VOICE)

I USED TO HATE THE lady described in Proverbs as "an excellent woman." Well, not really hate her, but all of her noble endeavors intimidated me. Any woman who rises before the sun, buys a field and plants a vineyard, helps the poor, sews her own clothes, and always honors the Lord is too perfect. How could I measure up?

When I complained to my pastor/husband, Kevin, about that perfect lady, he enlightened me. "These are her accomplishments over a lifetime," he explained.

Aha. Kevin's insight made me feel better. And when I read how Jesus treated women, I feel a lot better.

In an era when females weren't considered valuable, Jesus gave them dignity and significance. Instead of shaming the unclean woman who touched the hem of His robe to receive healing, Jesus spoke kindly to her, even calling her "daughter" (Mark 5:25–34). Jesus commended the mother who begged Him to heal her tormented child, saying, "You have great faith! Your request is granted" (Matthew 15:21–28, NIV). And the woman caught in adultery? Jesus told her, "Neither do I condemn you; go and sin no more" (John 8:3–11, NKJV).

Throughout His life, Jesus showed His esteem and love for women. I'm relieved and overjoyed that when I come to Him, I needn't bring a long list of accomplishments. He loves me for who I am, and that makes me feel excellent! —JEANETTE LEVELLIE

FAITH STEP: *Thank Jesus that in His eyes you are valuable, capable, and loved, not just for your accomplishments but for who you are.*

TUESDAY, APRIL 18

"Can a mother forget the baby at her breast and have no compassion on the child she has borne? Though she may forget, I will not forget you! See, I have engraved you on the palms of my hands; your walls are ever before me." Isaiah 49:15–16 (NIV)

I FOUND A HILARIOUS PICTURE online the other day. A mom, trying to get things done, had tucked her six-month-old baby inside her shorts. The baby looked completely content as its feet dangled through each of the mom's leg openings. I texted the photo to my nieces, Aly and Claire, who have babies. In response, they sent me selfies of their own. Claire gripped the back waistband of her yoga pants, while her son was secure in front of her. Aly's daughter fit perfectly inside the front of her shorts. Both babies were snuggled next to their moms, completely at ease and trusting, despite not having a clue what was going on. Being close is what moms and babies are all about.

Being close is what Jesus is all about too. Sometimes when life is stressful, I don't know what's going on. I don't know if Jesus is still near. I can't feel His presence, hear His voice, or see Him working. I wonder if He has forgotten me. But Jesus loves me more than a mother loves her child. He won't forget me. My name is engraved on the palms of His hands. He is with me no matter what I'm doing, where I go, and even when I don't have a clue what is going on. —SUSANNA FOTH AUGHTMON

FAITH STEP: *Write the scripture reference Isaiah 49:15–16 on the palm of your hand today as a reminder that Jesus has not forgotten you. He is always with you.*

WEDNESDAY, APRIL 19

A joyful heart is good medicine, but a broken spirit dries up the bones.
Proverbs 17:22 (NASB)

MORNING SUNSHINE STREAMED THROUGH THE entry window. I squinted and yawned and headed for the kitchen and the coffee maker. Some people wake up perky. Not me.

Even though I wasn't all in for the day yet, those sunbeams shined with hope. It was the first morning in several when my cold symptoms weren't dragging me down. Carrying a steaming mug to the front porch, I sank onto an Adirondack chair and drank in the warmth of the sun and the brew.

Thank You, Jesus. I'm making it a priority to reacquaint myself with simple pleasures—namely, the pursuit of joy. Every moment has potential for joy, and I'm determined to find all the happiness I can.

Jesus didn't let happy times pass Him by either. In fact, it's easy to envision Jesus enjoying a great party. Luke 7:34 states that the Son of Man came eating and drinking, which sounds to me like someone who enjoyed life and everyday pleasures.

I gazed into our yard and drank it all in as I sipped my steaming brew with flavored creamer—a gentle breeze, birds singing in the trees, squirrels scurrying, flowers in bloom, sidewalks for meandering, bike paths for exploring, and my cold symptoms subsiding.

I finished my coffee and smiled. My body inched toward healing as my heart expanded with happiness over an ordinary day. Finding joy really is medicinal. —ERIN KEELEY MARSHALL

FAITH STEP: *What are some of your favorite simple joys? Write them on a sheet of paper and list ways they are good medicine for your heart.*

THURSDAY, APRIL 20

". . . first take the plank out of your own eye, and then you will see clearly to remove the speck from your brother's eye." Matthew 7:5 (NIV)

I'VE BEEN BLESSED TO NEVER have had any known enemies. Sure, there have been people over the years that I've disagreed with or didn't click with. Nonetheless, I always treated each one with respect. I believe that we should love and pray for our enemies.

Right now, as a troubling divide continues to widen in our country, I find myself labeling "the other side" my "enemy." I bring those on the other side into my prayer time, pleading with Jesus to do whatever is necessary to change their hearts to draw our world back to Him.

But one day as I sat at Jesus's feet, He revealed that when I use the words "us" and "them," *I* am feeding the divide. Such terms assume one side is right and the other is wrong. Each time I succumb to that kind of divisive thinking, pitting people against one another, the plank in my eye grows bigger.

As a carpenter, Jesus knows a thing or two about splinters. To remove them, we need clear vision. He's helped me see that it's not just the speck in the eyes of others that are splintering our country but also the plank of malice in mine. First, I need to remove the obstacle that prevents me from seeing with open eyes and heart. Then I can pray for Jesus to remove the speck from the eyes of others. With clear vision and clean hearts, together—with Jesus as our guide—we can bridge the divides that separate us. —CLAIRE MCGARRY

FAITH STEP: *During the next conflict you experience, examine your own heart for any plank that needs to be removed.*

FRIDAY, APRIL 21

Words from the mouth of the wise are gracious, but fools are consumed by their own lips. Ecclesiastes 10:12 (NIV)

I COULDN'T BELIEVE MY EYES as I read the comment on a social media post. An acquaintance was extremely upset by something she thought I'd said. Clicking on the original post, I released the breath I'd been holding.

Another woman with my name had said harsh words, and I'd been tagged by mistake. It hurt my heart to see the abrasive things the other Tricia had said. I quickly untagged myself and said a prayer for the situation.

With social media, it's easy for me to hide behind a screen and spout whatever is on my mind or place blame, whether warranted or not, on others. But the Bible states that true wisdom is considering our words and caring for the person or people who are listening.

Before I post, I like to ask myself if I'm saying the right thing, to the right person, at the right time. Can my words hurt and offend others? Will my words draw others toward me and my faith in Jesus or will my comments push them away?

Some people will be offended by anything I say, but speaking, writing, or posting with wisdom and grace goes a long way in bringing unity instead of division online and in real life too. —TRICIA GOYER

FAITH STEP: *Before you post a comment on social media, pause and pray. Make sure your words are gracious and wise.*

SATURDAY, APRIL 22

Unless the LORD builds the house, the builders labor in vain. Unless the LORD watches over the city, the guards stand watch in vain. Psalm 127:1 (NIV)

IN SOME RESPECTS, I'VE LIVED like an atheist for much of my Christian life. Wait! Before you wonder if I'm a spiritual impostor, hear me out. You see, despite my love for Jesus, I acted as though everything that happened—or didn't happen in my life—depended on me. What's worse, despite all my Bible reading, prayer, and praises, I thought I could somehow manipulate the events in my life by my own effort. That's not grace. That's not faith. That's the world's way. My way.

The Bible tells me plainly that apart from Jesus, I can do nothing (John 15:5). Yet, I had this idea that I had to make all the best decisions to ensure the right outcomes, as though I could even determine what the right outcome was in the first place. If what happened was not what I wanted or expected, I'd assume I'd failed or sinned, and it was all my fault.

After making the mistake of leaving Jesus out of certain parts of my life, I've come to the conclusion that I now embrace and believe wholeheartedly. Jesus *really is* entirely sufficient (2 Corinthians 12:9). He pours out His grace in the everyday way I so desperately need, especially on those days when I think I can do it myself and try to live like an atheist. —ISABELLA CAMPOLATTARO

FAITH STEP: *Look up the definition of an atheist in the dictionary. Consider whether you are counting on your wisdom, effort, or good judgment in dealing with a particular issue or if you are depending on Jesus.*

SUNDAY, APRIL 23

Just as a body, though one, has many parts, but all its many parts form one body, so it is with Christ. 1 Corinthians 12:12 (NIV)

MY OLDEST SON, GIDEON, BEGAN playing cello in sixth grade and was often required to play "living room concerts" for us in order to prepare for school performances. During his last living room concert of junior high school, he put his bow in his lap midway through his second song and stared at his sheet music for an uncomfortable amount of time. "I have eight measures of rests right now," he finally explained. "Just pretend you can hear the other instruments playing."

Later that week, when I heard him perform the same composition with the full school orchestra, it was an entirely different experience, completely devoid of any awkward moments. This time, I barely noticed when his cello went silent because the music continued with violins, violas, and basses. As each musician followed the conductor, what would have been individual sounds combined together into a beautiful melody.

It made me think about how Jesus creates each of us with special gifts and abilities for the specific purpose of serving Him. In my quest to serve Jesus with all my heart, I sometimes forget that I was never meant to serve Him in isolation or to meet every need myself. Instead, I am part of a greater body of believers, with each of us serving Jesus according to His perfect timing for our lives. When I follow Jesus like a musician follows a conductor, even my time of rest contributes to the greater song of His glory. —EMILY E. RYAN

FAITH STEP: *What gifts has Jesus given you to serve Him? Ask Him if now is a time for rest or action.*

MONDAY, APRIL 24

For I will restore health to you, and your wounds I will heal, says the Lord, because they have called you an outcast: "It is Zion; no one cares for her!"
Jeremiah 30:17 (NRSV)

MY HUSBAND, HAL, IS VERY particular about his coffee mugs. He says coffee just doesn't taste as good unless it's in the right cup. His favorite mug is one he received as a gift from the diaconate ministry with the words, "Serving with the joy of Jesus" on one side.

So when Hal broke that mug, I expected him to have a moment of anguish, then proceed to throw away the pieces, select another cup, and move on. That's what I would have done.

Imagine my surprise the next day when I opened the kitchen cabinet. There was the coffee mug! Hal had used Super Glue to repair the handle, which had broken into three pieces. The cup wasn't as perfect, but it was still functional. Hal continued to use it and enjoyed his morning brew from his (still) favorite cup.

It's a good thing that Jesus doesn't cast me aside or throw me away when I'm broken. Every time I look at that less-than-perfect mug, I'm reminded that even in my brokenness I still have purpose. Jesus saved me through the great sacrifice of His life and gave me a chance to live and fulfill my purpose. He always picks up my broken pieces and puts them back together so that I can keep serving Him and others, despite my brokenness and flaws. You might say Jesus is my Super Glue. —BARBRANDA LUMPKINS WALLS

FAITH STEP: *Who can be encouraged by your story of brokenness? Tell that person how Jesus saved you and repaired the broken pieces of your life. Remind them that no matter how broken, they are worth saving.*

TUESDAY, APRIL 25

Then he showed me the river of the water of life . . . flowing from the throne of God and of the Lamb down the middle of the city's main street. . . .
Revelation 22:1–2 (CSB)

FOR WEEKS, MY HOUSE RATTLED as thunderous heavy equipment dug up our street. The hundred-year-old water main had become so badly perforated with leaks that the ancient pipe was beyond repair. We were finally getting a much-needed new water main.

My little town has no shortage of water. A prominent river flows through it, while a network of creeks, natural springs, and underground streams weave their way throughout town. In opposition to this abundance of fresh water, I'm contemplating how to dramatically reduce and limit our usage. Not only is conserving water a responsible practice, but also my husband and I are planning on doing some off-grid camping—aka boondocking—where we won't be connected to a municipal water supply.

Contemplating water usage, my thoughts naturally turn toward Jesus and the contrast between physical water and the Living Water He provides. One is finite. The other is infinite. It's possible for physical water to be in short supply, causing me to want to conserve or economize my usage. During those times, I'd be reluctant to use more than a quick sprinkle of water for washing hands or dishes. But Jesus is never in short supply. He's unlimited. Jesus invites us to immerse ourselves in and soak up the Living Water He provides.

It's reassuring to me that when it comes to Jesus, there's no need for conservation. Rather, He calls us to be saturated with the free-flowing, abundant Water of Life. —CASSANDRA TIERSMA

FAITH STEP: *Pour yourself a glass of water. While drinking it, envision being saturated with Jesus, the Living Water.*

WEDNESDAY, APRIL 26

I sought the Lord, and he answered me; he delivered me from all my fears.
Psalm 34:4 (NIV)

MY TWO-YEAR-OLD GRANDDAUGHTER, LEXI, IS frightened by loud noises. We dare not turn on the kitchen blender or use the coffee grinder without warning her first. We can't use the vacuum cleaner when she's in the room. When someone mows the lawn, she needs to stay inside.

Lexi recently noticed the sound of the furnace running. She wondered what was making that sound, so I carried her into the utility room.

"This is the noisemaker. It's called a furnace," I said softly.

Her grip on me tightened, but she didn't cry, so I pointed out the washing machine and dryer and explained how helpful they were to her mommy. Then she saw the vacuum cleaner parked against the wall. Her body stiffened.

"Go out," she said, pointing toward the door. "Make me feel better." I comforted her, hugging her tight.

Children aren't the only ones who struggle with fear. Before Jesus died, He told His disciples not to be troubled or afraid (John 14:1). He promised to send the Holy Spirit to be with them. He also promised to leave them with a gift—peace of mind and heart (John 14:26–27).

His words hold true for us today. Just as I comforted Lexi over her irrational fears, Jesus comforts me when I feel afraid. Whether my fears are rational or justified, He hugs me tight. —GRACE FOX

FAITH STEP: *What are you afraid of? Complete this sentence: "Because Jesus is with me, I will no longer fear _____."*

THURSDAY, APRIL 27

I will praise the Lord, who counsels me; even at night my heart instructs me. Psalm 16:7 (NIV)

TEACHING A TEEN TO DRIVE may be the reason ibuprofen was invented. Each teen driver in our family brought his or her own set of curiosities to the process. One feared nothing. One feared everything. One was a natural. Six were not.

The most recent new driver in the family "invited" me to ride with her as she logged hours behind the wheel. She prefaced the invitation with, "I don't like anyone trying to teach me something while I drive. Don't give me instructions unless someone's life is in danger, okay?"

She might have meant it sincerely, but as I climbed into the passenger seat, my conclusion was that my life probably would be in danger at some point during our drive.

How can an inexperienced driver learn without instruction? She'd read the manual. I guess she thought that qualified her as an expert behind the wheel. Maybe she thought she merely needed an adult to witness her driving and not an experienced authority to guide and help her get better.

And then I gulped. Have I ever treated Jesus like that? Have I assumed that because I frequently glance at the Bible, the manual, I don't need His help? That I can take it from here? Have I acted as if I am perfectly capable of navigating the roadways of life without the voice of Jesus in my ear telling me to slow down, speed up, swerve, brake, pull over?

A song comes to mind: "I Need Thee Every Hour." And I'm not ashamed to admit that I do, especially while riding with a teen driver. —CYNTHIA RUCHTI

FAITH STEP: *Consider this prayer for your day: Jesus, I'm awaiting Your instructions. Amen.*

FRIDAY, APRIL 28

O LORD, make me know my end and what is the measure of my days;
let me know how fleeting I am! Psalm 39:4 (ESV)

MY HUSBAND AND I ENJOY avocados. But catching the opportune chance to enjoy them is an ongoing challenge. When we buy them, they're hard and unripe. Each morning, we expectantly and gently squeeze every one to see which, if any, are ready to eat.

But no matter how diligent I am, sometimes I miss that optimum moment, and an avocado becomes too soft. When I cut it open, the fruit is smudged with bitter gray.

Their brief window of perfection makes me think of my life. I have limited days to serve Jesus here on earth, but distractions cause me to forget that truth. I get busy with work, worries, or projects that consume my thoughts, time, and energy. When I'm too preoccupied, I can miss ripe opportunities to be Jesus's hands and feet to a hurting world.

Just as avocados ripen at different moments, all believers are equipped with various skills and abilities throughout their lives. In different seasons, one might be a student, a teacher, or a preacher. We all go through many changes as we grow into the people Jesus created us to be.

The Psalmist writes that our time on earth is fleeting. That encourages me to ask Jesus where He wants me to serve today and to be alert to His guidance. The way Jesus helps each of us to ripen is never the same, but the goal is—to provide fruit by sharing the tasty truth that Jesus's love is always in season. —SHARON HINCK

FAITH STEP: *With a notebook in hand, ask Jesus to reveal ways you can use this valuable day to serve Him.*

SATURDAY, APRIL 29

. . . deliver us from evil. . . . Matthew 6:13 (KJV)

I'M CONTENT WITH ALMOST ALL of the words Jesus used when instructing His disciples how to pray. Apparently, like many of us, they had been uncertain they were doing it right. Jesus countered that one's heart, attitude, and approach needed to be right, rather than specific words (Matthew 6:5–8). I appreciate the "hallowed be thy name" part and the "thy kingdom come, thy will be done" portion of the Lord's Prayer. I lean on "give us this day" and quickly ask forgiveness for my transgressions.

But yesterday I was stuck on a less comfortable phrase that, despite being a prayer directive from Jesus, is one I've slid over too lightly. "Deliver us from evil." There it was on the page before me. It did not say, "grow complacent with evil, because, after all, it's everywhere." Jesus didn't suggest turning a blind eye to evil, or in contrast, giving up in despair because evil is rampant. He asked us to pray to be *delivered* from evil, a Greek word *rhýomai* that means "rescue," or "deliver me to Yourself and for Yourself."

Some people, young and old, within my circle have let the evil of this world form their opinions, shape their thinking, mess with their theology, and draw them into habits and patterns and illogic that are the opposite of God's good. Jesus emphasized the importance that we pray to be rescued or delivered (us and them) from evil.

I don't yet know what that means in full, but I'm committed to praying as Jesus taught, for myself and for those I so deeply care about. —CYNTHIA RUCHTI

FAITH STEP: *Think of someone you love who has succumbed to evil. Rather than worry, earnestly pray.*

SUNDAY, APRIL 30

"He who believes in Me, as the Scripture has said, out of his heart will flow rivers of living water." John 7:38 (NKJV)

THE WILLAMETTE VALLEY BAKED IN the midst of a heat wave, so I spent the morning watering the garden. As I bent to place the sprinkler in one of its last positions, I noticed several of my primroses looked terrible. Their leaves had wilted, and the blooms withered.

We'd placed these flowers at the edge of a flower bed, surrounding a fountain. As I investigated, I discovered that some of the plants lay just beyond the radius of the water's spray. As other parts of the yard soaked up life-sustaining moisture, these blossoms waited just inches away, shriveled and dying. I repositioned the watering system, making certain the entire area was covered. I'd noticed the problem and made the necessary adjustment just in time.

Before I found my way to Jesus and drank of His Living Water, I was like those parched annuals. I existed on the fringe, unnoticed and love-starved. I sensed that some of my acquaintances were happy. Whatever they had, I wanted—and needed—badly. But the mysterious contentment they possessed seemed to tease at me, as if just out of reach.

Then one day, a friend invited me to her Bible study. That was the beginning for me. As Jesus made His home in my heart, healing waters fed my soul, first in gentle droplets, then in buckets. The river of life runs through me now, and I will never thirst again (John 4:10). —HEIDI GAUL

FAITH STEP: *Purchase a small houseplant to care for. As you feed and water it, watch it thrive just as we do under Jesus's care.*

MONDAY, MAY 1

"Has not my hand made all these things, and so they came into being?" declares the LORD. "These are the ones I look on with favor: those who are humble and contrite in spirit, and who tremble at my word. Isaiah 66:2 (NIV)

ONE OF MY FAVORITE NECKLACES is shaped like a butterfly, its wings filled with glittering beads that resemble genuine peridots. While I paced and prayed one morning, I glanced down and noticed the metal frame of the necklace had broken in two places. *Rats.*

I thought I'd ask my husband to fix it with special glue he uses to repair everything from ceramics to shoes. But when I looked closer, I realized the cracked places were visible only from my perspective.

Sometimes I feel too broken for Jesus to use me and my life. I look at others with their seemingly perfect, powerful ministries and think I'll never have it all together like they do. But that's when Jesus whispers to my heart, "No one sees your broken places but Me, dear lamb. You are valuable and precious, even though you're not perfect."

All of the disciples, Jesus's twelve closest friends, had glaring faults. Yet, He used them to turn the world upside down. Not because they were perfect, but because He empowered them despite their brokenness.

Jesus doesn't expect me to be perfect either. He loves me with my imperfections and brokenness. As I examined the crack in my necklace, I decided not to have my husband repair it. I wanted to wear it just as it was. It sparkled with beauty despite its flaws.

I did too. —JEANETTE LEVELLIE

FAITH STEP: *Find a broken item in your house. Ask Jesus to show you a use for it, just as it is.*

TUESDAY, MAY 2

Let us then approach God's throne of grace with confidence, so that we may receive mercy and find grace to help us in our time of need.
Hebrew 4:16 (NIV)

A LOVED ONE RECENTLY REMARKED that my son Pierce was graceful. When I asked her to explain, she said he moved with elegance, delicacy, and beauty. People have said I'm a gracious hostess. This translates into my desire for guests to feel comfortable and cared for. That kind of grace, in movement and action, is not always entirely easy for me to explain in words, but I know it when I see it.

It's also hard for me to wrap my mind around the spiritual concept of grace. Simply put, grace is unmerited favor. It's a spontaneous gift—unexpected, undeserved, and totally free. Nothing I can do or say can earn it, nor do I deserve it. My effort can't gain it, no matter how good and righteous I am. Grace is bestowed, granted, given from Jesus. Jesus freely offers His grace through His blood and therefore provides those who believe in Him with the forgiveness of sins (Ephesians 1:6–7).

I can duplicate grace in my movements or the graceful actions of a hospitable hostess, but to mirror the grace of Jesus, I must put aside my desires. I must love those who seem unlovable. Forgive those who've done the unforgivable. Unselfishly serve those I'd rather not and do what's in the best interest of others. Just like Jesus graciously did for me. —ISABELLA CAMPOLATTARO

FAITH STEP: *What does grace mean to you? Think about an instance where you could have shown Jesus's grace to someone else, then pray for guidance that you remember to do that in the future.*

WEDNESDAY, MAY 3

So then, let us not be like others, who are asleep, but let us be awake and sober. 1 Thessalonians 5:6 (NIV)

ON SPECIAL OCCASIONS, MY HUSBAND makes me eggs Benedict for breakfast. It's an undertaking of love—with a lot of steps and plenty of cleanup afterward. Recognizing the special treat for what it is, I stop whatever I'm doing so I can be in the moment for that first bite. As it passes my lips, I close my eyes to increase my sense of taste. I savor every flavor and texture: the crunchy English muffin, the juicy Canadian bacon, the fluffy poached eggs, and the creamy hollandaise sauce. It's like a symphony of flavors perfectly blended together.

Once I've taken that first bite, however, the magic begins to fade. It got me wondering why.

After much thought, I determined the fault lies with me. I only stop to focus on that very first bite. Then I multitask throughout the meal, eating while resuming whatever I was doing or thinking about before. Yet in my distraction, I still expect every bite to be just as delicious. How can it be when my senses are no longer heightened, and I'm no longer fully receptive?

Funny how eggs Benedict taught me why the marvelous things in my life often lose their flavor: my beautiful home, my wonderful family, my good health. To savor my blessings, I must remain alert. I can't grow gluttonous and sleepy with expectation or live my days in a daze of activity.

Jesus is cooking up something wonderful. I want to taste the deliciousness of every moment. —CLAIRE MCGARRY

FAITH STEP: *Give your full attention to something you previously cherished. Write in your journal how your experience rekindled the wonder and awe you previously missed.*

THURSDAY, MAY 4

. . . We have seen his glory . . . who came from the Father,
full of grace and truth. John 1:14 (NIV)

I'VE QUOTED IT, BELIEVED IT, counted on it, and taught it. Jesus was "full of grace and truth." Today, though, it's resonating in a new way.

Some people are full of themselves, full of baloney, up to their eyeballs in work, full to the brim with ideas, or have had it "up to here" with their kids/boss/neighbor. But Jesus? He was full of grace and truth. At the same time. If we're to grow into Christ-likeness, logic tells us the same mix of truth and grace should be our lifelong goal.

All truth and no grace is religiosity. All grace and no truth is misguided. It's a beautiful, awe-inspiring, divine blend that warranted the description of Jesus in Scripture. It's the same blend that sets a person apart in this truth-challenged, grace-challenged world of ours, one not all that different from the culture of Jesus's time.

How does that change my approach to life? It's what's on my heart as I rehearse those words: *full of grace and truth*. Won't it mean that every interaction—with friends, strangers, family, church family, store clerk, antagonist—should be firmly rooted in truth and gentled by grace? How does it change my approach to me? I failed again. Messed up. Spoke too harshly. I was impatient. Truth in me would have to agree. All true. Grace in me would forgive myself, be kinder to myself, and view myself through Jesus's eyes.

Lord, may Your grace and truth never grow out of balance in me.
—CYNTHIA RUCHTI

FAITH STEP: *Which is racing in the lead in your life—grace or truth? Make it your prayer to, with His power, be as full of both as Jesus.*

FRIDAY, MAY 5

And my God shall supply all your need according to His riches in glory by Christ Jesus. Philippians 4:19 (NKJV)

JERSEY STOOD STILL IN FRONT of the bowl I'd filled with kibble that morning. Only weeks ago, the tinkling of dry food hitting the cat's ceramic dish summoned him like a dinner bell. The scraggly white stray with black patches of fur (like Jersey cattle) had found me on my front porch enjoying a spring evening. Most likely, someone had dumped him near our rural home.

My heart couldn't resist his hungry meows, so I fed the little guy from the stash I kept for visits from my grandkitties. Which, of course, as anyone who has ever fed a stray cat knows, made me the new owner of a cat. The next morning, Jersey devoured a can of wet food. And so began his mealtime routine: gravy-covered, canned morsels in the morning, hard food for strong teeth at dinner. Until now.

Jersey looked down at the dry pieces in his bowl, then up at me. The question in his eyes was clear: *Are you serious? Where's the yummy wet stuff I'm supposed to get?* How could he turn up his whiskers at a meal he once so desperately needed? Funny how quickly he forgot.

Funny how quickly I forget too. Many times I've cozied up to Jesus with my incessant cries, only to act all finicky afterward, forgetting how He blessed me. Or I complain if my need wasn't met the way I had anticipated. Honestly, what could be better than *His riches in glory* supplying my needs? So purrfectly. —KAREN SARGENT

FAITH STEP: *What blessings from Jesus have you overlooked or underappreciated? Take a moment to thank Him for always meeting your needs.*

SATURDAY, MAY 6

Praise be to the God and Father of our Lord Jesus Christ! In his great mercy he has given us new birth into a living hope through the resurrection of Jesus Christ from the dead. 1 Peter 1:3 (NIV)

NOTHING COULD HAVE PREPARED ME for the FaceTime call that Friday morning. My mother had just been diagnosed with an emergency, life-threatening condition. The doctor gave her twenty minutes to discuss her course of treatment with family. When Mom's face appeared on my phone screen, I knew she'd already made her decision. She explained the risks involved in immediate surgery and the low likelihood of cure. Mom wanted to let nature take its course.

Hospice was called, and immediate family members took turns sitting at Mom's bedside day and night. We held her hand and told her we loved her and would miss her.

My pain was intense. At the same time, I felt an undeniable sense of anticipation on Mom's behalf. She'd placed her faith in Jesus in her childhood and walked in relationship with Him her entire life. She was ready to move from earth to heaven. She longed to experience its glories, be reunited with loved ones, and meet Jesus face-to-face. It was only a matter of time until He came to take her home to be with Him forever.

Jesus granted her heart's desire exactly one week after that phone call. I grieved but not without hope. Because Jesus conquered death, I didn't say goodbye. I said, "See you later, Mom." —GRACE FOX

FAITH STEP: *Meditate on a loved one who has passed from this life into heaven. Ask Jesus to give you a glimpse of what they may be experiencing in eternity with Him.*

SUNDAY, MAY 7

Open my eyes that I may see wonderful things in your law. Psalm 119:18 (NIV)

THIS SATURDAY MORNING, I AM standing in front of my church to direct visitors to a vaccination clinic we're hosting. During a lull, I turn to admire the beloved red-brick building I've entered and exited hundreds of times over more than three decades.

As I look up, I notice a stone tablet sitting high at the top of each of the two stately pillars at the entrance. Each tablet is inscribed with scripture—one is Psalm 27:1; the other is John 3:16. I'm amazed I've never noticed the tablets before.

Maybe I've not seen them because I'm often rushing in or out and I fail to slow down enough to take in my surroundings. Also, I rarely stand still at the entrance, so I don't have the viewpoint needed to see what's up above me.

I've had the same experience when reading a familiar passage of Scripture. It can be the creation story in Genesis, the Israelites leaving Egypt in Exodus, or the miracles of Jesus in Matthew. When I slow down and take time with the passage, often something different catches my eye. I may read in a new version or be in the midst of a trial. Jesus uses both to change my perspective and open my eyes to see in a new way. In the process, I spiritually grow and mature.

I've learned that I can meet Jesus through the scriptures and through my life experiences. He is there to give new sightings of Himself in myriad ways. I just need to be on the lookout for it and look up. —BARBRANDA LUMPKINS WALLS

FAITH STEP: *How has Jesus opened your eyes to Him in a new way?*

MONDAY, MAY 8

Praise be to the God and Father of our Lord Jesus Christ, the Father of compassion and the God of all comfort. 2 Corinthians 1:3 *(NIV)*

RAIN WAS PREDICTED IN THE forecast again today. We'd already had four days of gloom. It was starting to deeply affect my energy level and attitude. I was desperate to see the blue of the sky and feel the warmth of the sun.

Suddenly, the temperature dropped, changing the moisture into snow—the mystical kind with white, fluffy flakes that gently blanketed the earth in a kind of hush. My mood transformed just as quickly. The child in me came alive, and pure glee bubbled up. Like a giddy kid, I was enchanted by the wonder of it all.

In dark days, when I yearn to find and feel the Son, Jesus shows up. The temperature of my circumstances may be uncomfortably high, but just like the same moisture is present in both rain and snow, the same grace waits for me in both sorrow and joy. As I shift my perspective, I see His goodness and grace falling all around, despite my situation.

Like the child within me is awakened by an unexpected snowfall, His peace and grace change my perspective when I trust in Jesus and wrap myself in His warm blanket of love. —CLAIRE MCGARRY

FAITH STEP: *Envision yourself wrapped up in a blanket with Jesus. Record in a journal the words He speaks to you in your circumstances. If you know someone who is struggling, try to be the sun in their gloomy day. Deliver a meal, send a Thinking of You card, make a phone call, or send a text to share Jesus's comforting blanket of love.*

TUESDAY, MAY 9

I want you to recall the words spoken in the past by the holy prophets and the command given by our Lord and Savior through your apostles. 2 Peter 3:2 (NIV)

OUR CITY CONSTRUCTED A CORDONED-OFF boardwalk along a road near an area of wetlands. At both ends of the boardwalk, signs warn, "Slippery when wet." Those entering the wooden path had fair warning. In the middle of the special path, there is an overlook to pause and watch herons and red-wing blackbirds. Another bold sign at that spot again alerts people the boards can be slippery.

My husband and I chuckled about the redundancy. Since one can only enter the boardwalk from either of the two ends, walkers have already been warned. What good does a sign in the middle do?

But the truth is, when a path is hazardous, we might need another reminder. People are quick to forget; I know I am.

I've noticed the same need for reminders in my spiritual life. I know Jesus. I know He loves me. So why do I need all the repetition of prayers, hymns, church services, Bible reading, fellowship, sacraments? Because Jesus knows that I so easily forget.

He has called believers to remember Him in various ways. When the path of life gets slippery, He reminds me to keep my eyes fixed on Him. —SHARON HINCK

FAITH STEP: *Create a reminder today to turn your thoughts to Jesus. It could be a Post-it on a mirror, a rubber band on your wrist, or an alarm that rings to remind you to stop, pray, and keep your eyes fixed on Him.*

WEDNESDAY, MAY 10

God is our refuge and strength, an ever-present help in trouble.
Psalm 46:1 (NIV)

WITH THE LARGE FAMILY WE have, I created an online, ready-made, grocery shopping list. With one click, all of the typical items we buy are put into our virtual cart, and I scan down the list to see if there is anything we *don't* need.

Recently, I've created a "Hoping List." These are scriptures that I turn to when my hope is gone. When I am discouraged, I read verses that remind me that the Lord delivers me out of my troubles (Psalm 34:17–19) and He is close to the brokenhearted (Psalm 147:3). When I am overwhelmed, I read that I can cast my burdens to the Lord (Psalm 55:22). When I am weary, I am reminded that those who wait on the Lord shall renew their strength (Isaiah 40:31).

I find hope by exchanging my worries with the truth in God's Word. Scripture reminds me to turn to Jesus, to still my thoughts, and to trust Him (Colossians 3:2). Hope isn't limited to my own resources. Instead, I can tap into Jesus's abundance anytime. God's Word doesn't cost a penny (unlike groceries). Just as my online shopping list is accessible to me anytime day or night, so is my Hope.

My "Hoping List" reminds me that even though I sometimes get low on hope, replenishing it is only an arm's length away in my Bible, and Jesus is only a prayer away. —TRICIA GOYER

FAITH STEP: *Create your own "Hoping List." Write down the scriptures noted in this devotion and more of your favorites. Keep this list in a place that you can turn to often, whenever you run out of hope.*

THURSDAY, MAY 11

Through him all things were made; without him nothing was made that has been made. In him was life, and that life was the light of all mankind. The light shines in the darkness, and the darkness has not overcome it. John 1:3–5 (NIV)

ONLY FOUR OTHER GUESTS OCCUPIED the oceanfront hotel that starless night, and I assumed they lay dreaming of seashells and breaching whales. It was half-past three as I opened the room's window to allow the seaside sounds entry. In the midst of the blackness outside, the inn had installed a floodlight facing the sea. It highlighted the waves, changing them from onyx to midnight blue, the foam a soft shade of gray, the tide high in an eloquent show of nature's passion.

A seagull flew out over the water, followed by three more. Then the entire flock circled, a fluid ballet on the wind, a ribbon of life skimming the seaway. As they headed north, my throat tightened and my eyes blurred with tears.

Something extraordinary had occurred, possibly the most beautiful event I'd ever experienced. Jesus had touched me with a glimpse of the divine wonder of His creation. As the Master applied careful strokes to His living canvas, He'd chosen to share this secret treasure privately with me.

Later, I tried to explain the sacred moment to my spouse, but words couldn't capture the magnitude of the gift I'd received. I'd been graced. And I'll never forget it. —HEIDI GAUL

FAITH STEP: *When has Jesus graced you with a magnificent sight? Journal those memories for reference when you feel your hope take flight.*

FRIDAY, MAY 12

My health fails; my spirits droop, yet God remains! He is the strength of my heart; he is mine forever! Psalm 73:26 (TLB)

I SUFFER FROM SEVERE MIGRAINES and sometimes have transient aphasia, commonly called "migraine babble," meaning I speak gibberish. One spring, our daughter-in-law, Erin, went into labor at twenty-nine weeks' gestation. Due to cord prolapse, she lost the baby. Our family was devastated.

My tiny grandson's death wrenched me back thirty years. Our three-year-old son, Blake, had died suddenly from meningitis.

I'm usually strong in a crisis, but the sadness, grief, and sudden emotional trauma sent me into a tailspin. Reliving Blake's death was devastating, but contemplating the journey that lay ahead for my son and his wife was worse. I felt a migraine coming on. Distraught, I cried, *Lord, I can't do this!* Suddenly, my words came out garbled. Not only was my heart breaking, but I also had a severe migraine.

While my migraines with aphasia normally last ten to fifteen minutes, this one went on for hours. My husband took me to the emergency room. Undergoing scan after scan, I revised my plea from *I can't do this!* to *Jesus, help me!*

On the cold exam table with monitors beeping, Jesus whispered, "I'm here." Peace washed over me. I went home soon thereafter; all tests were normal.

With Jesus's help, my husband and I would rise above our own grief and recall depending on Jesus during our journey of losing a child in order to counsel and support my son and his wife. We'd all make it knowing help was only a whisper away. —PAT BUTLER DYSON

FAITH STEP: *Is there something in your life you feel like you can't do alone? Ask Jesus for help—He's waiting to hear from you.*

SATURDAY, MAY 13

"The LORD himself goes before you and will be with you..."
Deuteronomy 31:8 (NIV)

SPRING WAS PUSHING UP THROUGH the remnants of a long Midwest winter. We'd recently moved from our home in Arkansas to this house in Indiana. I'd never experienced so many months of cold weather. But this morning, I noticed miniature daffodil buds brightened my flower bed. Nearby, tulip shoots showed their greenery too. I couldn't believe it! Gifts of nature that my Savior knew would surprise and delight me when I doubted.

I love the first sightings of spring bulbs. When crocuses poke through the dirt, I anticipate daffodils soon to come. When those emerge, I know tulips are on their way. I've always wanted a plethora of them, but we'd never stayed in the same house long enough to get them well established in the yard.

When our family made this big, out-of-state move, we felt Jesus leading us to this area and this specific property. But through the long, cold months, my faith grew as frozen as the ground. Now seeing my favorite flowers were already planted here, just waiting to greet me, was confirmation that we were right where Jesus wanted us to be.

I wanted to know what was beneath the surface of our current experience, asking Jesus for a tomorrow that bloomed brighter. These simple spring flowers would grow into perennial faith anchors to thaw any doubts I may have.

Take heart this morning. Jesus knew those bulbs would surprise me come spring. Jesus has blessings in store for you too.
—ERIN KEELEY MARSHALL

FAITH STEP: *Seal a written prayer request in an envelope with a date to open in one year. Watch how God moves in you and the situation. You may be surprised!*

MOTHER'S DAY, SUNDAY, MAY 14

Charm is deceptive, and beauty is fleeting; but a woman
who fears the LORD is to be praised. Proverbs 31:30 (NIV)

MY MOTHER FULFILLED A HOST of roles in my growing-up years: seamstress, chauffeur, cook, nurse, cheerleader, guidance counselor, and more. The majority of her positions changed as my siblings and I grew up, left home to pursue our dreams, and started our own families, but Mom's role as intercessor remained until she started her final journey toward heaven.

Mom was a woman of prayer. This irked me when I was a teenager who wanted to follow the desires of my heart, rather than do what was right. The last thing I wanted to hear was, "Grace, I'm praying that you'll listen to Jesus and change your ways." I knew Mom's prayers were powerful. Fighting them was pointless.

I was a freshman in Bible college before I began to appreciate the seriousness with which Mom embraced her intercessory role. She prayed me through the fear of making new friends, writing research papers, and auditioning for choir. She cried out to Jesus on my behalf when I sought summer employment and when a broken engagement broke my heart. Later, she pleaded for my health and safety as I moved to Nepal in my early twenties, newly married and naïve about cross-cultural life.

I knew I could count on Mom to pray me through whatever challenge I faced. This filled me with courage and gratitude. Of all the roles she played, intercession bore the greatest significance. After all, that headstrong teenager finally came around. Thanks, Mom! —GRACE FOX

FAITH STEP: *Write a thank-you note to your mother or someone who prays for you.*

MONDAY, MAY 15

---

*"I have told you these things, so that in me you may have peace.
In this world you will have trouble. But take heart! I have
overcome the world." John 16:33 (NIV)*

"YOU *WILL* HAVE TROUBLE." NOT, "you may have trouble," or "you'll have trouble if you do this and that." We *will* have trouble. Can I get an "Amen"?

I've had more trouble than many and less trouble than others. Some of the trouble was out of my control. With my remarkable parents, who struggled with mental illness and addiction, trouble was bound to happen. Having a child with Down syndrome brought trouble in the form of health challenges. But my troubles are nothing compared to those of my Jesus.

Jesus was preparing to face trouble the likes of which the disciples never imagined when He spoke these words in John 16. He'd not yet faced his trial or suffered the mocking, beating, and degradation at the hands of the Jews and the Romans. He hadn't been abandoned by most of his followers or betrayed by His disciples, who professed to love Him. He hadn't experienced the undeserved pain, anguish, and death on the cross.

Despite the cruelty and injustice that awaited Jesus, the perfect, sinless Son of God tells the disciples to have peace. He warns of guaranteed trouble in this fallen world, but the good news is that He has overcome the world. Not that He *will*, but He *has*. Past tense.

No matter what worldly trouble I'm currently in or I'm about to face, I can have peace. I have Jesus's promise—the promise I *will* face troubles, and the better promise that because of Him, I *have* already overcome them. —ISABELLA CAMPOLATTARO

FAITH STEP: *Inventory your troubles. Pray about each one in the past tense as though it has been solved, thanks to Jesus.*

TUESDAY, MAY 16

Instruct the wise and they will be wiser still; teach the righteous and they will add to their learning. Proverbs 9:9 (NIV)

I'VE EXPERIENCED THE CASTING PROCESS for a prosthetic arm numerous times in my life, yet never six times in one day. Alabama State University needed a patient model with upper-extremity limb loss. Being born without a left elbow, forearm, and hand, I allowed prosthetics students to practice making arms for me.

The first student covered my torso and legs with plastic to protect my clothes. He slipped a tight, cotton sleeve over my upper arm and secured it with a chest strap. Then, he dipped some plaster bandaging in warm water and wrapped it around my arm and shoulder. As the plaster dried, he applied pressure to ensure a snug fit. After ten minutes, he wiggled the cast free from the cotton sleeve and pulled it off.

Each student repeated the steps, and by the sixth one, plaster speckled my shirt, pants, shoes, and hair. I also discovered a few spots on my face. But I extended grace to the young men and women because they were learning—and learning can be messy. I knew someday they'd become skilled prosthetists, helping patients like me.

In the same way, Jesus offers me grace while I am learning—and I am always learning. I know I won't ever fully grasp the lessons in His rich Word. I expect I'll make a mess of things occasionally, even though my intentions are good. Grace gives me a chance to clean up today's messes and try again. With practice, like those prosthetics students, I'll eventually get better too. —BECKY ALEXANDER

FAITH STEP: *Have you unintentionally caused a mess recently? Thank Jesus for His grace as you learn and plan your do-over.*

WEDNESDAY, MAY 17

"For I know the plans I have for you," declares the Lord,
"plans to prosper you and not to harm you, plans to give you hope
and a future." Jeremiah 29:11 (NIV)

I RECENTLY JOINED AN ONLINE women's group whose purpose is to help women discover a two-word mission statement. I logged in to a website and answered a series of questions. From my answers, I received "Inspire Hope" as my mission statement. I was skeptical, but after further exploration in our sessions, I was surprised at how suitable the word was for me.

Hope has been a consistent theme through my life. When I was in college, my password to draw funds out of my account was "hope" because I hoped I wasn't overdrawn. The painful memory of my older alcoholic brother, who committed suicide, instilled in me the crucial need of hope for life. I believe his lack of hope for his future led to his lack of desire to continue living.

Jeremiah 29:11 is a favorite verse because God promises to give us hope and a future. I've consistently tried to share Jesus's message of eternal hope and hope for our here and now, especially after the tragic loss of my brother. Thanks to my online group, I'm clearer on my mission to inspire hope. Not a hope that runs out, like the money in my checking account often did, but the eternal hope Jesus graciously offers us. That's something I can bank on! —JEANNIE BLACKMER

FAITH STEP: *Write the passage from Jeremiah 29:11 on a notecard and give it to someone who you think might need hope today.*

THURSDAY, MAY 18

But because of his love for us, God, who is rich in mercy,
made us alive with Christ . . . Ephesians 2:4–5 (NIV)

ONE OF THE THINGS I miss because of my current work schedule is playing the piano for our local high school choir and high school musicians who prepared solos, duets, and ensembles for regional and state competitions.

I don't consider myself an accomplished pianist, so the privilege of accompanying them and being by the students' side during competition came with its share of stress. But I enjoyed being exposed to a wide range of music from classical to pop. I also enjoyed being with these teen musicians. Not just musical connections with them, but emotional and hormonal highs and lows. Off-key, off-tempo, and unpracticed for some. Soaring and stirring performances for others.

I remember one of my favorites was a Gregorian piece in Latin—a duet by two very accomplished young female voices. Tears fell on the piano keyboard as I tried to hold it together while I played and they sang Andrew Lloyd Webber's version of "Pie Jesu." I can hear their emotion-rich performance in my mind, even now.

I knew *Jesu* was Latin for Jesus, but not until today did I look up the English translation for the rest of the lyrics. My tears are falling again. "Merciful Jesus, Merciful Jesus, Merciful Jesus, Merciful Jesus, who lifted the world's sins, grant us peace." Others translate it as "Sweet Jesus" or "Faithful Jesus."

Both the song and its intent remind me of the grace, mercy, and faithfulness that radiate from Jesus and my never-ending need for Him. —CYNTHIA RUCHTI

FAITH STEP: *If you were to set your thoughts about Jesus to music today, what would the song communicate about Him?*

FRIDAY, MAY 19

Let your conversation be always full of grace, seasoned with salt, so that you may know how to answer everyone. Colossians 4:6 *(NIV)*

LAST WEEK, WHEN MY DAUGHTER suffered a severe head cold, she temporarily lost her sense of smell. She said it made cooking difficult because she was unable to discern one seasoning from another. Chili powder and other heady spices were odorless to her, causing her to believe they'd be flavorless and of no use.

Matthew 5:13–14 says we're the salt and light in the world. I take this to mean we are always to do good and be a positive influence in the world by being morally upright and sharing the message of Jesus. This seems a daunting responsibility. I can recognize "salt and light," which is spiritual maturity, in others around me. But in myself? Not always so much.

During a recent searching conversation with my friend Brooke about spiritual maturity, she volunteered a simple, but astute, observation. She pointed out that one often has to go through a lot of challenges to become a well-seasoned, spiritually mature individual.

Just like my daughter's inability to perceive the fragrant aroma of spices didn't mean they were flavorless or unusable, I, too, am sometimes unable to see how Jesus intends for challenges He allows in my life to flavor my development as a believer and make me more mature.

Even though I may not always recognize my own spiritual salt and light, I trust my Heavenly Chef Jesus with the seasoning necessary to bring out the best in me. —CASSANDRA TIERSMA

FAITH STEP: *Thank Jesus for seasoning you with His Grace. Write down specific ways you can be salt and light in the world today.*

SATURDAY, MAY 20

*For God does speak—now one way, now another—though
no one perceives it. Job 33:14 (NIV)*

"DIDN'T YOU HEAR THEM?" MY husband asked when I returned from a morning walk. He was talking about the cicadas, flying insects that had invaded our section of North America. That spring, billions of them had surfaced. Seeing the swarms litter the streets and grassy areas made me think of the plague of the locust that God sent to persuade Pharaoh to let the Israelites leave Egypt (Exodus 10:4).

I hadn't yet heard the buzzing that morning, but later the next day, I detected some low chirping. Then the sound got louder. Finally, the racket from the crickets-on-steroids was nearly deafening—like someone was mowing the lawn. Constantly. When I went outside, I saw cicadas flying around, covering sidewalks, some dead and some alive. There was no mistaking their presence now.

That's sort of like how Jesus speaks to me. I sometimes ask to hear from Him when I need guidance, and there's complete silence. Nothing, zilch, nada. Then there are times He will speak in a still, small voice, and I question if it's really Him. The voice will start to get louder as I receive confirmation through the Bible, other people, nature, or many other creative ways the Lord uses to let me know what Jesus is saying to me.

As I listened to the incessant clatter of the cicadas, I couldn't help but wonder, *Jesus, are You speaking to me through these annoying insects?* I quieted my soul, despite the clatter, and waited to hear from Him. —BARBRANDA LUMPKINS WALLS

FAITH STEP: *Is Jesus using something annoying or unusual to get your attention? How do you recognize His voice when He speaks to you?*

SUNDAY, MAY 21

We all live off his generous abundance, gift after gift after gift....
John 1:16 (MSG)

I ATTENDED A THREE-DAY CHRISTIAN renewal weekend several years ago. We needed to leave our phones behind, but other than that, I didn't know what to expect. I was surprised by the many small kindnesses shown to the participants. Held in a rustic campground, our luggage was waiting in our rooms soon after we arrived. I found encouraging notes or little gifts in my seat after breaks. I was so touched by the tiny, repeated kindnesses that happened to me there. I felt seen, valued, and loved.

People can be rather indifferent to each other in our culture. I know I get caught up in my own little world and what I need to do as I go about my day. As if I'm on a mission, I sometimes fail to notice those around me. I stay separate. Alone.

Jesus didn't act like that. If he needed to be with God, he withdrew and prayed, but when Jesus was with people, he was *with* them. He saw them. He paid attention. He noticed the widow dropping her mites into the offering (Luke 21:2). He saw the grieving mother whose son's funeral delayed his journey (Luke 7:12–14). Jesus gave her what she wanted and needed most: the gift of life for her son.

Gifts touch us. Love gets people's attention.

Jesus, help me connect with others. Love them through me.
—SUZANNE DAVENPORT TIETJEN

FAITH STEP: *Next time someone crosses your path, be present. Look at them. You might try giving them a token in addition to your presence. Buy a few $5 coffee gift cards or collect some pretty things to keep in your purse and share when an occasion arises.*

MONDAY, MAY 22

When you obey my commandments, you remain in my love . . .
I have told you these things so that you will be filled with my joy.
Yes, your joy will overflow! John 15:10–11 (NLT)

ONE OF MY FRIENDS CONNECTS with me periodically and always asks the same question: "Are you still enjoying life on the sailboat, or are you ready to move back into a house?" My answer never changes. "Moving onto a sailboat wasn't something we did by our own volition. We did it because Jesus said to do it, and we're here to stay until He tells us otherwise."

My friend cannot fathom how I can live in tiny quarters with few earthly belongings and remain happy, especially in winter. Truthfully, I can't understand it either apart from Jesus giving me joy.

Jesus promised His disciples that He would fill them with overflowing joy if they obeyed Him. I've experienced the fulfillment of this promise. I constantly marvel at the opportunity to build friendships with people whose lifestyle and beliefs are much different from mine. Knowing them enriches my life. So does finding contentment apart from material possessions and seeing how Jesus takes care of life's little details, such as reserving a washer and dryer for me in the marina laundromat when I'm pressed for time.

Sometimes Jesus asks us to do things considered radical. Obedience may or may not be easy, but the payback is amazing. I wouldn't trade the joy I've experienced by following Him for anything. —GRACE FOX

FAITH STEP: *Are you holding out on obeying Jesus in any area of your life? If so, ask Him to give you a desire and the ability to do what He says.*

TUESDAY, MAY 23

. . . that the sharing of your faith may become effective by the acknowledgment of every good thing which is in you in Christ Jesus. Philemon 6 *(NKJV)*

TODAY, I'M PAINTING THE LITTLE library my daughter and son-in-law built for our yard and, ultimately, for the neighborhood. I can't wait for neighbors to come by and take a book or leave a book.

I want the structure to complement our historic home, so I'm adding a few touches to its styling—some Victorian trim, a cedar-shake roof, and colors that match our house. I'll set it up near the rosebushes bordering my quiet lane. With every brushstroke, I'm contemplating which titles to place on the shelves. I have more than enough to fill it.

This wonderful gift, so well-chosen for a lover of the printed word, houses a responsibility along with the books I'll place inside. Every title and word will need to balance with my ethics, or better still, my faith. Will this cheery yellow structure see a lot of activity? I hope so. It all depends on how its visitors view the treasures found inside.

This little library mirrors the way I want to project my faith. Matthew 12:35a (NIV) says it well. *A good man brings good things out of the good stored up in him.* Do the words I say reflect grace? Does my lifestyle? Am I able to share my treasure—Christ in me—in a manner that makes others crave Him for themselves?

Like my library, I want to be always open and share all I have. After all, Jesus in me may be the only Bible some people ever read. —HEIDI GAUL

FAITH STEP: *Share some of your favorite books with others. Then share the real treasure within you—Jesus.*

WEDNESDAY, MAY 24

Therefore, as God's chosen people, holy and dearly loved, clothe yourselves with compassion, kindness, humility, gentleness and patience.... And over all these virtues put on love, which binds them all together in perfect unity. Colossians 3:12, 14 *(NIV)*

As soon as they're old enough, I assign my kids chores to help out around the house. My youngest, Jocelyn, is currently responsible for sorting the laundry. After school, she has to dampen a few cloths, toss them into the dryer with the clothes that have been sitting there, and turn the dryer on for a few minutes to fluff the load and get the wrinkles out. Then, she sorts the clothes into piles according to their owner, all while being sure not to wrinkle them again. Once she delivers the piles, each person is responsible for folding and putting away his or her own clothes. It is such a joy to walk into my laundry room and find the baskets and dryer blissfully empty!

Sometimes, the juggling act of parenting, maintaining a household, and writing from home can feel an awful lot like an overflowing laundry basket to me. That's when I know I need to cycle in some extra time with Jesus. Despite laying a jumbled and wrinkled mess of problems at His feet, He spins it, gets the wrinkles out, and fluffs me back to life. After a few moments together, I'm sorted out, more ready to clothe myself with compassion, kindness, humility, gentleness, and patience. Being with Jesus is never a chore. —CLAIRE McGARRY

FAITH STEP: *The next time you're doing laundry, use it as an opportunity to pray and let Jesus help you sort it all out.*

Thursday, May 25

"He must become greater; I must become less." The one who comes from above is above all; the one who is from the earth belongs to the earth, and speaks as one from the earth. The one who comes from heaven is above all. John 3:30–31 (NIV)

LAST FALL, I WAS INVITED to speak at a retreat for my women's group at our new church. I was a little nervous. It is one thing to speak to a group of unknown people, but if my presentation didn't go well, I'd have to see these women again.

I've shared before, even once at the church where my husband, Scott, used to be the pastor. "Once" is the key word here. It was a small group. No one laughed at my stories. Scott said he'd heard them before. (I reminded him that I always laugh at his stories even though I have heard them many, many times.) Then there was the lady in the back row who fell asleep, head thrown back, mouth gaping open. I was uncomfortable, sweaty, and embarrassed.

In spite of that disastrous time, I continue to accept speaking engagements. But the reason I do it is because I feel Jesus wants me to. As His follower, I keep my words focused on Him and His words. His truth. His glory. Not mine.

So now whenever I stand in front of an audience, no matter how small or how well I know them, I'm comfortable because Jesus is there with me, standing right next to me—even if someone falls asleep. —SUSANNA FOTH AUGHTMON

FAITH STEP: *In what area of your life do you need more of Jesus and less of you? Ask Him to help yield your focus and your life completely to Him and His will.*

FRIDAY, MAY 26

*Gracious words are like a honeycomb, sweetness to the soul
and health to the body. Proverbs 16:24 (ESV)*

AS A BEEKEEPER, I'M GRATEFUL for every teaspoon of honey I collect and consume. I also enjoy giving it away, knowing how healthy it is. Honey is a miraculous substance. Did you know it was found in the tombs of the Egyptians, thousands of years old, and still edible? When kept properly, honey never spoils.

It's used for medicinal purposes such as healing infections and alleviating allergies. Honey contains water, vitamins, minerals, and necessary enzymes to give the body energy, making it one of the only known foods with all the ingredients to keep us alive.

Proverbs 16:24 compares our words to honey. Words are also life giving. Many scriptures admonish us to use our tongues wisely. In Proverbs alone, more than seventeen verses direct us to use words for healing, hope, and life.

Jesus spoke many kind and healing words during His time on earth. He complimented a Centurion's faith before healing his sick servant (Matthew 8:5–13). He commended the persistent Canaanite woman's great faith as she pleaded for her daughter's healing (Matthew 15:28). And He praised Mary, Martha's sister, for choosing to sit and listen to Him rather than anxiously laboring (Luke 10:38–42).

Like honey, gracious words have a miraculous impact on those with whom we speak. I intend to use kind words to encourage those around me and point them to Jesus, who is the ultimate salve for our souls. I want to offer gracious words freely, just as I give away jars of honey. Honey and Jesus—two sweet treats, healthy for body and soul. —JEANNIE BLACKMER

FAITH STEP: *Give someone an unexpected and sincere compliment today.*

SATURDAY, MAY 27

. . . under his wings you will find refuge . . . Psalm 91:4 (NIV)

A POND AT THE EDGE of a nearby town is often a good place to spot swans. Swans are so elegant, so beautiful, and so full of life lessons. How much like baby swans, cygnets, we humans are!

Away from their mom or dad, cygnets are virtually defenseless. If a baby is separated from its parents in the early weeks, its ability to procure food diminishes, too, because the parents lead their offspring to food sources.

Cygnets can't afford to get too cold or too hot. They often shelter from direct sunlight beneath their mother's wings. Or they "burrow" underneath her feathers or stand in her umbrella-like shade, since Mom can sleep standing up. If the water in which the cygnets swim is too cool, they can climb onto the adult swan's back. Interestingly, the parent doesn't actively assist in the baby's climbing aboard. Instead, the parent stops swimming and ensures its tail is lowered so it's flat to the water. The cygnet then climbs up between the wings to a position behind the adult's neck.

From there, a cygnet can watch what's going on around it. When tired, it can snuggle in the warm space between the parent's wings and sleep. When I read Psalm 91, I'm moved by the comparison.

Jesus, I want to stay close to You, since you are my Protector. You point me to where I find my soul's nourishment, shade me from the excess heat of life, and warm me with Your closeness. Thank You for sheltering me beneath Your wings! —CYNTHIA RUCHTI

FAITH STEP: *Do swans show up in your neighborhood? The next time they do, offer a prayer of gratitude for the wonder of creation and the shelter of His wings.*

SUNDAY, MAY 28

Jesus Christ is the same yesterday and today and forever. Hebrews 13:8 *(NIV)*

WHEN MY ADULT DAUGHTER, MELISSA, who'd had an endoscopic procedure, asked if I had any soft food she could eat, I found a container of chocolate pudding at the back of my fridge. Melissa's eyes closed in ecstasy as the cool chocolate slid down her sore throat. Casually turning the carton over in her hands, she screamed, "MOM, THIS PUDDING EXPIRED TWO YEARS AGO! Are you trying to poison me?"

Melissa and her sister, Brooke, delight in rummaging through my pantry and fridge, searching for expired items, and apparently with good reason. Once they found a carton of milk that had an expiration date from the previous day. From their shrieks of horror, you would have thought they'd seen a rat.

Thankfully, Jesus doesn't have a use-by date. Sometimes, when life gets hectic and tasks overwhelm me, I forget to spend time with Him. On days like the other morning when I had to rush my cat to the vet, I neglect Him altogether. But most days, I gather my Bible, my prayer journal, and my devotional books and settle down on the couch where we always meet. Jesus is right there next to me—abiding in mercy, grace, and love.

I'm thankful that His love never expires, His grace never turns sour, and His mercy is always fresh. —PAT BUTLER DYSON

FAITH STEP: *Do you struggle with a consistent time with Jesus? If not, thank Him for being a constant in your life. If so, ask Jesus to help you be more consistent, beginning right now, and meet Him right where you are.*

Memorial Day, Monday, May 29

Do nothing out of selfish ambition or vain conceit. Rather, in humility value others above yourselves, not looking to your own interests but each of you to the interests of the others. Philippians 2:3–4 (NIV)

Years ago, I visited my brother-in-law during his basic training, and I was enthralled. The barracks filled my vision, an army of identical dormitories lined up like soldiers ready for battle. How could anyone feel comfortable in such a sterile environment? Like the anonymous caserns where the soldiers resided, their lifestyles also reflected a monotonous uniformity and discipline.

But the individuals walking the grounds were unique in invisible ways. While one might struggle with physical pain, another battled homesickness. As one spent sleepless nights praying for courage, another celebrated a promotion. So many differences, yet they all shared one characteristic—a willingness to defend the freedom of America, their beloved country above all else. I left the fort impressed.

Jesus possesses that depth of love and shares it freely. When He sacrificed His life, He ensured my citizenship in heaven, preserving my life for eternity. Because He put me first, I've found shelter in Him.

Today, I honor my loved ones—and soldiers throughout our country's history—who've given up their time, energy, uniqueness, and, for some, their very lives. Like Jesus, they have humbled themselves to be part of a greater whole.

I don't need to worry about losing my freedom, now or ever. I can trust the armed forces—and Jesus—to protect me. I am safe and sound, body and soul. —Heidi Gaul

Faith Step: *Make it a habit to thank those in uniform for their service. If you know a soldier or veteran, reach out and show your gratitude today.*

TUESDAY, MAY 30

He covers the sky with clouds; he supplies the earth with rain and makes grass grow on the hills. Psalm 147:8 (NIV)

I STEPPED OUTSIDE FOR MY morning walk and saw dark clouds forming to the west. It had been an unusually wet spring, and I was tired of the constant threat of rain ruining my routine. *Surely I can beat the shower this time,* I thought as I turned away from the clouds and began my three-mile route.

Ten minutes later, I felt the first sprinkles and quickened my pace, but after another half-mile, the storm was upon me. "Jesus, help me get home fast," I whispered, but I immediately sensed an unexpected answer to my prayer.

"No, meet Me here."

Here? In the middle of a storm? I laughed at the irony. Of course Jesus wanted me to meet Him here. He's in the middle of every storm. I slowed my steps and heightened my senses.

As I felt the thick drops of water drenching every inch of my body, I thought of how Jesus had washed away my sins and whispered a prayer of thanks. When a clap of thunder boomed behind me, I was reminded that sometimes I must obey the sound of Jesus's voice through Scripture, even when I cannot see where He's leading me. And later, when I saw lightning flash in the distance and braced myself for thunder that never came, I remembered that Jesus's silence can never be interpreted as His absence. He's in the middle of every storm, ready to walk through it with me. —EMILY E. RYAN

FAITH STEP: *Next time it rains, try meeting Jesus in the storm. If it's safe, step outside and walk in the rain.*

WEDNESDAY, MAY 31

*And He said to them, "Follow Me, and I will make you
fishers of people." Matthew 4:19 (NASB)*

AS HIGH SCHOOL GRADUATION APPROACHED, I found myself trying to teach my son all of the life skills I felt he still needed to learn before he left for college. Once I showed him how to do something new, I expected him to immediately apply that knowledge and be proficient. Clearly, my expectation was unrealistic.

I can be impatient with other people's development. Thankfully, Jesus doesn't respond the same way. When He recruited His disciples, they were not instantly the scholars, preachers, missionaries, teachers, evangelists, and martyrs that I read about in the Bible. In fact, they were self-centered (Matthew 18:1–4), unreliable (Matthew 26:36–45), and hot-tempered (Matthew 26:47–54). It was only after they followed Jesus, made mistakes, and learned tough lessons along the way that they developed into the "fishers of men" He was training them to be (Matthew 4:19).

Just like Jesus was patient with the pace of His disciples' growth, I must be patient with my son. As much as I wish my accelerated training prepared him for every possible scenario that will come his way, I recognize that he'll benefit from facing life's challenges, making his own decisions and learning from his mistakes. —ERICKA LOYNES

FAITH STEP: *Write down all of the expectations you have of yourself and others. Even if your expectations are reasonable, make a promise to create a safe space and extend godly grace for all of you to grow in Jesus.*

THURSDAY, JUNE 1

I know that there is nothing better for people than to be happy and to do good while they live. Ecclesiastes 3:12 (NIV)

I CALL MY MOTHER A few times each week to check in with her. Mom lives in an assisted living community. Our conversations always start the same way. "Hi, Mom. How are you doing?" But one day, her reply caught me off guard.

Instead of answering, "I'm doing just fine," Mom said, "I'm happy as a hot dog!" We both erupted with laughter. "I have my health. I have a nice, clean place to live and good food to eat," she said. "What more could I ask for? Honey, I'm so wonderfully blessed."

A good hot dog certainly makes me happy, so Mom's giddy, unconventional reply made perfect sense to me. My octogenarian mother recognizes the blessings in her life, both large and small. Like the writer of Ecclesiastes, she's wise in not taking life's simple pleasures for granted—health, shelter, and food, as well as the precious memories of her life as a wife, mother, and godly servant. Mom also knows that there's joy and satisfaction in knowing and following Jesus.

I often pray with Mom before we end our phone chats. I thank Jesus for her life and ask that He continues to bless and protect her. And I pray that I, too, will continue giving thanks to Jesus and be satisfied with my life as I age—as happy as a hot dog, just like Mom. —BARBRANDA LUMPKINS WALLS

FAITH STEP: *Make a list of what simple pleasures and spiritual blessings make you happy.*

FRIDAY, JUNE 2

Having gifts that differ according to the grace given to us, let us use them:
if prophecy, in proportion to our faith; if service, in our serving; the one
who teaches, in his teaching; the one who exhorts, in his exhortation;
the one who contributes, in generosity; the one who leads, with zeal; the
one who does acts of mercy, with cheerfulness. Romans 12:6–8 (ESV)

I WAS READY TO PULL out my hair! My internet connection was intermittent, and I'd been on the phone for more than an hour troubleshooting with technical support. Unfortunately, I'm not the most tech-savvy person, and following suggestions for a fix only made matters worse. Finally (I imagine because they deemed me hopeless), the cable company rep agreed to send out a technician.

A clean-cut young man knocked on my door. Bright-eyed and brimming with enthusiasm and professional courtesy, he quickly identified the problem. Once he made the repair, he tested his fix to ensure it worked.

Seeing people operate within their gift, doing what they love and are graced to do, is exciting. Some tasks I do with dazzling effectiveness and joy. Others, like technology, are not my passion. I haven't a smidgen of gifting and it shows.

In Christ, all believers have different spiritual gifts. Jesus has graced me to do many everyday tasks like being cheerful, compassionate, kind, and generous. Not everyone is meant to serve in children's ministry, live in the mission field, preach on street corners, or repair technology. When I'm properly connected to the ultimate source, Jesus's power, my passion and gifts are used for His glory. —ISABELLA CAMPOLATTARO

FAITH STEP: *Are you struggling to serve God? Ask Jesus to connect you in finding the gift with which you're graced.*

SATURDAY, JUNE 3

I will give thanks to the Lord with my whole heart; I will recount all of your wonderful deeds. Psalm 9:1 (ESV)

THE WORD *RECOUNT* HAS ECHOED through my mind this past year. As the whole world focused on life during and after quarantine, our family had pressing issues that had nothing to do with a worldwide pandemic. We discovered our teen daughter needed more help for emotional trauma than we could give. As awareness of her needs increased, I became desperate for help. I sought counselors and programs to help my daughter. I also sought counseling help for myself.

In my need for help and answers, I made a list of all the ways Jesus has helped and guided our family. No matter how challenging things have been, Jesus has never failed us. When I feel emotionally, mentally, and physically exhausted, recounting Jesus's provision has helped me to hang on when I wanted to give up.

Another thing worth recounting is the fact that Jesus is worthy to be praised no matter how hard life is at any given moment. As Psalm 86:12 (ESV) says, "I give thanks to you, O Lord my God, with my whole heart, and I will glorify your name forever."

The best way to understand how Jesus can help and guide us is to look back to all the ways He's helped and guided us in the past and to praise Jesus even when things are hard. —TRICIA GOYER

FAITH STEP: *Make a list of three ways Jesus has helped and guided you or your family this past year. Then spend three minutes thanking and praising Jesus—glorifying His name.*

SUNDAY, JUNE 4

"The wind blows wherever it pleases. You hear its sound, but you cannot tell where it comes from or where it is going. So it is with everyone born of the Spirit." John 3:8 (NIV)

OUR CONGREGATION WAS HOLDING AN outdoor service in front of our church building. Pastoral personnel and the music team stood on a platform. The day was sunny, and my heart was full as I worshiped.

Then the wind picked up. A few sheets of music blew off the music stands. Staff scrambled to gather them and return them to the instrumentalists. Stronger gusts rattled nearby trees. One music stand tipped over. More pages scattered. My gaze followed a sheet of music as it swirled higher and higher, over the rooftop of the church.

In spite of the challenges, our service continued. Soon it was time for the Scripture reading. A volunteer opened her Bible and read the sermon theme for the day, "The wind blows wherever it pleases."

The congregation chuckled at the appropriateness of the verses, but I also felt a tingling awareness.

Jesus told Nicodemus about the bold and unrestrained work of His Holy Spirit in John 3. Sometimes, He goes places we don't expect. He often stirs a new calling in our hearts. He disrupts the ordinary and invites us to share in His work.

Like our windy worship service, I may sometimes have to hold on to my hat when the Holy Spirit is working in my life. But one thing's for sure, when Jesus is near, His presence never fails to sweep me off my feet. —SHARON HINCK

FAITH STEP: *Step outside and watch for signs of the wind. Ask Jesus to show you ways that His Spirit is moving in your life.*

MONDAY, JUNE 5

So, leaving them again, he went away and prayed for the third time, saying the same words again. Matthew 26:44 (ESV)

I FELL YESTERDAY. PHYSICALLY, NOT spiritually. It's been a long time since I'd hit the ground hard like that. I used to fall several times a day, a decade ago, following a neurological injury that left me deaf in one ear and often feeling dizzy. Doctors tried to diagnose it, but they never could. They prescribed medicine and sent me home.

The most helpful treatment was vestibular rehabilitation (balance training). Through repetition of a series of exercises, the connections between my brain and body were reinforced. I went from many falls a day to weeks and finally months between falls.

Yesterday's fall resulted from squatting too long while observing my bees, then standing and turning all at once, instead of in two separate motions, as I'd been taught in balance training. I scraped a knee and banged an elbow, along with my cheekbone and forehead. I hadn't done my vestibular exercises for a long time. And I wasn't following the principles I'd been taught.

There's a purpose behind repetition, whether it is for emphasis, validity, or retention. Drawing a line over and over darkens, deepens, and broadens it. This happens to the nerves in our brains and bodies too. What is initially softwired—a fleeting connection of neurons—becomes hardwired with repeated use.

Jesus often repeated himself. His story is told in four Gospels from different perspectives. He prayed the same hard Gethsemane prayer three times, using the same words. Repetition is good, and as I know well, helps with keeping balance. —SUZANNE DAVENPORT TIETJEN

FAITH STEP: *Read a responsorial Psalm (like 118 or 136) out loud. Hear the rhythm of the repetition as you pray.*

TUESDAY, JUNE 6

Very truly I tell you, my Father will give you whatever you ask in my name. Until now you have not asked for anything in my name. Ask and you will receive, and your joy will be complete. John 16:23b–24 (NIV)

FOR AS LONG AS I can remember, I've heard people in my faith circles end their prayers with, "In Jesus's name, amen." I've done the same thing, often with little thought about what that really means. Things changed when I was researching and writing a Bible study about the names of God.

I learned that the name "Jesus" means "the Lord is salvation," but the Bible contains more than two hundred other names to describe Him. One of my favorites is "Shepherd." A good shepherd provides pasture for grazing. He ensures protection from pests that would "bug" his sheep and prevent them from getting proper rest. He'll do everything possible to help them thrive because he cares about them.

Understanding a shepherd's role helps me better understand Jesus's role in my life. This, in turn, influences my prayers. I admit that I'm like a helpless lamb dependent on His provision for daily needs, for wisdom in relationships, and for guidance in making decisions. I confess my need for His protection from outside forces. I cry out for a greater awareness of His presence and a keener ability to recognize His voice when He speaks to me.

Praying in Jesus's name is no longer a rote tradition for me. There's power in His name, and I want to access it. —GRACE FOX

FAITH STEP: *List as many names for Jesus as you know. Circle one, then pray to Him from the perspective of that name today.*

WEDNESDAY, JUNE 7

If you listen carefully to what he says and do all that I say,
I will be an enemy to your enemies and will oppose those
who oppose you. Exodus 23:22 *(NIV)*

WE'RE IN THE MIDDLE OF an Indiana cicada summer. The flying beasts are everywhere and they're loud. While I acknowledge the miracle of their seventeen-year hatch cycle, I wish they'd have self-awareness and stop offering so much unsolicited input.

The world can be a noisy place, and I'm not just speaking about bugs. I'm bombarded with sensory overload, as opinions, beliefs, and ideas zoom my way and dive-bomb me out of nowhere, just like those noisy, annoying cicadas.

Processing information in the media, social media, or even in conversations with friends or family members can become especially difficult if I sense mixed motives behind someone's words. This noise can spin my thoughts and cause confusion to the point that I might feel off-balance.

The enemy of my soul is noisy too. When he can't derail me with obvious lies and overt tactics, he works overtime in covert, subversive ways and I might not recognize him immediately. In the cacophony of chaos, I sometimes get caught off guard.

It's easy to forget that I was created to thrive in peace and truth. One of my favorite steadying habits is intentionally making time to listen to the quiet. I slip away from the television, my telephone, and my family to find a secluded spot to be still with Jesus. Only when I spend quiet time with Him do I find that nothing bugs me, not even those annoying cicadas. —ERIN KEELEY MARSHALL

FAITH STEP: *Stillness isn't easy to find in life's busyness. Be intentional and schedule a time to be still as you would with other priorities.*

Thursday, June 8

But as for me, I will watch expectantly for the Lord; I will wait for the God of my salvation. My God will hear me. Micah 7:7 (NASB1995)

ALL FOUR GOSPELS RECORD THE presence of the women who stood watch during Jesus's crucifixion. These devoted followers had traveled with Him and ministered to His needs. Now they stood helpless to intervene, their hearts breaking from sorrow. A couple of women stayed on after almost everyone else had left the scene. Mary Magdalene and Mary, mother of James and Joseph, watched Jesus's body being taken down from the cross and wrapped in linen. They followed to the tomb where He was buried and saw the stone rolled across the opening.

Sometimes faith means watching and waiting. Even after all hope has been lost. Even when it seems as though our world has crumbled and there's nothing to wait for. A frightening medical diagnosis, a broken relationship, sudden loss of a loved one, or financial ruin. During these times, we show our trust in Him by quietly waiting and watching to see what He will do.

The women's loyalty to Jesus brought great rewards on Sunday morning when they went to the tomb to anoint His body. They were the first to hear the news of the resurrection and to see the risen Savior. I wonder if I would have persevered in their situation. I admire their stubborn faith that would not let go. After all, that's the only appropriate response to a love that won't let me go.
—DIANNE NEAL MATTHEWS

FAITH STEP: *Have you despaired of waiting for an answer to a need or a deep longing of your heart? Repeat Micah 7:7 as a prayer and tell Jesus you're watching to see what He will do.*

FRIDAY, JUNE 9

Then an angel appeared to Him from heaven,
strengthening Him. Luke 22:43 (NKJV)

DOCTORS CIRCLED THE HOSPITAL BED where my husband awaited a diagnosis. Initial testing was complete. "Acute myeloid leukemia," the lead doctor stated. Russ was admitted to the cancer center for a month. We were crushed. We didn't want the cup we'd been handed. Only three weeks prior, Russ had retired from law enforcement and hung up his uniform for the last time. Now he was weak and defenseless in a flimsy hospital gown. Despite my best efforts to encourage him, he felt utterly alone.

Sometimes I did too, even though I knew my Savior watched with compassion. Utterly alone, Jesus asked that His cup be taken from Him in the Garden of Gethsemane (Luke 22:42).

Interestingly, Gethsemane means "olive press." Just as olives are pressed and crushed to extract their oil, Jesus agonized under the crushing weight of the sins He would bear to the point of sweating blood. Though God did not take the cup from Jesus, He did send an angel to strengthen His Son.

And Jesus sent an angel to Russ too. Joe arrived, rolling a chemo IV pole identical to my husband's down the hall. Joe loved Jesus, farming, and basketball. The two men never ran out of things to talk about, or laugh about, during their daily visits.

When we wish the cup would pass from us, Jesus doesn't leave us to bear it alone. He may send a person, like Joe, or a Bible verse at just the right moment, or a new message in a worship song we've sung before. No matter what cup we're given, we never drink it alone. —KAREN SARGENT

FAITH STEP: *Look and listen for the variety of ways Jesus strengthens you throughout your day.*

SATURDAY, JUNE 10

He cuts off every branch in me that bears no fruit, while every branch that does bear fruit he prunes so that it will be even more fruitful. John 15:2 (NIV)

MY NEIGHBOR HEIDI RECENTLY TOOK a new job at a gardening center and is now on a mission to rescue plants in need of a little TLC. She knows I have a green thumb, and yesterday, she gave me a needy salvia plant to see if I could save it.

Salvia usually has perky green leaves and bright purple flower spikes, but part of this one was wilted, and the other part had turned crispy brown. After a good soak in the kitchen sink overnight, I gently cut away the dead leaves and charred blossoms. Water, sunlight, and nutrients from the soil could now work toward restoration.

Jesus does the same with me. When areas of my life are not thriving or growing the way they should, He removes or cuts them back. Often this feels devastating. Pruning sometimes comes in the form of a job loss, enduring family issues, divorce, financial ruin, health scares, a desperate diagnosis, or even death of a loved one. While Jesus doesn't necessarily cause painful events, He often uses them to prune me and help me grow past my selfishness, pride, coveting, bitterness, and self-sufficiency. Jesus prunes me because He loves me. He wants me to grow and flourish in Him—and for Him.

Just as I dramatically cut back the salvia to help it grow, the Master Gardener is always working in my best interest to help me grow too. —SUSANNA FOTH AUGHTMON

FAITH STEP: *Looking back, can you see areas of your life that have been pruned? How has Jesus turned the pain of that experience into growth?*

SUNDAY, JUNE 11

Rejoice always, pray continually, give thanks in all circumstances; for this is God's will for you in Christ Jesus. 1 Thessalonians 5:16–18 (NIV)

I SURVEYED THE LAWN. DOZENS of buttery-yellow flowers bore witness to my neglect. Dandelions. Some had already gone to seed, their fluffy white heads teasing, as if waiting for the child in me to pull a stem and blow. I fought the temptation, despite a list of wishes I'd love to have made.

I know well the trouble that comes when I fixate on desires. One hunger begets another—and another. Soon, I'd focus on my wants. Shoes calling to me from the shop; dream vacations beckoning. There were many ways I let Jesus know His plan for me wasn't quite enough.

Had I done that too much lately? Had I forgotten the myriad blessings Jesus has already granted me? He has given me a world filled with joy and love and a treasure so vast that no amount of wishing is ever needed. Eternal life. It took root the day I found Him and will culminate when I see His blessed face in heaven.

I looked at the weed bobbing in front of me, its golden head stretched toward heaven. Dandelions grow wherever the wind takes them, thriving and spreading even in the toughest environments. They don't require coddling.

How could I be more like this sturdy weed, especially when I'm drawn by temptation? By thanking Jesus and communing with Him through prayer. By lifting my head, heart, and hands to Him, spreading His love far and wide, just like dandelion seeds. —HEIDI GAUL

FAITH STEP: *Make a wish list of desires. Beside each one, write a blessing or favor you've instead received. Thank Jesus that no matter what you want, He is enough.*

MONDAY, JUNE 12

"You heavens above, rain down my righteousness; let the clouds shower it down. Let the earth open wide, let salvation spring up . . ." Isaiah 45:8 (NIV)

SOMEONE RECENTLY SHARED THE PRAYER hack of setting several smartphone alarms as a reminder to routinely think about Jesus throughout the day. Initially, the idea of hearing several blaring alarms turned me off. The sudden, jarring noise always catches me off guard and evokes stress. My shoulders tense up, and I'm worse off than before. Regardless, the idea kept ringing in my mind.

I have a solid morning prayer routine, but the peace I found there quickly unraveled as the day progressed. I decided the alarm idea was worth a shot. I ruled out every ringtone until I listened to chimes. Comforting, soothing, and melodious, it was a call to prayer that I'd like to answer.

Every day at 9 a.m., 12 p.m., 3 p.m., and 6 p.m., the beautiful tone now sounds on my phone. When I hear the gentle tinkle of the bells cascading, I imagine Jesus's mercy and grace showering down on me. I stop whatever I'm doing and pray that raining grace on whomever comes to mind. Whether it's a friend in crisis, one of my kids who's struggling, my husband hard at work, or myself with frayed nerves, I visualize each soaking in that grace like thirsty flowers. Each time I hear the alarm, my soul is refilled, and my sanity is saved knowing that no matter what the next few hours hold, Jesus will ring in showers of His goodness and blessings on me too. —CLAIRE MCGARRY

FAITH STEP: *Find a ringtone on your cell phone that evokes peace. Set a few alarms as reminders to stop during the day and pray to Jesus.*

TUESDAY, JUNE 13

Through him we received grace . . . Romans 1:5 (NIV)

AFTER LIMPING BY WITH AN ancient septic tank, we realized the time had come to update to a mound system, or so the county told us. We've been waiting almost nine months now. We had to save a long time to afford it. Then when we had the money in hand, it was too late in the year to dig and ensure that grass seed would have time enough to grow over the mound before the winter freeze. We waited through the long winter for spring. But it was too wet of a spring to dig then, and spring, as it sometimes does in Wisconsin, kept one foot in winter for months. We waited for the company's schedule to open up. And we're still waiting.

I'm reminded of other seemingly interminable waits we've endured—no kitchen for four months during an exchange from the '70s-style cabinets to the current-century cupboards. We waited from January to July once to have water restored after a pipe in our well froze. We waited twenty-seven years for new carpeting on the stairs to the second floor. We waited four decades to remodel this old house for better traffic flow.

But here's the glory. It is possible to wait with grace. Jesus, the epitome of grace, waits *with* us. Although Jesus didn't use the word grace, He *is* grace and the giver of grace. He keeps us sane, calm, occupied, at peace, and content despite the circumstances when we choose to invite Him into our waiting times. We can, because of Him, wait with grace. So much better than the impatient, anxiety-ridden alternative. —CYNTHIA RUCHTI

FAITH STEP: *"Well, what are you waiting for?" is a common expression. Ask yourself today a more meaningful, "Who am I waiting with?"*

WEDNESDAY, JUNE 14

I know, my God, that you test the heart and are pleased with integrity....
1 Chronicles 29:17 (NIV)

I DIDN'T EXPECT DRAMA IN the parking lot. Three spots were open in a row, so I pulled in the center one. I remained in the car for a few minutes, checking messages on my phone. When an SUV parked to my left, I glanced up briefly and continued reading. Then, *wham!* I jolted at the impact of metal slamming into metal. My head spun left to see the heavy SUV door resting against the mirror of my Volkswagen. I glared through the window at a woman in the passenger seat. Her mouth formed an "O," and she slapped her hand over it. She yanked her door back a notch and climbed out. I got out too.

"Oh! I am so sorry!" the woman exclaimed. "I didn't know anyone was in there."

"Well, that's not really the point, is it?" I asked. "I don't want my car banged up."

"Oh, no, no, no. Your car isn't hurt at all," she said.

Fortunately, I was slow to speak that day, only thinking of "things I should have said" later. I gave the woman grace, just as Jesus has done for me on many occasions. She never admitted wrongdoing or showed any remorse, but she gifted me with a life lesson of great value: "Integrity is doing the right thing when you don't have to—when no one else is looking or will ever know" (Charles Marshall).

The big scratch on my little car reinforces that truth—and Jesus's grace—each time I take a drive. —BECKY ALEXANDER

FAITH STEP: *Invite Jesus to test the integrity level within your heart. Ask Him to reveal new ways you can please Him today.*

THURSDAY, JUNE 15

---

*Therefore, as God's chosen people, holy and dearly loved,
clothe yourselves with compassion, kindness, humility, gentleness
and patience. Colossians 3:12 (NIV)*

MY DEAR FRIEND VIVIEN HAD died, and I was selecting an outfit to wear to her visitation. Viv was an impeccable dresser. Her clothes were fashionable and well-tailored, her jewelry tasteful. To honor my friend, I wanted to look sharp. I chose navy pants with navy kitten heels and a silky top in a pattern of navy, rust, and gold. A new pair of navy earrings completed my ensemble. As I got dressed, I prayed for Jesus to give me words of comfort for Viv's children.

I stepped out of the car at the funeral home and straightened my clothes. When I looked down, I was horrified! My pants were black instead of navy. Too late to go back and change, I slunk inside.

Viv's daughter met me at the door. Before I could offer any words of comfort, she said, "I can't tell you how much Mom appreciated your visits, phone calls, and cards, especially after she got sick."

We hugged as I told her how much I loved her mother. Moments later, Viv's son was by my side. He thanked me for caring about Viv's dog and for helping her with home repairs. I signed the guest book, watched the video of Viv's life, and left.

In the car, Jesus whispered, *Really, Pat, are your clothes what mattered to Viv's kids?* I was ashamed of my shallowness. Right then, I updated my spiritual wardrobe—my outfit didn't matter, but kindness was always in fashion. —PAT BUTLER DYSON

FAITH STEP: *Take a look at your spiritual ensemble and write down how you are clothed in compassion, kindness, humility, gentleness, and patience. Nothing you wear matters more.*

FRIDAY, JUNE 16

Bend down, O LORD, and hear my prayer; answer me,
for I need your help.... Give me happiness, O LORD,
for I give myself to you. Psalm 86:1, 4 (NLT)

AS AN AUTHOR, I LOVE vibrant verbs. So as I read the early verses of Psalm 86 today, my writer mindset noticed all those calls to action. David asks God to bend down, hear, answer, protect, save, be merciful, and bring joy. Pondering the life of Christ, I realized that David's prayer was answered for all of us in Jesus.

In the Gospels, we see Jesus bending down to touch and heal. He listens to people's needs. He removes the disabilities of the blind and lame. He protects the woman about to be stoned. He saves us all by His death on the cross. He shows mercy to Peter after his denial. And He brings all of humankind eternal hope with His resurrection.

Jesus shows immense love for us with every grace-filled verb I can think of. He moves in practical and tangible ways to guide, comfort, and forgive.

Reading about His life makes me want to follow Him and serve others in tangible ways. Perhaps I can stoop down to tie a child's shoes. Or listen to a friend who is lonely. Guard the reputation of a member of my congregation by not listening or responding to gossip. I can show grace to an acquaintance who made an annoying comment. Maybe I will bring joy with a surprise card or gift to someone who is lonely.

Today I want to respond to Jesus's love with active verbs as I invite Him to live through me. —SHARON HINCK

FAITH STEP: *Read Psalm 86 and highlight all the verbs you notice. Choose one and serve others with that tangible action today.*

SATURDAY, JUNE 17

Fathers, do not provoke your children to anger, but bring them up in the discipline and instruction of the Lord. Ephesians 6:4 (ESV)

MY KIDS WANT THEIR CHILDREN to grow into capable, responsible members of society. With that in mind, one of their parenting techniques is to post chore charts on the fridge. Chores are assigned based on kids' ages and abilities. A four-year-old might be told to help empty the dishwasher, while a seven-year-old might be expected to feed the chickens and put them in their coop for the night.

My kids would never blindly assign chores to be done independently by children incapable of performing them. Doing so would be unkind and would guarantee failure. They train their children before turning them loose to do their work on their own. This gives their little ones the best opportunity to succeed.

Jesus tends to us like responsible parents tend to their children. He would never thrust us into a position where we're guaranteed to fail. He brings experiences into our lives to train and mature us. He prepares us along the way for greater responsibilities in building His kingdom or for entrusting us with hardships that will refine us and make us more like Him.

As our heavenly Father, Jesus cares for us. Protecting and loving, He helps us flourish just as parents help their children. We can rest assured Jesus will provide us with all the training we need to succeed on this journey of life. —GRACE FOX

FAITH STEP: *Envision Jesus sitting beside you right now. Imagine yourself cradled in His arms or sitting on His lap. Thank Him for lovingly training you and being with you, especially when you've learned hard lessons.*

FATHER'S DAY, SUNDAY, JUNE 18

My feet have closely followed his steps; I have kept to his way without turning aside. Job 23:11 (NIV)

As I OPENED MY EYES in the early morning light, I heard the familiar sound of my husband shuffling around the house in his slippers. I immediately thought of Hal's father who did the same thing. Dad Walls lived with us for the last four years of his life before the Lord called him home to heaven. My father-in-law, who was in his late nineties, used to drag his feet slowly when he walked.

While Dad Walls was with us, I started to notice how much my husband was like his father. Not only did they walk and talk alike, but the two also had similar body types and idiosyncrasies. I marveled at how Hal's parents knew to wait until my husband was born to name him, instead of his older brother, Hal Jr. My Hal is indeed the spitting image of his dad.

My father-in-law set a good example for my husband and his nine other children as a believer in Jesus and follower of God's Word. Much like Job, who experienced tragedy and sickness during his life, Dad Walls declared he would follow Jesus and remember His goodness all the days of his life.

What a legacy for a parent to leave for his children. My own father did the same for our family. I know how important it is to closely follow Jesus and walk in His footsteps. While I can never fill Jesus's shoes—or even those of my earthly father—I can and will strive to follow in His footsteps. —BARBRANDA LUMPKINS WALLS

FAITH STEP: *Write down the ways you are leaving footprints like Jesus for a family member or another to follow.*

JUNETEENTH, MONDAY, JUNE 19

Therefore if the Son makes you free, you shall be free indeed.
John 8:36 (NKJV)

OF ALL THE GRIEVOUS TRAVESTIES for those who were enslaved in our country, one stands out as an additional tragedy. The history of it is embedded in the celebration known as Juneteenth, which commemorates General Order No. 3 by Union Army General Gordon Granger, proclaiming freedom from slavery in Texas, a declaration made on June 19, 1865 (hence, Juneteenth). Many months after legislation was passed, and almost three years after Lincoln's Emancipation Proclamation, slaves in Texas were still in bondage. Finally, on June 19, federal troops arrived in Galveston to take control of the state and ensure that all enslaved people were set free. Freed months earlier, although most did not know it, they were still held in unlawful bondage as slaves.

Juneteenth is now celebrated widely as a day to remember, reflect, and to move forward. It's the oldest nationally celebrated commemoration of the ending of slavery in the United States, and is often marked by sermons, guest speakers, picnics, and family gatherings.

My heart is heavy for those who *ever* lived enslaved or who had ancestors who were slaves. It's an especially heartbreaking injustice that people remained in slavery just because they had not been informed of their freedom—freed already but not living free.

Likewise, some people don't know they have been declared free from their bondage to sin and their redemption was purchased by the blood of Jesus. It's up to me, and all of us as Jesus followers, to fight injustice and to proclaim the freedom that is offered in Him. —CYNTHIA RUCHTI

FAITH STEP: *What still holds you chained? Spread the Good News about Jesus and choose to live in the freedom He bought for you.*

TUESDAY, JUNE 20

Cast but a glance at riches, and they are gone, for they will surely sprout wings and fly off to the sky like an eagle. Proverbs 23:5 (NIV)

BECAUSE BALD EAGLES NEST NEAR our home, I often see them fly by our kitchen window. But only for a moment and then they're gone, just like a recent offer we received on a property we were hoping to sell. The first day after we listed it, a bid for more than the asking price arrived. I found myself daydreaming about living on a boat and scuba diving off the coast of Belize, updating my out-of-date wardrobe, and taking my husband, Zane, out for a fancy dinner. I glanced at riches. (Well, more than glanced.)

The next day the buyer rescinded his offer. Interest rates were going up, and he couldn't make financial sense of it. *Poof*—the riches sprouted wings and flew away like the eagles that darted past my window. I was disappointed the sale fell through, but even more disappointed with myself for time spent imagining how the money would change my life. I know better. Jesus is the only true source of provision, and He will never leave me.

When the rich young ruler asked Jesus what he needed to do to inherit eternal life, Jesus told him to sell everything and follow Him (Mark 10:17–27). The young man went away sad because he couldn't let go of his wealth. Jesus knew the lure of worldly possessions would cause some not to follow him.

Riches—or anything we put our trust in other than Jesus—can fly away, just like eagles. But Jesus is here to stay. —JEANNIE BLACKMER

FAITH STEP: *Write a prayer in your journal today proclaiming your trust in Jesus because He will never "fly away."*

WEDNESDAY, JUNE 21

Be diligent in these matters; give yourself wholly to them, so that everyone may see your progress. 1 Timothy 4:15 (NIV)

THE SUN RISES AND SETS, the moon shines in the sky, and the world continues its rotation around the sun. As the seasons advance, days lengthen from one to the next, the change imperceptible but undeniable. And then at last, the summer solstice arrives. The longest day of the year.

This has fast become one of my favorite days, and I get excited. As an avid gardener, it represents the heart of the growing season to me. Seedlings stretch skyward, bees bounce from blossom to blossom, and the sun shines bright. Within weeks, harvest will begin.

As I considered Earth's slow but steady change and how it benefits my plants, I sensed an invitation from Jesus. Maybe I could turn certain behaviors around gradually, just as our planet does. This approach to self-improvement might be more successful than my failed New Year's resolutions. I decided to give it a try.

Like my garden, I allowed myself ample time and nurturing as I battled established habits. I watched for and celebrated every sign of growth. Instead of punishing myself for setbacks, I focused on growing for Jesus, with Jesus, and through Jesus. I learned to offer myself—and others—the same grace He's shown me. But more than that, I worked toward a spiritual harvest rooted in love, one rich with fruit (Galatians 5:22–23). One that is everlasting.
—HEIDI GAUL

FAITH STEP: *Find small changes you can make toward self-improvement. Keep daily records of your transformation, like a growth chart, as you grow in, through, and with Jesus.*

THURSDAY, JUNE 22

His disciples asked him, "Rabbi, who sinned, this man
or his parents, that he was born blind?" "Neither this man nor
his parents sinned," said Jesus, "but this happened so that the
works of God might be displayed in him." John 9:2–3 (NIV)

WHEN I SPEAK OF ISAAC, my son with Down syndrome, some people murmur the comfort they think I need or encourage me as though I'm enduring an awful hardship. I don't take offense (anymore). They don't understand, nor did I, at first. I realize many people don't get that Isaac is a gift of grace to our family and that I have been allotted grace to be Isaac's mom.

In Jesus's day, it was a common belief that in Jewish culture birth defects, other physical abnormalities, suffering, and trials were caused because somebody somewhere sinned. But Jesus sets the disciples straight by using the man's blindness to teach them about faith, grace, and glorifying God.

A bounty of love, joy, fun, and innate wisdom, Isaac teaches me about unconditional love every day. He meets a deeply personal need in me as I rely on my faith to parent him. Are there challenges? Sure. Being a mom is never easy under any circumstances, but Jesus has uniquely graced me with the ability to be Isaac's mom. Through His power, I have the perfect combination of qualities and failings to meet any challenge I may face.

Isaac bestows unmerited favor and grace on me every day. Because of him, I understand the work of Jesus better. And there's no sweeter gift. —ISABELLA CAMPOLATTARO

FAITH STEP: *Ask Jesus to help you receive the gift of grace He's provided for a particular mission and show you how to discern the work of God through situations that seem like challenges.*

FRIDAY, JUNE 23

I love the LORD because he hears my voice and my prayer for mercy. Because he bends down to listen, I will pray as long as I have breath! Psalm 116:1–2 (NLT)

AS A MOTHER OF MANY (ten children), I find myself on my knees every day in prayer. I have adult children who need prayer for work and relationships. I have teens who need prayer as they plan for their future and discover their unique, God-given identity. I have elementary-age children who need prayer for school and friends. The more family members, the more needs.

Taking the needs of my loved ones before Jesus is more than simply rattling off a prayer list. It starts by humbling myself before Him. When I humble myself, I turn over my worries and trust that Jesus *is* the answer. I know He will hear, provide, and bless me.

The word "bless" was influenced by the Hebrew word *brk*, which means to bend, which implies kneeling. I envision this picture when I pray, Jesus—Lord of the universe—bending down to my level to hear and help me.

I've always felt there was something remarkable about praying on my knees. Now I understand that whenever I kneel to pray, my faith is strengthened because I'm blessed. My faith also grows as I realize Jesus bends near to listen. No prayer or request or need is too great or too small for Jesus. He only asks that I humble myself and bring them all to Him.

There's no greater blessing than realizing He's bending near to hear, provide, and love me. —TRICIA GOYER

FAITH STEP: *Bow your head or kneel before Jesus in prayer. As you pray for yourself, your family, and your friends, picture Jesus bending down to listen.*

SATURDAY, JUNE 24

My soul [my life, my very self] clings to You;
Your right hand upholds me. Psalm 63:8 (AMP)

THE SHEEP IN MY LONG-AGO flock were excellent followers. I sometimes gave them treats but not often enough they would count on them. I hoped to create a strong relationship between shepherd and animal. I wanted the ewes to see me as a provider and protector, the source of their safety and well-being, and not some sort of sheep Santa—only good for handouts.

Many in the herd trusted me, and I believe they saw me as their source and protector. They alerted quickly, noticing my presence, while staying in place, their bodies relaxed. They looked toward my face, not my hands.

Farah was one of my most memorable ewes. When I entered the pasture, she trotted over to greet me. Like a puppy, she dogged my steps—following hard after me. If I sat down on a hay bale to rest, Farah leaned against my thigh, closed her eyes, and dozed when I stayed a while. When she did that, I wanted to sit with her as long as I could, pat her chest, even feel her heartbeat. Our relationship grew strong as we spent quality time together, shepherd and sheep.

I want to come to Jesus like Farah came to me. I want to enjoy being in His presence, sit with Him for some quality time, and expect nothing from Him in return for my devotion. I want my Good Shepherd to feel my heart beating with His. *Help me follow hard after Jesus and love Him well.* —SUZANNE DAVENPORT TIETJEN

FAITH STEP: *Imagine yourself in a pasture sitting with the Good Shepherd. Not trying to understand or asking anything, just spending time in His presence.*

SUNDAY, JUNE 25

Whatever your hand finds to do, do it with all your might...
Ecclesiastes 9:10 (NIV)

I'D RECENTLY RETIRED AS A high school English teacher, and I wanted to use my newly acquired time to glorify Jesus. But I had so many choices: pursue publishing a book of my own, volunteer with the youth at church, lead a women's Bible study, take on freelance writing or editing assignments. The possibilities excited me, but which should I choose?

I prayed Jesus would take me out of the equation, that He'd send someone to ask me to serve in a way that fit me just right because exploring the options on my own felt like I was playing Whack-a-Mole. Ideas flooded my mind, but the Lord remained silent.

Weeks later, I promised Jesus if He would show me the door, any door, I'd walk right through it. In my mind, I imagined His exasperated response, "You have so many doors. Just pick one already!" At first, I chuckled. Then I realized maybe Jesus was waiting on me.

Suddenly, a highlight reel of recent conversations played in my mind. Four people from church had reached out to me, expressing their desire to write stories. Were they asking me to serve in just the right way and I missed it?

The next week, I walked through one of those doors Jesus pointed out to me. I met with my pastor to plan and schedule a writing workshop. —KAREN SARGENT

FAITH STEP: *What door is Jesus opening for you? Walk through it today.*

MONDAY, JUNE 26

Whether you turn to the right or to the left, your ears will hear a voice behind you, saying, "This is the way; walk in it." Isaiah 30:21 (NIV)

FOR YEARS, MY SISTER, ELAINE, has asked me to pray for her son, my godson, Brendon. As he seemingly drifted from one college to another, struggling to find his path in life, her heart ached. Brendon jumped from one major to the next, dropped out of college for a while, traveled around the United States, and volunteered for some overseas mission work. When he finally graduated from his third university with a degree in communications and media, he was still uncertain of what job he envisioned having.

Elaine recently sent me a video of Brendon being interviewed on Facebook while on a Christian mission in Lebanon. When prompted by the reporter to recount his faith story, Brendon went on to explain how at each college and seeming detour along the way, Jesus used new friends and experiences to take him from crawling in his faith journey, to walking, and ultimately running to the arms of Jesus. Brendon is so in love with our Savior now, he wants a job following Jesus full time, devoting his life to be His disciple.

What looked like years of random wandering to my sister and me was actually the divine route that Jesus had mapped out for my beloved nephew. I'm thrilled to know my godson has finally arrived at the most perfect destination of all: the feet of Jesus. —CLAIRE MCGARRY

FAITH STEP: *Show an extra dose of kindness to those who outwardly seem to be wandering. Pray that, like Brendon, they will listen to the inward voice of Jesus telling them which way to go at each turn.*

TUESDAY, JUNE 27

*Remain in me, as I also remain in you. No branch can bear
fruit by itself; it must remain in the vine. Neither can you bear
fruit unless you remain in me. John 15:4 (NIV)*

I DON'T KNOW MUCH ABOUT gardening, but I love how flowers brighten up a home. So I planted daisies, flowers I was told could flourish in a hot climate. At first, they were lush and vibrant. But soon, I got busy and forgot to water my flowerpots. Eventually, the daisies withered and died. Later, I found one stem was even separated from the root. How did I expect anything to grow without water?

In John 15, Jesus told the disciples to stay connected to Him in order to thrive. He was the "vine," their life source, and they were his "branches." As branches, they would produce "fruit." They were "offshoots" of the Savior. Since Jesus's ministry was productive, their ministries would be productive too. How they lived their lives directly reflected their connection to Jesus.

Just as I became too distracted to tend to my flowerpots, I sometimes find myself neglecting my time with Jesus. I might not pray for a few days. I set aside my Bible reading for a few weeks. Over time, I stop growing spiritually and start feeling as dry and wilted as my daisies. But Jesus has given me a way to revive simply by reconnecting with Him. Through spiritual disciplines such as praying and reading the Bible, I become rooted in Him. Remaining in Jesus allows me to be fruitful. As I grow in Him, I might even try my hand at growing flowers again. —ERICKA LOYNES

FAITH STEP: *This week, do an inspection of your life and assess what kind of fruit, if any, it is producing.*

WEDNESDAY, JUNE 28

You will keep in perfect peace those whose minds are steadfast, because they trust in you. Isaiah 26:3 (NIV)

PICTURE-TAKING IS A PASSION MY husband and I share, especially macro and close-up shots. Macro photography is taking a picture of something small and showing it as larger than it truly is.

As we walk through our garden with cameras in hand, we focus on specific blooms. In one image, a red rose's delicate petals fill the frame edge to edge, its intricate beauty visibly enhanced. In another, a bee nestles into a different blossom's pollen. Its legs coated yellow, its important task is now magnified in our hearts.

The main reason I love this form of photography is that it makes a solitary item the point of interest. No distractions like cars driving by, the accumulation of mud on the side of the shed, or any other sights that can confuse or clutter the background. The finished photo is a lone, calming flower. Nothing else dilutes the image.

Sometimes life seems like a bewildering jumble of distractions, be it bills, illness, or even an unkind word directed toward me. My thoughts stray away from my focus—Jesus and His beautiful, multi-faceted creation. At times, it is easy for negativity to envelop me with anger, depression, or jealousy.

But Jesus is like the calming lone flower. With Him as my solitary point of interest, there are no distractions. I read Isaiah 26:3 and know Jesus will provide me peace as I keep my focus on Him. Picturing Him, alone, His perfect peace is magnified. —HEIDI GAUL

FAITH STEP: *Set aside an hour to place your complete focus and attention on Jesus, to pray or read Scripture, or both. Magnify Him and give Him glory, rejoicing in the peace that flows over you.*

THURSDAY, JUNE 29

But you are a chosen people, a royal priesthood, a holy nation, God's special possession, that you may declare the praises of him who called you out of darkness into his wonderful light. 1 Peter 2:9 *(NIV)*

MY HUSBAND, SCOTT, IS A pastor, and together we have shared his ministry for twenty-three years. I'd taught Sunday school and was on the worship team before we married, so being a leader at church has shaped my life. It's who I am. How I define myself.

Two years ago, we left the San Francisco Bay area church we'd planted fifteen years earlier and moved to Idaho. Scott took a position in a large company to follow his passion for marketing. But the 180-degree turn left me feeling uncertain what my next step would be. Ministry, paid or not, was my career. I went from leading on the platform to sitting in the pew.

I felt like I was having an identity crisis. If I wasn't a pastor's wife or in ministry, who would I be in our new church?

As I mulled this over with Jesus, a realization dropped into my mind. My identity was not in *what* I did but *whose* I am. Pastor's wife or not, I am just me—God's creation, chosen and loved by Jesus, a royal priesthood, a daughter of the King.

I'm called to share His love and praise Him whether I'm in an official ministry or not. My title has changed, but my identity has not. I am His. And that's enough. —SUSANNA FOTH AUGHTMON

FAITH STEP: *Write down what you do, your jobs, accomplishments, and duties— how you see yourself. Pray over the list and ask Jesus to show you whose you are and how He sees you.*

FRIDAY, JUNE 30

*Walk with the wise and become wise, for a companion
of fools suffers harm. Proverbs 13:20 (NIV)*

AFTER READING THIS PROVERB, I made a mental list of wise people
I could spend time with. Then the realization jumped to mind that
Jesus is the wisest companion anyone could have. But how do I
walk with Him? What does that look like on a practical level?

First, I can walk with Jesus through descriptions of His actions
in the Gospels. I can read about what mattered to Him, how He
responded to each situation, how He showed His love.

Second, I can spend time with others in the body of Christ—His
church. Although none of us live out the love of Jesus perfectly, I often
see glimpses of His nature in others. Jesus appears in the generosity
of a friend who gave a gift to cheer me, in the companion who can
empathize with my pain but doesn't let me wallow in self-pity, and
in the tenderness of someone who cries with me in my grief. Each
person in the body of Christ can lead me to "walk with the wise."

Third, I can turn to Jesus in prayer each day, in every experience
I face, and discover His guidance. His Spirit counsels and guides
me when I deal with a conflict at work, a decision in my family, or
habits I want to change.

I've embraced this proverb with new enthusiasm. I plan to explore
every way I can to walk with Jesus and hopefully grow wise like
Him. —SHARON HINCK

FAITH STEP: *Think of a situation for which you need wisdom. Through Scripture,
fellowship, and prayer, ask Jesus to walk with you in this circumstance and help
you be wise.*

SATURDAY, JULY 1

You shall walk in all the ways which the LORD your God has commanded you, that you may live and that it may be well with you . . .
Deuteronomy 5:33 (NKJV)

AS MY SOON-TO-BE TWENTY-TWO-YEAR-OLD DAUGHTER and I waited in the checkout line, I scanned the merchandise displays for impulse purchases. A bright, green-striped beach bag caught my attention. It would be perfect for our upcoming family vacation.

The tote was well constructed with room for towels, sunscreen, and snacks. I put the straps on my shoulder and remembered the days of traipsing through the shifting, white sand to a vacant spot down the beach, away from the crowd. When my daughter was young, her feet would sink in the deep sand. She struggled to walk as she tried to keep up with her father and me.

"Walk where Daddy stepped," I said, as I bent down to her eye level and pointed to where her father's footprints burrowed out the sand. She stretched her thin legs, hopping and jumping to match his stride. I followed behind, also taking advantage of the path my husband had made. It was easy and effortless for both my daughter and me.

Placing the beach bag on the checkout counter, I looked up at my daughter, who stands a head taller than me. She can now forge her own path through the deep sand, but my hope is that we both remember how much better it is to walk in the footprints of the One who goes before us. —KAREN SARGENT

FAITH STEP: *Encourage a child or young person in your life to walk in Jesus's footsteps.*

SUNDAY, JULY 2

When they saw the courage of Peter and John and realized that they were unschooled, ordinary men, they were astonished and they took note that these men had been with Jesus. Acts 4:13 (NIV)

MY HUSBAND AND I ARE happily married, but the "happy" part didn't happen automatically. Early in our marriage, I blurted out my emotions without considering their impact. I was quick to judge his actions while making excuses for my own behavior. I would spend hours on tasks that consumed me, overworking and leaving very little time for us as a couple. Even though I was overly sensitive to his constructive criticism, I knew I needed to change. I wanted a second chance.

The Peter in Acts is very different from the Peter in Matthew. In Acts 4, Peter courageously and unapologetically preaches the gospel of Jesus, while back in Matthew 26, he denied knowing Jesus. So what made the difference? Jesus gave Peter a second chance. Peter learned from his mistake and reconciled with Jesus (John 21:15–19).

Change isn't easy. We all make mistakes. It took practice and prayer, but, fortunately, after twenty years of marriage I'm a different (and, more importantly, a better) wife today than I was when I first married. I'm open to asking for and accepting feedback. I show more empathy toward my husband's perspective. I take time to think before I speak and try to be fully present when we're together. I'm thankful to my husband, and Jesus, for second chances. —ERICKA LOYNES

FAITH STEP: *Do you need a second chance? Stop dwelling on your mistakes. Instead, forgive yourself, reflect on what you have learned, and have the courage to change.*

MONDAY, JULY 3

Even if my father and mother abandon me, the LORD will hold me close. Psalm 27:10 (NLT)

ONE OF MY FAVORITE THINGS is when I see my little children climbing onto my husband's lap or snuggling by his side. Even though my youngest kids are ten and eleven years old, they want to sit near him, especially during family movie night. They like being close to their dad because of the relationship that he's built with them. Years of providing for them, hugging them, and listening to them have created a special closeness.

These moments are significant to me because I never had that type of relationship with an earthly father. Growing up, I didn't know my biological father and my stepdad was aloof and distant. Thankfully, I've discovered that I can draw close to my Heavenly Father. As I pray, I picture myself climbing onto His lap. Because I know He cares, it brings me peace and my heart floods with joy and love to imagine my Heavenly Father holding me close.

Even if we have felt abandoned by our fathers, mothers, or other family members, I know we can always trust that Jesus is forever faithful. Just as I picture little children turning to Jesus, I can turn to Him in the same way. Whenever I feel alone, I imagine climbing up into His lap. Jesus puts His arms around me, holding me close and loving me. —TRICIA GOYER

FAITH STEP: *Picture yourself drawing near to Jesus. Can you see yourself climbing onto His lap and allowing Him to hold you close? Pause and find peace there.*

INDEPENDENCE DAY, TUESDAY, JULY 4

It is for freedom that Christ has set us free. Stand firm, then, and do not let yourselves be burdened again by a yoke of slavery. Galatians 5:1 (NIV)

PICNICS AND FIREWORKS, MOSQUITO BITES and the scent of sunscreen—all conjure the memory of July 4th gatherings. I'm so grateful for the freedom I enjoy in my country. Liberty is a treasure worth celebrating with noisy fireworks and rousing marches from a local band.

But there is a far more amazing freedom that I've been gifted because of the grace of Jesus. I am free to be loved by my Creator, free of the penalty of sin, free of a sense of worthlessness that tries to dog my steps. And I'm free from the fear of death.

Galatians reminds me to stand firm in that freedom. Like the people in Galatia, I slip into thinking I need to do more, that perhaps Christ's grace isn't enough. I take on burdens that aren't mine to carry and forget the sufficiency of Jesus. I struggle to trust He has truly forgiven me for my mistakes.

So while I indulge in watermelon and corn on the cob, I'll also remember the deeper liberty of Independence Day. Shackles fall away. Doubts are swallowed up by joy. Grace gives my heart wings.

In Jesus, I am truly free. And that's something to celebrate.
—SHARON HINCK

FAITH STEP: *Blow a horn, use a noise maker, applaud, and cheer. Celebrate your freedom in Christ today.*

WEDNESDAY, JULY 5

When Jesus spoke again to the people, he said, "I am the light of the world. Whoever follows me will never walk in darkness, but will have the light of life." John 8:12 (NIV)

ENGINE TROUBLE ON OUR SAILBOAT caused unexpected delays. My husband and I arrived at the mouth of the Fraser River as the wind was calm and the sun was setting. At dusk, we motored upriver. It was nearly impossible to see hazards in the water, but we had to keep going so we could find a place to moor.

I pulled out our big light. Gene steered the sailboat while I stood on the deck holding a three-thousand-lumen spotlight (equivalent to the light of three thousand candles). Steel navigational buoys located fourteen hundred feet apart dotted the length of that section of the river, marking the lanes in which incoming and outgoing vessels traveled. Colliding with one could seriously damage a hull, which is the body of the boat. My task was to find these markers and shine the light on them so Gene could steer away from them. Trying to navigate the river without that light would have been treacherous, foolish, and nearly impossible.

Jesus knew that navigating life successfully in spiritual darkness was impossible for mankind. He loved us so much that He came to earth and died for us (John 3:16). He revealed Himself as the light of life (John 1:4). He unveiled the enemy's tactics and lies so we could steer clear of them (James 4:7). I can't imagine navigating life apart from the light of Jesus any more than I can motor safely upriver in the dark. —GRACE FOX

FAITH STEP: *Recall an instance in which Jesus saved you from a potentially painful situation.*

THURSDAY, JULY 6

*Yet give attention to your servant's prayer and his plea for mercy,
LORD my God. Hear the cry and the prayer that your servant is
praying in your presence this day. 1 Kings 8:28 (NIV)*

*GOOD MORNING FROM THE BRONX! Hello from Birmingham, Alabama!
Praise God from Houston! Greetings from Dubai!* People from around
the world dial in to my church's daily 7 a.m. prayer call. Monday
through Friday, I hear familiar voices joyfully bidding each other
good morning before the prayer leader mutes the phone line and
starts with his or her own welcome and a short devotional before
beginning our time in prayer.

It's great to start my day in communal prayer with like-minded
believers who know the power of coming together before the Lord.
We pray for all sorts of things—healing for loved ones, courage to
face the day, protection of our leaders, peace in our country, safety
for our children, restoration of relationships, unwavering faith, and
more. The prayer leader will often unmute the line for a few seconds during our fifteen minutes together so we can collectively call
out the names of people or situations we want to lift up to Jesus,
trusting that He will answer us in due time. I don't know who's saying what in the cacophony of voices, but I know that Jesus hears.

Whether I'm alone in my bedroom or among hundreds of people on
the phone, I have confidence that the lines of communication are always
open with Him. Jesus hears us all. —BARBRANDA LUMPKINS WALLS

FAITH STEP: *Call a friend or relative to join you in prayer today.*

FRIDAY, JULY 7

Don't worry about anything; instead, pray about everything. Tell God what you need, and thank him for all he has done. Philippians 4:6 (NLT)

MY SON AND I WANTED to catch a movie at our town's waterfront park. At the end of a busy day, we ran late, and all the nearby parking spots were taken. When Isaac, who has Down syndrome, gets tired or loses patience, he'll dig in his heels and go no further, even if it's something he really wants to do.

Laps around the various lots yielded nothing, and parking far away wasn't an option as I had chairs to carry. I started to feel anxious and prayed because I was out of ideas.

Thank You, Jesus! I finally found an open parking spot, but it was far enough away to make it a struggle with beach chairs and now-grumpy Isaac in tow. I got out of my minivan and popped open the trunk, wondering how we'd manage.

"Isabella, is that you?"

My friend Tammy and her husband, Tim, were walking their dogs. I didn't know they lived nearby. I explained our plight.

"Our golf cart is right around the corner," Tammy said, as Tim darted down the street to retrieve it.

Moments later, Tim pulled up, loaded our chairs, and delivered Isaac and me to the perfect spot in the grass to watch the movie. I marveled how Jesus answered my prayer in a way I never imagined. I wanted a close parking space, but a wheeled cart was even better. I was out of ideas, but Jesus was not. —ISABELLA CAMPOLATTARO

FAITH STEP: *Next time you run into a problem, make prayer your first resort instead of your last.*

SATURDAY, JULY 8

*Now to him who is able to do immeasurably more than all we ask
or imagine, according to his power that is at work within us, to him
be the glory in the church and in Christ Jesus throughout all generations,
for ever and ever! Amen. Ephesians 3:20–21 (NIV)*

FOR MY DAUGHTER JOCELYN'S TENTH birthday, I bought her a cotton-candy machine and several different flavors of floss sugar. Ever since, she's been making cotton candy as often as she can.

It's mesmerizing to watch the colored sugar slowly melt and then suddenly become a whisper-thin thread that she spins into a cloud. But when moisture hits it, even a drop of liquid, the cottony puff melts.

I've been guilty, at times, of having faith like the cotton candy that Jocelyn makes. When I meld my will into Jesus's, beautiful things happen. I find myself floating on a billowy cloud of His grace, overjoyed with all He's blessed me with. But when I start to float along on my successes, forgetting to routinely ground myself in Him, my ego begins to inflate. I get puffed up with self-importance and start taking credit, and the glory, for what Jesus is doing through me.

In that me-focused state, I rely on my own resources instead of His. But as soon as any stress or chaos comes my way, the cloud I'm floating on dissolves under the pressure, just like Jocelyn's cotton candy when water hits it.

Cotton candy is a sweet treat, but it lacks nutrition, substance. So does cotton-candy faith. —CLAIRE MCGARRY

FAITH STEP: *Copy Ephesians 3:20–21 onto a note card. Put it somewhere visible as a reminder to point the praise in the right direction for your next success.*

SUNDAY, JULY 9

". . . We do not know what to do, but our eyes are on you."
2 Chronicles 20:12 (NIV)

I HAVE A JEWELRY ARMOIRE with a full-length mirrored front. It's made to hang on a wall, but it hasn't been mounted yet because there's always something more immediate on the to-do list. For now it sits on the closet floor.

Recently, I found a solid-wood, full-length mirror at a neighborhood sale. Like the other one, it rests on the floor, waiting to be mounted in the hallway for my kids to use.

There is nothing wrong with either mirror, but neither is positioned to best serve its purpose. Unless you're two feet tall, you can't see your full image without squatting, lunging, or other comical antics.

Likewise, it's nearly impossible to see the truth of a situation without having a clear view of the whole picture. I may get derailed by fact, opinions, or emotions, but I can count on Jesus to show me what's really going on. He also sees how much I don't see. My ignorance and shortsighted wisdom aren't surprising to Him, even though it's sometimes eye-opening to me.

As I grow in my faith in Jesus, I'm understanding more and more the blessing of not seeing what to do on my own. Instead, I mirror His response. Jesus always has a complete view. —ERIN KEELEY MARSHALL

FAITH STEP: *What circumstance do you need to see as fully as Jesus does? Ask Him for His view of the situation.*

MONDAY, JULY 10

*He replied, "Blessed rather are those who hear the word
of God and obey it." Luke 11:28 (NIV)*

SOMETIMES JESUS SPEAKS THROUGH CURIOUS circumstances or people. I shouldn't be surprised. Throughout the Bible, animals or objects became instruments for communicating important truths. A talking donkey, for instance (Numbers 22:28).

While watching a musical competition on television, I felt Jesus tugging on my heart. And from what some might consider an unlikely source—Snoop Dogg. The iconic hip-hop rapper, actor, media personality, and businessman served as a guest coach, helping the singing contestants grow stronger and more polished for their next performance. In his inimitable way, Snoop made this simple but profound comment: "I love giving information to those who sponge it up."

Doesn't that sound like something Jesus would say?

Jesus spent much of His ministry trying to turn humans into sponges who would listen to truth and soak it up, then be willing to be squeezed out so the teachings would land on others. Many followed Jesus, including the disciples, hanging on to His every word, but not letting it soak in and reach the depth of their souls. For many of His closest followers, they didn't become true sponges until after His death and resurrection. Their greatest transformations happened after Christ rose from the dead. Another layer of sponge-ness developed in them with the coming of the Holy Spirit after Jesus had returned to heaven.

Thanks to Snoop Dogg, I have a new way of expressing my listening to Jesus—sponge it up. —CYNTHIA RUCHTI

FAITH STEP: *As you read God's Word today, think of yourself as a sponge. Let it soak in far deeper than your brain. And get ready to squeeze it out to others.*

TUESDAY, JULY 11

Therefore, since we are surrounded by such a great cloud of witnesses,
let us throw off everything that hinders and the sin that so easily entangles.
And let us run with perseverance the race marked out for us, fixing our eyes
on Jesus, the pioneer and perfecter of faith. For the joy set before him
he endured the cross, scorning its shame, and sat down at the
right hand of the throne of God. Hebrews 12:1–2 (NIV)

MY SON, WILL, RECENTLY GRADUATED from high school. It was a glorious day. "Pomp and Circumstance" played through the loudspeakers. The graduates filed past us, two by two. Our family cheered for Will as he walked by. But he didn't acknowledge us. He stared straight ahead, his eyes fixed on the stage.

Will's senior year has been full of ups and downs. Senior retreat. Sickness. Makeup work. Finals. Senior trip. It had all led to this moment. The journey to graduation wasn't what he expected, but Will had done what he set out to do. We cheered when he received his diploma. I cried a little.

Like Will's last year of high school, my journey on this earth has been unexpected, full of ups and downs, but Jesus shows me how to make the best of it and get through. Just as Will had his eyes fixed on graduation, I fix my eyes on Jesus as I persevere. As I shake off hindrances, He teaches me how to overcome trials and sin that test me. Jesus is cheering me on as I pass each milestone. I look forward to the day I will graduate into His loving arms.
—SUSANNA FOTH AUGHTMON

FAITH STEP: *Meditate on Hebrews 12:1–2. Ponder the great grace and hope that Jesus offers you as you journey toward your heavenly commencement.*

WEDNESDAY, JULY 12

Each time he said, "My grace is all you need. My power works best in weakness." So now I am glad to boast about my weaknesses, so that the power of Christ can work through me. 2 Corinthians 12:9 (NLT)

I TURN THE RADIO ON when I'm working in the kitchen, mostly for company. I don't usually listen intently, but my ears perked up when I heard the question posed by a honey-voiced announcer: "Who have you disappointed today?" Being slightly compulsive, I made a list in my head.

I didn't get to the grocery store, so I was out of my cats' favorite food. Ditto milk for my husband, Jeff. I was late getting home, so the pest-control technician had to wait before he could spray my house. I didn't get a card in the mail for my sick friend. I forgot to take the chicken out to thaw, so dinner would be pizza, again. I ate two candy bars instead of one protein bar. I forgot to return my daughter's Crock-Pot, as promised. I cut my devotion time short to ride my bike before it rained. I failed to return my library books. I neglected to vacuum. Feeling dreadful about myself, I figured a better question might be, "Who DIDN'T I disappoint today?"

In my heart, I knew the answer: Jesus! He knows my faults and my frailties. He sees when I fall short. He understands I'm trying, but I'm an imperfect person.

Jesus LOVES imperfect people! His grace, His power, works best in my weakness. He doesn't want me to beat myself up. Nothing I could ever do will disappoint Him. —PAT BUTLER DYSON

FAITH STEP: *Make a list of three people you didn't disappoint today. Feel free to include Jesus!*

THURSDAY, JULY 13

But with you there is forgiveness, so that we can,
with reverence, serve you. Psalm 130:4 (NIV)

I HOISTED A FULL LAUNDRY basket onto my hip and walked downstairs. While I matched socks and wrestled with fitted sheets, my children tackled their own chores. I was pleasantly surprised to see my two youngest working together nicely in the kitchen. "We're almost done," called my son from over the counter. "Everything's fine!"

I paused. Rarely do children volunteer that everything is fine unless it is most definitely *not* fine. I set the basket down and walked into the kitchen to investigate. My flip-flops stuck to the floor.

"What happened?" I cried, then noticed the empty powdered sugar container lying on its side. A thin layer of white residue blanketed the tile like a dusting of fresh snow.

"We tried to clean it up!" My son's eyes brimmed with tears. "But the water made it sticky." I sighed and searched for the mop. If they had just come to me when the mess first happened, I could have kept it from becoming bigger.

As I scrubbed, I realized how I'm often like my children when I make messes in life. Instead of running to Jesus right away, asking for help and forgiveness, I try to fix my mistakes myself, but it only makes matters worse.

Mopping the sticky floor, I decided to come clean with Jesus too. I confessed my inclination to hide my secret mistakes and shout "everything's fine," instead of first seeking Him when I get myself in a mess. —EMILY E. RYAN

FAITH STEP: *Think of a small mistake that has grown into a big mess by not turning it over to Jesus. Ask Him to forgive and help you before it gets out of control.*

FRIDAY, JULY 14

But blessed are your eyes because they see, and your ears because they hear. For truly I tell you, many prophets and righteous people longed to see what you see but did not see it, and to hear what you hear but did not hear it. Matthew 13:16–17 (NIV)

AFTER ENDURING A PARTICULARLY DIFFICULT spring, a friend suggested I focus on a summer of praise. Instead of asking Jesus for something or thanking Him for blessings, she encouraged me to look for and honor His attributes in nature.

Before I went for a walk each morning, I'd slip my smartphone into my pocket. When I noticed something beautiful or interesting, I'd snap a picture of it and ponder what it showed me about Jesus.

A large stone reminded me He was my firm foundation. A delicate wildflower spoke to me of the gentleness of Jesus. A bush laden with berries made me think of His generosity.

As I stopped to notice the beauty around me, I began to have new eyes to see. I learned to praise Jesus for who He was and not for what I wanted from Him. I realized that although I couldn't see Him in the same way that His disciples could when He walked the earth, Jesus was truly present. He revealed His love, His mercy, His power in myriad ways.

Now when my circumstances look bleak, I pray for eyes to see Him at work, and for His vision of hope for the people I love. Snapshots of Jesus are all around me. —SHARON HINCK

FAITH STEP: *While walking outside or simply sitting in nature, take a picture that speaks to you about an attribute of Jesus. Ask Him to show you how He's working in your life today.*

SATURDAY, JULY 15

So anyone who becomes as humble as this little child is the greatest in the Kingdom of Heaven. Matthew 18:4 (NLT)

OUR TEENAGE GRANDDAUGHTER, GRACE, CLEANS our house to earn extra spending money. But when I correct her or show her how I want something done, she responds with grimaces and loud sighs. "Oh, all right," she says. Although she complies, her reluctant attitude hurts me.

I can't help but miss little three-year-old Gracie, the younger version of my granddaughter who lives in my mind. When I asked that darling girl to pick up her toys or brush her teeth, she chirped, "Okay!" and ran off to obey.

As I mused about these changes, Jesus showed me that Grace wasn't the only one who needed an attitude adjustment. How many times has His Spirit prompted me to change my plans and follow His lead? When He asked me to serve Him in a way I'd not anticipated, did I drag my feet, stall for days or weeks, and finally comply, only out of duty, not love? Did that hurt Him the way Gracie hurt me?

I want to respond to Jesus's leadings like that darling three-year-old in my mind with a cheerful "Okay!" instead of a reluctant, "Oh, all right."

I still drag my feet at times, but I'm learning to be thankful and cheerful for His voice encouraging me to obey Him willingly.
—JEANETTE LEVELLIE

FAITH STEP: *Next time Jesus whispers in your heart, try saying "Okay!" and feel the joy.*

SUNDAY, JULY 16

Truly the light is sweet, and it is pleasant for the eyes to behold the sun. Ecclesiastes 11:7 (NKJV)

As a child, milk made me gag, so I drank as little as possible. When I grew up, I cut it entirely from my diet. That's why I wasn't completely surprised by the unfavorable results of my bone density test. I assumed Dr. Schuster would tell me I had to drink the white stuff. But instead, he said, "Get lots of sunshine and eat lots of ice cream. Sunshine for vitamin D and ice cream for calcium. Both together can strengthen your bones."

"Will you put that in writing?" I asked. Dr. Schuster opened his prescription pad and wrote: "Sunshine transdermal QD, ice cream PO QD." Translation? Sunshine on my skin every morning and ice cream in my mouth once a day.

We physically need sunshine. Sun exposure initiates the production of vitamin D in our skin. Vitamin D helps our bodies absorb calcium. Calcium, in turn, travels to our skeletal systems to ensure healthy, strong bones. Sunshine also provides emotional benefits. We've all experienced it—the sun pops out, and our spirits become bright. According to science, spending time in the sun triggers the release of serotonin in our brains. This chemical calms us, brings focus, and boosts our mood.

Ecclesiastes describes sunshine beautifully: The light is sweet, and the sun is pleasant for the eyes to behold. Jesus, the Son, created the rising sun. Daily I will seek the sun's rays to warm me on the outside, as I allow the Son to shine brightly within me. —BECKY ALEXANDER

FAITH STEP: *Find a sunny spot and enjoy a scoop or two of your favorite ice cream. Thank Jesus for another light-filled, sweet day of life.*

MONDAY, JULY 17

*Having heard about Jesus, she came up behind him in the
crowd and touched his clothing.* Mark 5:27 (CSB)

A FRIEND AND I WERE deeply engaged in conversation when she
attempted to *knock on wood.* The only trouble was, we stood in
front of our hundred-year-old church, which was built out of hand-
hewn stone. It's funny how this ancient superstition of touching
wood is still so ingrained, even in followers of Jesus. For the most
part, she doesn't practice other superstitious rituals. No throwing
salt over her shoulder or dabbing olive oil behind her ears, yet she
readily touches wood to ward off the loss of something positive and
good in her life.

This contrast between her professed faith in Jesus and her superstitious outward action has weighed on my heart and mind. In those
instances when she fears losing a blessing, shouldn't her automatic
response be to *touch Jesus* rather than touch wood?

Touch Jesus is what I want my go-to response to be in all circumstances. I want the same kind of deliberate, focused intent as the
woman in the Bible who pressed through the crowds of people to
touch His cloak, knowing that one touch would ensure her healing. And not just to touch Jesus as a superstitious ritual when I
think I might lose a blessing, but to stay *in touch* with Him at all
times. —CASSANDRA TIERSMA

FAITH STEP: *With a dry-erase marker, write "Touch Jesus" on your bathroom
mirror. Like the woman in the Bible who made it her top priority to touch Him,
make staying in touch with Jesus your focus for the day.*

TUESDAY, JULY 18

The Father loves the Son, and has given all things into His hand. John 3:35 (NKJV)

MY YOUNGEST DAUGHTER, RANDI, RECENTLY graduated from college and moved into her first apartment. As I sorted through the belongings she left behind, I found one of her favorite childhood books.

During Randi's senior year of high school, she was invited to read *The Kissing Hand* to a kindergarten class. The story features a young raccoon who is afraid to leave his mom and go to school. The mama raccoon kisses the inside of his paw and suggests he press his paw to his cheek if he misses her.

The thoughtful kindergarten teacher emailed a video of Randi as she read to the class. Once the book was finished, Randi confided to the students that she used to feel like the baby raccoon when she left her mom to go to school. And now, she felt that way again as she prepared to leave for college.

I wished I would have read that story to my daughter more often. I wish I would have kissed her hand when she was young—pressing a reminder of my love on her palm every day so Randi could see a concrete display of the love I have for her.

I know Another's hands who are imprinted with love. Nail-scarred from hanging on Calvary, the palms of Jesus represent a love so far-reaching, so unending, that I can't fathom it or escape it. And, that's my favorite story of all. —KAREN SARGENT

FAITH STEP: *With your finger, trace JESUS on your palm and press it to your cheek. Thank Him for His unfailing love.*

WEDNESDAY, JULY 19

The crowd demanded that they keep quiet, but they cried out all the more, "Lord, have mercy on us, Son of David!" Matthew 20:31 (CSB)

WHEN THE TWO BLIND MEN heard that Jesus was passing by, they cried out to Him for help. The crowd grew angry and tried to silence them. But the men refused to be intimidated. Jesus stopped and asked, "What do you want me to do for you?" The men answered they wanted healing. With a touch from Jesus, they could see.

Some of my favorite Bible stories show the rewards of perseverance. That's probably because I struggle with a tendency to give up too easily. A good example is spending time with Jesus and the Word early in the morning. I know what a difference this practice can make in my day. But I always seem to have a "crowd" trying to keep me from calling out to Him: the day's activities and appointments, pressing chores, other people, my own desires.

If I allow myself to be silenced and skip my special time of communion with Him, I miss out on all Jesus wants to give me. But if I persevere, I imagine Him asking the same question He asked the blind men: "What do you want me to do for you today?" A wise answer would be the same one those men gave Him: "Lord, let my eyes be opened." I want to live for Jesus, and I need His spiritual discernment to see and understand His will. That's a gift worth any amount of perseverance. —DIANNE NEAL MATTHEWS

FAITH STEP: *What is the one thing you most long for Jesus to do in your life? Determine that nothing will prevent you from calling out for His help and listening for His guidance.*

Thursday, July 20

*"Whoever belongs to God hears what God says. The reason
you do not hear is that you do not belong to God." John 8:47 (NIV)*

WITHOUT REALIZING WHAT SHE WAS saying, a toddler interrupted my prayer time with a friend. "Stop talking to Jesus!"

Yes, the child's need for a frozen treat was strong, but it's highly unlikely she had any concept of the weight or rudeness or ridiculousness of those words.

Or are they ridiculous?

Maybe that advice is wiser than it at first appears. My ratio of talking words versus listening words in prayer is often out of balance. Requests come naturally. There's no lack of needs to discuss with Him. But for me, the listening part of a conversation with Jesus gets shortchanged too often.

After giving the toddler a popsicle, we all went out on the deck. My friend and I resumed our prayer time, not talking to Jesus, but listening.

It took a while for the chattering in my brain to quiet down. I knew I was listening, not so much for a voice, but for impressions, inaudible whispers, the "still, quiet" kind of communication Jesus is known for. I heard a reminder, as a thought formed in my mind, of what a grace gift it is to be invited into the throne room of the King. That alone put me in awe and gave me something to ponder as I sat and listened to Him.

Stop talking to Jesus? Pretty good advice from a toddler.
—CYNTHIA RUCHTI

FAITH STEP: *Find a spot where pray-listening won't be interrupted. Consider writing down the impressions you gained from the unmistakable voice of Jesus.*

FRIDAY, JULY 21

When he had led them out to the vicinity of Bethany, he lifted up his hands and blessed them. While he was blessing them, he left them and was taken up into heaven. Luke 24:50–51 (NIV)

MY HUSBAND AND I HAVE enjoyed a growing friendship with a couple who live on a sailboat, like we do. When they leave the dock, they're usually gone for at least two weeks. Knowing from experience that boating can prove both pleasurable and miserable, we always send them off with well wishes: "Good luck! Take care. We hope everything goes well."

When Jesus ascended into heaven, He shared well wishes of a different sort with the disciples. He said nothing trite like, "Good luck. Take care. I hope everything goes well." Instead, He blessed them with words that would fill their lives with purpose—to go and make disciples of all nations and baptize them in the name of the Father, the Son, and the Holy Spirit. He commissioned them to teach new disciples to obey His commands. And then He promised to be with them until the end of the age (Matthew 28:19–20).

Can you imagine mankind's mess if Jesus had wished the disciples luck and then left them to figure out life on their own? I'm grateful that when He departed, He left with a blessing that applies to us today. I don't have to merely hope everything will go well. I have assurance that all will be well because He is with me. I don't need luck because I'm blessed. —GRACE FOX

FAITH STEP: *Count how many times you are tempted to use the word "luck" today. Thank Jesus for His presence and that nothing in your life depends on luck.*

SATURDAY, JULY 22

Because you are precious in my eyes, and honored, and I love you . . .
Isaiah 43:4 (RSV)

AFTER FORTY-PLUS YEARS OF MARRIAGE, I'm finally starting to understand that when my husband explains something to me in great detail, he isn't implying I'm stupid. Kevin is a pastor with the gift of teaching. He loves to impart knowledge. Period. His penchant for sharing facts has no relationship to my knowledge or expertise.

As a child, I repeatedly heard, "If I want something done right, I guess I'll have to do it myself," from a loved one. I translated those words as, "You are inept."

As an adult, I realize I've applied that same erroneous thinking to many interactions with others. I wrongly believed their words and treatment of me reflected my inherent worth.

But there's a big difference between saying, "This needs work" and "You are a failure." One addresses a mistake I've made that needs correction. The other attacks me as a person.

Learning to see myself through Jesus's eyes means separating my mess-ups from my value. Jesus thinks I'm worthy based on His love for me as His child. How He feels about me is not based on how well I sing, garden, cook, write a story, or preach a sermon.

So these days, when Kevin explains facts I already know I don't say, "Why do you think I'm so dumb?" I say, "Wow, that's fascinating. Tell me more!"

Jesus paid the same price for everyone—His blood. We are all precious in His sight, and that includes me, no explanation needed. —JEANETTE LEVELLIE

FAITH STEP: *Tell Jesus, "Thank You for the price You paid for me. Please help me love myself because I am precious to You."*

SUNDAY, JULY 23

For the flesh desires what is contrary to the Spirit, and the Spirit what is contrary to the flesh. They are in conflict with each other, so that you are not to do whatever you want. Galatians 5:17 (NIV)

AFTER WEEKS OF RESEARCH, I found the perfect spray to refresh my hair. I loved the sheen and moisture the hairspray gave my curls. But moments after using it, I felt stinging and saw burns and discoloration on my ears and forehead. Instead of discarding the spray, I sat it on the shelf. I really didn't want to throw it out. I liked what it did to my hair. As irrational as it sounds, I hoped I could think of a way to keep using it, even though it burned my skin.

The lure of temptation can be irrational too. Jesus used Scripture to take control of the situation when He was tempted in the wilderness (Matthew 4:1–10). He used God's Word to fight against the enemy and prevail during those forty days.

Like Jesus, I have access to the same powerful Word, the Bible, that will rebuke the enemy. By memorizing scriptures, I can speak God's Word and resist the sparkle and shine that the enemy uses to cover up the pain and suffering on the other side of temptation.

Even though I loved the sheen and moisture that hairspray gave my curls, I resisted the temptation to try it again and threw it in the trash can. —ERICKA LOYNES

FAITH STEP: *Memorize scriptures and use them to fight against temptations that the enemy puts in your path. Resist the urge to give in by surrendering yourself completely to Jesus.*

MONDAY, JULY 24

Therefore do not worry about tomorrow, for tomorrow will worry about itself. Each day has enough trouble of its own. Matthew 6:34 (NIV)

I ANSWERED MY PHONE THAT first day of Isaac's summer camp. My son's counselor told me that Isaac, who has Down syndrome, didn't want to join the group and was refusing to budge.

Isaac went to the camp last year and liked it. Maybe he was being slow to warm up in the situation. I gave her some tips and hung up. Anxiety crept onto my shoulders.

She called again, minutes later. Isaac still refused to move to the next activity at the park. She was going to give it a bit more time and get back to me. Anxiety erupted into full-blown worry, and questions crowded my mind. *Was he miserable? Were the counselors exasperated with him? What if he was dismissed from the camp? Was this a mood or would he act like this the rest of the summer? Should I rush there and pick him up?*

As thoughts about what might happen consumed me, another question popped into my mind. *What should I do, Jesus?* I stopped, took a deep breath, and a peaceful trust enveloped me. There was nothing I could do, but I knew Jesus would help Isaac and equip the counselors to deal with the situation.

Twenty minutes later, the camp secretary called to say Isaac had joined the group and was having fun. I had nothing to worry about, thanks to Jesus. —ISABELLA CAMPOLATTARO

FAITH STEP: *Next time you feel even a hint of worry, don't let it run wild. Stop right where you are and pray, then let Jesus take it from there.*

TUESDAY, JULY 25

When the sun came up, Jesus was standing on the beach,
but they didn't recognize him. John 21:4 (MSG)

AS A BEEKEEPER, I'M FASCINATED by bees. Each is a separate organism but is a member of the hive, which itself resembles an organism. The bees' changing roles parallel human development: first as larva, fed by others; then workers, advancing through the ranks as housekeepers, caregivers, undertakers, builders, packers, fixers—even controlling the temperature in the hive. Some bees guard the hive, while others finally graduate to fieldwork, becoming scouts and foragers.

These outdoor bees buzz close while I sit near the hives observing them. Individual bees fly within a few inches of my face, flitting from side to side, zigzagging downward in a plane four inches from my nose. It seemed like they were scouting me!

I researched this and discovered they were doing just that. Scientists have discovered that bees see a pixelated image of the human face and recognize their beekeeper.

Humans aren't always astute as bees. Soon after Jesus rose from the dead, there were several times when his followers had trouble recognizing Him. Mary mistook Him for the gardener (John 20:15). Cleopas and his companion on the road to Emmaus didn't know who He was immediately (Luke 24:28). The disciples didn't quickly recognize Him from afar as they fished (John 21:4).

Since I visit my bees unveiled, they see and know me. In the same way, Jesus is present to me. I can always know Him through His Word, listening for His whisper, by prayer, and spending time in His presence. —SUZANNE DAVENPORT TIETJEN

FAITH STEP: *Close your eyes and imagine Jesus with you face-to-face. Keep that image before you as you come to Him in prayer.*

WEDNESDAY, JULY 26

Your love has given me much joy and comfort, my brother, for your kindness has often refreshed the hearts of God's people. Philemon 1:7 (NLT)

THE WEEK HAD FELT A month long: too much work, projects that I couldn't finish, and flare-ups of health problems. And just when my husband and I were making headway with a financial goal, our furnace broke down and needed replacing. When Sunday rolled around, I wanted to pull the quilt over my head and stay in bed. But I knew that church was where I needed to be—what I needed most.

Sure enough, the hymns about Jesus lifted my spirits. Smiles of friends brought joy. Words of Scripture fell on my parched heart like water. The pastor's sermon shared wisdom and encouragement. Each person participating in the service offered kindness by their presence, and that kindness brought refreshment. My soul was quenched.

Refreshment is a beautiful, grace-filled word. It's an oasis in the desert, the sheltered rest stop along the freeway, the safe haven for a bruised and battered heart. The kindness of God's people filled my tank and changed my perspective. It restored hope. No matter how many difficulties the last week had held, I was strengthened and even eager to tackle the days ahead.

As I savored being refreshed, Jesus stirred a new resolve in my soul. I wanted to bring this grace and encouragement to others. Like the offer of an ice-cold drink on a summer day, my church-going experience inspired me—the best way to refresh myself was to refresh others first. —SHARON HINCK

FAITH STEP: *List three people you know who are struggling. Think of creative ways to give them kindness and grace that will refresh their soul and spirit.*

THURSDAY, JULY 27

So do not throw away your confidence; it will be richly rewarded.
You need to persevere so that when you have done the will of God,
you will receive what he has promised. Hebrews 10:35–36 (NIV)

I LAUGHED OUT LOUD FROM inside the public bathroom stall. Here's why: A sign affixed to the stall door read: "Don't flush paper towels, sanitary products, or your dreams down the toilet."

I felt validated and uplifted by finding important advice in a most unlikely place. The rest of the day, the unexpected words of encouragement swirled around in my mind. I mean, who hasn't, at one time or another, had a dream that got flushed down the toilet?

I've had many dreams and made many plans to achieve them throughout my life. Some have come to fruition. Some have not. Sometimes circumstances beyond my control bring my dream to an anticlimactic halt, and the dream I envisioned dies. I abhor the heartbreak and disappointment of a dream not coming true; however, that's entirely different from giving up on a dream. When I've not followed a dream, for whatever reason—maybe it took longer than I thought it should or I didn't have the confidence—a part of my spirit was laid to rest too. I lost hope along with that dream.

When Jesus plants a dream in my heart that will honor and glorify Him, I don't want to flush it away just because I may feel scared, inadequate, or unequipped. No matter how long it takes, I must keep my hope and dream alive. My confidence to achieve the dream isn't in me, but in the Dream Maker, Jesus. —CASSANDRA TIERSMA

FAITH STEP: *Has Jesus put a dream on your heart? Write it down. Ask Him to give you confidence.*

Friday, July 28

One who has unreliable friends soon comes to ruin, but there is a friend who sticks closer than a brother. Proverbs 18:24 (NIV)

Once a month, my friend Christa and I meet in downtown Boise. We grab coffee and gluten-free donuts and talk as we walk down the tree-shaded greenbelt along the Boise River. The coffee is delightful, the donuts are delicious, the walk is idyllic, but it's the conversation I look forward to most. Kids. Husbands. Ministry. Work. Family. Connecting with Christa on a regular basis strengthens our friendship. We can tell each other anything, and we support, encourage, and point each other toward Jesus. When you find a friend like that, you don't let go.

Jesus isn't letting go of me, either. In spite of all my mess-ups and weaknesses, He chooses to call me friend. Imagine! Just like my friendship with Christa, I can tell Jesus anything too. Kids. Husbands. Ministry. Work. Family. No subject is taboo. Unlike Christa, Jesus already knows everything that's going on with me, and He knows how to best advise me in every circumstance.

Just like my friendship with Christa, to build my relationship with Jesus, I must make time for Him. Anywhere, anytime is perfect to connect with Jesus. He's the best friend I could ever ask for, and when you find a friend like that, you don't let go. —Susanna Foth Aughtmon

---

Faith Step: *Just as you would spend time with a human friend, Jesus wants to spend time with you. Make a breakfast, brunch, or lunch date with Him today. Envision Him seated next to you as you talk and listen.*

SATURDAY, JULY 29

You discern my going out and my lying down; you are familiar with all my ways. Psalm 139:3 (NIV)

GOING FOR WALKS IS AN easy way for me to get some exercise. Before I head out the door, I gather my keys, phone, and identification. I don't map out a route; I just go where the spirit leads me. Although I'm walking in our neighborhood, my husband leans toward caution. He wants to know which direction I'm headed so he can find me in case of an emergency or if I'm gone too long. "You need to be safe!" he says.

I wanted to have the freedom to roam the streets *and* address my husband's concern about my safety. As a compromise, I use my phone's "share my location" feature that allows him to track me and see my whereabouts in real time.

In Psalm 139:7–8 (NIV), King David recognized that God sees and knows all. He asks, "Where can I go from your Spirit? Where can I flee from your presence? If I go up to the heavens, you are there; if I make my bed in the depths, you are there."

Jesus doesn't need a GPS signal to locate me. He knows where I am physically, mentally, spiritually, and emotionally. I may think Jesus isn't aware of the envy, resentment, or anxiety I may be feeling, but who am I fooling? Certainly not Him. Whether I share with Jesus or not, He knows my location and my heart. I can't hide or get lost. Walking with Him, I'm always safe. —BARBRANDA LUMPKINS WALLS

FAITH STEP: *Read Psalm 139 out loud and write the ways you are encouraged by knowing Jesus is always with you.*

Sunday, July 30

"Now My soul is troubled, and what shall I say? 'Father, save Me from this hour'? But for this purpose I came to this hour. Father, glorify Your name."...John 12:27–28 (NKJV)

DURING LUNCH WITH SEVERAL LADIES, my friend Mischelle passed around a few books she'd finished reading. I flipped through a small gift book called *The Red Sea Rules: 10 God-Given Strategies for Difficult Times* by Robert Morgan and then put it back on the table. The last thing I needed was another item on my to-read list. But Mischelle urged me so sweetly to take it home that I finally dropped it into my bag. Little did I know how timely its message would be.

Later that week, I read Rule #2: *Be more concerned for God's glory than for your relief.* The chapter focused on how God had led the Israelites to a point between the Red Sea and the Egyptian army for the purpose of displaying His glory. I jotted down a few main points, but apparently my mind wandered a bit. Instead of writing *The Lord devises ways of turning difficulties into deliverances and problems into praise*, I wrote *problems into panic*. I crossed out *panic*, but my hand started to write it again! I intentionally marked through the letters and deliberately wrote the word *praise*.

As a psychology major, I might be tempted to call that a Freudian slip. But I believe Jesus was preparing me for a catastrophic storm I'd soon face. Weeks later, Jesus helped me focus on His glory by turning problems into praise in the midst of a major hurricane that would normally have ignited panic. —DIANNE NEAL MATTHEWS

FAITH STEP: *The next time you face a difficulty, ask Jesus to help you praise Him as you wait for deliverance.*

MONDAY, JULY 31

"I tell you the truth, anyone who doesn't receive the Kingdom of God like a child will never enter it." Then he took the children in his arms and placed his hands on their heads and blessed them. Mark 10:15–16 (NLT)

MY TWO-YEAR-OLD GRANDDAUGHTER, AMELIA, AND her parents recently came to stay with us. My daughter, son-in-law, and granddaughter live out of the country, so I was able to share a lot of new foods with Amelia. We discovered she loves yogurt-covered raisins, cheese crackers, and popsicles. Each time I asked Amelia if she wanted to try something new, she opened her mouth wide. As her nana, she trusted me. And because I love her, I never took advantage of her trust. Instead, I made sure I offered delicious foods that I thought she would like.

When it comes to my relationship with Jesus, I, too, must be childlike: trusting, fearless, and always full of hope. I must believe that Jesus desires the best for me and that He has good plans for my life (Jeremiah 29:11). When seeking the Kingdom of God, I must give up the things I find comfortable to understand Jesus has more for me than I could ever hope for or imagine (Ephesians 3:20).

Just as I offer tasty treats to my sweet granddaughter and she opens her mouth wide, Jesus desires to give His good gifts to me. I need only to open my hands, and heart, to receive them. —TRICIA GOYER

FAITH STEP: *Next time you are with a child, consider a good gift you can offer, such as a kind word, a special treat, or a few coins. As you experience joy in the giving, imagine how much Jesus enjoys giving to you.*

TUESDAY, AUGUST 1

. . . your Father knows what you need before you ask him.
Matthew 6:8 (NRSV)

I EAT MY BREAKFAST STRAIGHT from the tree outside the back door, savoring sweet, succulent fruit until I've had my fill. Thinking I'd planted an ornamental shade tree, I was surprised when it turned out to be a fruiting mulberry tree. Had I known, I never would've planted a berry tree so near an entrance to our home. Berries tracked in on shoes are notorious for staining carpets.

In our old garden, I'd enjoyed eating fresh, purple-black mulberries straight from the tree, planted in a hedgerow far from the house. *This* tree, though—which hitched a ride as an interloper in the pot of a poplar tree—turned out to be a *white* mulberry tree. Now, each time I eat fresh white mulberries straight off this unexpected blessing of a tree I am reminded of how the Lord knows me, how He knew I'd miss the fruit of my old mulberry tree. And He provided—not just a mulberry tree, but a *white* mulberry tree. So it wouldn't track in dark purple berries to stain the floors.

Every day, Jesus provides me with countless unexpected blessings before I even know what I need. I had no idea that a white mulberry tree would be perfect outside our back door. Now, picking fresh mulberries and popping them into my mouth is a seasonal reminder of how Jesus, in His infinite wisdom, continually provides for my needs and wants, often before I know what they are. And that's a tasty delight, indeed! —CASSANDRA TIERSMA

FAITH STEP: *Commit this part of Matthew 6:8 to memory: Your Father knows what you need before you ask Him.*

WEDNESDAY, AUGUST 2

And may you know his love, even though it can't be known completely. Then you will be filled with everything God has for you. Ephesians 3:19 *(NIRV)*

I WAS ALMOST DONE WITH a sewing project when I realized I had sewn an entire seam, and it didn't hold because the bobbin thread had run out. I stopped everything, rewound the bobbin with fresh thread, and began sewing again.

It reminded me of when I first taught myself to sew. I called my sister in frustration. "What is a bobbin and is it really even necessary?" She laughed and explained that the thread from the bobbin loops with the thread from the main spool to secure the stitches in place. "You could sew without it, but the fabric wouldn't hold together. All of your stitches would unravel."

This is the image that comes to mind when I feel unraveled myself. It's like I'm going through all of the right motions, but nothing is sticking. All my efforts are in vain and nothing I do has staying power. It's then that I remember to "check my bobbin." Have I given so much of myself that I've become empty? Have I forgotten to replace that which has run out?

When the answer is "yes," I know I have to pause and rewind. Not "rewind" as in "go backward," but "rewind" as in "wind again." Replenish. Refill. Restock. I rewind by spending time with Jesus and reflecting on how much He loves me. I read Scripture. Pray. Walk. Listen. Sing. Only with Him do my efforts have staying power once again. —EMILY E. RYAN

FAITH STEP: *Make a list of five ways you can rewind with Jesus, then do one of those today.*

Thursday, August 3

"A new command I give you: Love one another. As I have loved you, so you must love one another." John 13:34 (NIV)

I AM VERY CLOSE TO my younger sister, Andrea. We are good friends, and we often joke that we were forced to be this way. Mom didn't allow us to argue as children, and she always stopped put-downs or unkind remarks—even when it was clear we were kidding. I didn't understand why my actions and words were problematic. From what I observed, spats and sibling rivalry were the norm with my friends in their families. Regardless, Mom's expectation for how we treated each other held us to a higher standard.

When Jesus walked the earth, He had a higher standard too. His behavior contradicted the eye-for-an-eye culture He lived in (Matthew 5:21–48). Murder was a terrible sin, but anger with another broke God's law to the same degree. Adultery was punishable by death, but lustful thoughts were adultery of the mind. Jesus contradicted the common idea to love neighbors and hate enemies by commanding we love our enemies and pray for those who persecute us.

Though the rules society had were widely accepted, Jesus introduced this revolutionary concept for those who followed Him back then. That standard is still in place for those of us who follow Him now. Certain conduct and language may be tolerated today, but Jesus followers are called to a higher standard—to embrace this commandment and the sacrificial love of Jesus by extending love to everyone, always. And that includes siblings. —ERICKA LOYNES

FAITH STEP: *Read Matthew 5:21–48 and reflect on the high standard Jesus calls us to. Do your actions seem like normal behavior? If they don't, have the courage to change and look more like Him.*

FRIDAY, AUGUST 4

Don't be selfish; don't try to impress others. Be humble, thinking of others as better than yourselves. Philippians 2:3 (NLT)

MY YOUNGEST DAUGHTER AND HER husband hung two bird feeders in their yard. Small birds like wrens, finches, and sparrows visited daily. Crows came, too, and tried to reach the seeds with their beaks, but they were too large.

As I visited her one day, my daughter felt pity for the crows, so she placed several pieces of bread on the deck. Two feathered friends came to investigate the moment she retreated into the house. One bird grabbed two chunks in its beak and then perched on the deck rail to swallow them. The second bird waited its turn and then did the same thing. That's when the first bird behaved like a bully, using its beak to pry open the other bird's beak and yank bread from its mouth.

The word "selfish" came to mind as I watched the show. There was plenty of food for both, but one crow instinctually insisted on satisfying its own needs at the other's expense. The second bird's well-being meant nothing to the first.

Humans have a natural instinct toward selfishness, too, so Jesus came to show us a better way. He gave up His rights as God, became a servant, and died a criminal's death on the cross for our well-being. He demonstrated selfless grace. I want to do the same by setting my own desires aside and looking out for others whose needs are greater than mine. I want to behave like Jesus rather than follow my instincts like the local crows. —GRACE FOX

FAITH STEP: *Feed some birds today. As you do, ask Jesus to bring you an opportunity to selflessly share with a person in need.*

SATURDAY, AUGUST 5

He stilled the storm to a whisper; the waves of the sea were hushed.
Psalm 107:29 (NIV)

THIS MORNING WHEN I TURNED on the news, there was a hurricane approaching the East Coast, massive forest fires in California, earthquakes, shark attacks, and epidemics. I clicked off the television thinking the world had become like all the worst disaster movies rolled into one.

Life can feel stormy sometimes. There are the big-picture waves affecting the world at large. As my viewing of the news showed me, those calamities can be frequent and troubling.

There are rumbles of thunder for me too. I worry about my husband's cancer, my kids who are out of work, the progression of a loved one's Alzheimer's disease. My boat is tiny, and the waves are big. Lightning crackles and fear churns in my heart.

Until I remember Jesus.

The same Jesus who spoke from the boat when His disciples battled huge waves on the Sea of Galilee speaks to the scary things in my life too. The same Jesus who rose victorious to grant the world salvation promises that He is with us and is completing His purposes no matter how stormy the world looks.

The sea of struggle remains. I'm still worried about my husband's cancer, my kids who are looking for jobs, and my loved one with Alzheimer's disease. But I've been in the boat with Jesus long enough to know the howling wind stills to a whisper in obedience to His command. As I let Him speak to my own troubled heart, I find those waves are calmed inside my soul as well. —SHARON HINCK

FAITH STEP: *Draw some waves and label them with storms you are facing. Ask Jesus to calm the storm and give you peace.*

SUNDAY, AUGUST 6

*And God raised us up with Christ and seated us with him in the
heavenly realms in Christ Jesus. Ephesians 2:6 (NIV)*

MY HUGE FEMALE CAT, POKEY, loves to sit in my lap while I watch
TV. She curls her extra-large body with practiced precision. Rarely
is there more than a stray foot hanging off my lap, until Dr. Phibes
shows up.

We inherited Dr. Phibes—named for a sci-fi movie character—
from our son. When Ron moved from home into an apartment, he
left his cat behind. Now Dr. Phibes belongs to me. Wait. I belong
to him.

If Dr. Phibes decides my lap makes the perfect resting place, Pokey's presence doesn't faze him. He silently jumps on the sofa beside
me and inches his front paws onto the side of my thigh. Soon his
shoulders and front end have displaced half of Pokey. She glares at
him. But he keeps going. Little by little, Dr. Phibes scoots farther
onto my lap until he's pushed Pokey off.

I sometimes forget how big Jesus's lap is. If I hear a friend talk
about the favor Jesus did for her, I'm tempted to think, *Well. You
never did that for me, Lord.* Which is pretty catty.

Jesus reminds me that He has lots of room on His lap, plenty of
blessings, for all of us. I don't need to whine or feel left out. I just
need to climb up and ask. —JEANETTE LEVELLIE

FAITH STEP: *Close your eyes and imagine sitting on Jesus's enormous lap, with
many other believers sitting there too. Ask Him for a favor. He has plenty to go
around.*

MONDAY, AUGUST 7

All Scripture is God-breathed and is useful for teaching, rebuking, correcting, and training in righteousness. 2 Timothy 3:16 (NIV)

I BOUGHT A PLASTIC STORAGE bench with "some assembly required." My older son, Pierce, is fourteen, and I'm always looking for him to learn new skills. I briefly reviewed the instructions with him and a buddy, gave them the necessary tools, and stepped away, hoping they would sort it out as part of the learning process.

Not too far into it, I heard harrumphing and G-rated expletives. "Mom, this thing is broken! We have to send it back."

I smiled. I remembered I'd read in the instructions, "Before you send this back, please call us." I've put together many pieces of furniture, so I knew this was probably a case of user error. I read the directions out loud, and the three of us carefully walked through the steps together. They'd missed one. In a few minutes, the problem was solved. Moments later, they ran into another issue, but this time, I heard them talk through it.

How often have I built my life in this way? I hit a roadblock, throw my hands up in despair, and I'm ready to give up, before asking Jesus for help. How often have I failed to review my Bible, the ultimate instruction manual, to determine where I'd gone wrong or what to do next?

Today, that plastic bench sits on my patio, a reminder that the perfect handyman, Jesus, is standing by to help me assemble a life that works. After all, He was a carpenter. —ISABELLA CAMPOLATTARO

FAITH STEP: *Are you at a dead-end with a problem you can't seem to fix? Take some time to consult your biblical instruction manual and talk to the Carpenter.*

TUESDAY, AUGUST 8

Therefore he is able to save completely those who come to God through him, because he always lives to intercede for them. Hebrews 7:25 (NIV)

I WAS RAISED TO BE exceptionally courteous in my interactions with others. My mother instilled the importance of saying "please," "thank you," thinking of others before myself, and performing simple gestures, like greeting people. It was a wonderful introduction to the importance of manners, and I expected everyone I'd meet to behave in the same way. I eventually learned that everyone did not.

Over the years, I have developed a critical spirit when I don't sense benevolence in others. I can't name the number of times I have—loudly, I'm ashamed to admit—righteously corrected and shamed others when they, for example, rush through a door without holding it open for me or the people who were in front of me. My default tendency is to assume that their impolite behavior reflects rudeness.

How grateful I am that Jesus does not shame me in the same way I've shamed others. Despite my imperfections, inadequacies, and insensitivities, Jesus doesn't scowl, look down His nose, or wag a finger in my face. He graciously goes before the Father on my behalf to plead my case. Rather than judge me, He offers grace and forgiveness when I intentionally, or unintentionally, make mistakes.

When I think about it, telling someone he or she has shown bad manners is bad manners in itself. Shame on me for being so righteous and critical! Instead, I want to mind my manners and be like Jesus. —ERICKA LOYNES

FAITH STEP: *Next time you're tempted to shame someone, pray to react as Jesus would—with grace and forgiveness.*

WEDNESDAY, AUGUST 9

All the ends of the earth will remember and turn to the LORD . . .
Psalm 22:27 (NIV)

I'VE DEVELOPED THIS HABIT OF waving hello to people the minute I turn off the main road in my town and head for home. Even though I'm not in my neighborhood yet, I smile broadly and raise my hand off the steering wheel to greet couples (who are strangers to me) out for a stroll or kids (who I don't know from Adam) playing in their yards. I suppose I feel a shared sense of community with these near-neighbors. That's why I wave and smile at them through my car window.

After fourteen years, my hand automatically lifts to wave the minute I turn onto that road and start toward home. Once, while daydreaming behind the wheel, I caught myself waving at a delivery man and then a plumber. The gratifying thing is they both waved back!

It got me wondering if my faith reflex was just as strong. Did I automatically turn to Jesus when I needed help or the support of a friend? Sadly, my natural default was to rely solely on myself. Like an amnesiac, I kept forgetting how much Jesus was willing and able to be my source for everything.

The solution is similar to my pattern of waving. The more often I look to Jesus, the more automatic it will become to see Him in every circumstance. He's always beside me, no matter what road I'm on, awaiting me to wave hello to Him, too, and acknowledge His presence. —CLAIRE MCGARRY

FAITH STEP: *What positive action would you like to make automatic in your time with Jesus? Repeat that action as often as necessary until it becomes a habit.*

THURSDAY, AUGUST 10

The faithful love of the LORD never ends! His mercies never cease.
Great is his faithfulness; his mercies begin afresh each morning.
Lamentations 3:22–23 (NLT)

TWO BEAUTIFUL CHINESE HIBISCUS PLANTS are displaying all their glory on our deck this summer. Their bright yellow flowers attract hummingbirds, butterflies, and bees. My husband, Hal, and I enjoy watching the pollinators dart among the blooms. But what I find most interesting about the hibiscus is that each day a lovely bloom withers away—only to be replaced by another one the next morning.

The flowers bring to mind one of my favorite hymns, "Great Is Thy Faithfulness," and the song's lyric, "Morning by morning new mercies I see." For me, those blooms represent the new mercies granted to me every single day. My eyes opened this morning. *New mercy.* I'm able to get out of bed and move about. *New mercy.* Hal and I have good health. *New mercy.* My home is intact after heavy rains overnight. *New mercy.* I have food, shelter, clothing, and clean water. *New mercy.* No harm came upon us as we slept. *New mercy.*

The writer of Lamentations recognized that despite all the difficulties and disappointments he and his people had endured, he still has hope because of God's faithful love. Just as Jesus grants new hibiscus blooms to spring forth each day, He also allows His new mercies, His hope, to fall upon me. His mercies are a gift given daily, beautiful, fragrant, and full of promise, just like our hibiscus.
—BARBRANDA LUMPKINS WALLS

FAITH STEP: *Look around and take stock. What new mercies has Jesus granted you just since you've awakened? What words of thanksgiving will you offer Him?*

FRIDAY, AUGUST 11

"I am the vine; you are the branches. If you remain in me and I in you, you will bear much fruit; apart from me you can do nothing." John 15:5 (NIV)

THIS IS THE FIRST YEAR I've ever planted a vegetable garden. It's been a season of high excitement watching tomatoes, cucumbers, beets, onions, bush beans, snap peas, herbs, watermelons, blueberries, and squash grow. It has taken everything a while. Let's be honest. I was ready for tomatoes the day after I planted the four-inch-tall plants. Now the swirling vines are four feet tall. Heavy with tomatoes, they topple over their cages. The snap peas haven't made it into the kitchen. I just pop them straight into my mouth after picking. The cucumbers hide under the broad leaves, so I can't find them. This morning, I found seven in our little game of veggie hide-and-seek. The sunlight and water from the dripline have done their magic. I can't wait to see what I will find tomorrow.

When my life is hidden from Jesus, I don't often see the growth. On my own, it can take years, even decades, to start bearing the kind of fruit that He wants to see in me. Kindness? Gentleness? Self-control? These can be slow-yielding crops. Jesus is my sunlight and water. He nourishes me and helps me grow. Apart from Him, I can do nothing. But Jesus promises if I remain in Him, His life will flow through mine, yielding more growth than I could ever dream of harvesting on my own. —SUSANNA FOTH AUGHTMON

FAITH STEP: *Jesus wants you to grow into your full potential. Spend some time meditating on John 15:5. Ask Jesus to release the fruit of the Holy Spirit in your life as you remain in Him.*

SATURDAY, AUGUST 12

Now you are a wrecked ship, broken at the bottom of the sea. All your merchandise and crew have gone down with you. Ezekiel 27:34 (NLT)

AFTER ENJOYING A WEEKEND AT the coast, my husband and I headed home. As I drove along the highway, we spotted a large roadside sign. Its words read, "Life is a shipwreck. Sing in the lifeboat." We exchanged a glance and smiled, reflecting on the previous several months.

Together, we'd weathered a shipwreck of our own. After Dave suffered a life-altering accident, we slowed our pace. He needed to be taught a few basic skills and to learn appropriate emotional responses. Speech challenged him. Like a metaphorical bird, words perched at the tip of his tongue, then flew away before he could capture them.

I became versed in the true meaning of caregiving. Caring and giving. As I looked after Dave's needs, I saw in his eyes a new level of love—richer, more complete. Just as his trust in me grew, my faith in Jesus deepened.

I felt panic as waves crashed against our boat of the life we've made for ourselves. For a time, I wondered if the ship Dave and I sailed was sinking. But when I cried out, Jesus was there. He wasn't asleep, because God never sleeps (Psalm 121:4). He calmed our waves and guided our vessel to a safe harbor. This tempest hasn't drowned our faith. It strengthened it (Proverbs 10:25). Yes, we are singing in the lifeboat—singing praises to Jesus, our Captain, and we always will. —HEIDI GAUL

FAITH STEP: *Are you sitting in a lifeboat? Ask Jesus to settle the waves of your life and find rest on His calming seas. He'll never let you sink.*

Sunday, August 13

Precious in the sight of the LORD is the death of his faithful servants.
Psalm 116:15 (NIV)

How does the grace of Jesus show up in death and dying? The tragic loss of a friend's brother—young, vibrant, a living testimony to the love of Jesus—has me pondering that question. I trust Jesus, so I know He cares. Jesus was not unaware of the moment when the young man's foot slipped off the cliff.

What has both comforted and sobered me is the reminder that we are all in the queue to see the King. From the moment of our birth, we're part of the line that winds its way around the world and back. As time passes, we age, inching forward toward the moment when we stand in the King's presence.

Imagine waiting in line at a theme park for ninety years. In this case, though, our anticipation is worth the wait. And a lot of good things are happening while we're in the queue. We make friends, discuss ideas, marvel at the sunrises and sunsets. We build families, even. And create. And work. And play.

For some, the line seems too short. Far too short. The crowd hushes as the King rises from His throne and points to someone in line. "That young man," I imagine Him saying. "Let him come up here to the front of the line."

As we hold our own positions in the queue, we wonder if that's fair. Then we remind ourselves that the King personally called him. And we go back to waiting our turn. —Cynthia Ruchti

Faith Step: *Are you, or someone you care about, grieving the loss of a well-loved person? Cling tightly to the promise that Jesus cares more deeply than we can know.*

MONDAY, AUGUST 14

For the Son of Man came to seek and to save the lost. Luke 19:10 (NIV)

RIGHT ON TIME, I CONGRATULATED myself as I pulled into the parking lot for my yoga class. As I left my car, an SUV wheeled in beside me. A distressed-looking woman called, "I'm lost! Can you help me?"

I'd be late to class, but how could I not help her?

She had an appointment with a new doctor and couldn't find her office. Luckily, I knew the location. I told her to get back on the road, go three blocks, and look for a white building on her left. She sped away.

A person can be temporarily lost, as in confused about a location, or one can be a lost soul, wandering rudderless, without the direction of Jesus. Jesus told parables of the lost sheep (Matthew 18:12–14) and the lost coin (Luke 15:8–10). In both instances, the seeker would not give up until the missing item had been found. The Prodigal Son was lost, but when he found his way home, his father welcomed him with open arms (Luke 15:11–32). That's how Jesus is with us. He won't give up on us until we find our way home.

I've been lost directionally, and while it's frustrating, I can reprogram my GPS or stop and ask for directions. But being a lost soul is much worse. I've been both. When my young son died, I blamed Jesus and rejected Him, but He didn't turn away from me. After months of wandering aimlessly, I came back to Jesus, and He welcomed me home. —PAT BUTLER DYSON

FAITH STEP: *If you see someone is lost, either directionally or spiritually, reach out to them.*

TUESDAY, AUGUST 15

The eyes of the Lord are on the righteous and his ears are attentive to their prayer . . . 1 Peter 3:12 (NIV)

WE'RE HAVING AN EXTERIOR PAINTING project done this summer. I'd been doing a little project of my own, and because I'd procrastinated I didn't want to bother Jesus about it, even though I could really use His help.

It was a hot day, so I had the idea to offer the painter a glass of ice water. This isn't the first time Pat had painted for us. We found him through an acquaintance who told us he worked, during the school year, at a local Christian school, so I figured he was a believer.

He was high on the ladder, painting our shutters, when I stepped outside.

"How are you doing?" I called, looking skyward. "Want some ice water?"

Pat had brought his own water jug, but he was eager to tell me what had just happened. A group of wasps had been dive-bombing his head. With him being up on the ladder, I could only imagine how unnerving that felt.

"So I prayed. Jesus, this is a safety issue. Please stop them. Make them go away," he said, wide-eyed, his voice filled with awe. "And they stopped."

We talked for a few minutes about how amazing it was that Jesus cares about the small issues in our life. As I walked inside, I sent my own prayer skyward, knowing Jesus would help with my project too. I need only ask. —ERIN KEELEY MARSHALL

FAITH STEP: *Is there an issue you've kept to yourself because you feel like it's too small for Jesus? Write it down and prepare to be amazed when He answers it.*

WEDNESDAY, AUGUST 16

"But so that we may not cause offense, go to the lake and throw out your line. Take the first fish you catch; open its mouth and you will find a four-drachma coin...." Matthew 17:27 (NIV)

ONE NIGHT, DURING A VACATION with other couples, we played a foosball tournament. We giggled like kids as we clumsily twisted the metal rods affixed with soccer-like players, "kicking" a little ball back and forth, trying to score or block goals. It had been a long time since I had laughed so hard. God created us to play, and I don't think He wants that to lessen with age. But as life gets serious, playfulness diminishes; I know mine has.

When I read the story of the tax collectors who confronted Peter about paying taxes, I noticed a playful side to Jesus. When asked if Jesus paid taxes, Peter said, "Yes," then went to talk to Jesus. Before Peter could speak, Jesus answered his question. I imagine this had to make Peter smile. Jesus affirmed He would pay the taxes, and to prove it He sent Peter on a fishing excursion. Jesus told him to throw in his line and open the mouth of the fish he caught to find the money owed to the tax collectors. Sounds like a playful game to me—a strategically, uniquely designed, amusing activity for the fisherman. Perhaps Peter even laughed out loud when he opened the mouth of the fish.

Life is not all fun and games, but this story shows I need to create space for play in my life. So, we'll definitely plan a few more noncompetitive foosball games—or maybe I'll do a little fishing.
—JEANNIE BLACKMER

FAITH STEP: *Reflect on Jesus's interaction with Peter in Matthew 17:24–27, then plan a playful activity today.*

Thursday, August 17

All your children shall be taught by the LORD, and great shall be the peace of your children. Isaiah 54:13 (ESV)

RECENTLY TWO OF MY DAUGHTERS moved up from elementary school to middle school, and our church didn't have a Sunday school class for their age group. As I heard about the need for a teacher, something stirred within my heart. *Should this be something I consider?* I wondered.

Then, during my Bible reading, I was reminded of the peace that comes to children when time is taken to teach them in the ways of the Lord. *How would those middle school youth know about Jesus if someone didn't step up to teach them?*

I find it's easy to read a Scripture passage and allow it to make me feel warm and fuzzy, but opening my heart to teaching others has me worried. What if those I am teaching have questions and I don't have answers? What if I have to give up other activities that I enjoy to fulfill my commitment to them?

I remembered that Jesus doesn't ask me to do things perfectly. He only asks me to be willing and faithful. I often get so focused on the proper Bible lessons that I forget the whole point, which is to share about Jesus and bring others to know Him. Instruction is an avenue to help me connect my heart to His and to others. *Lesson learned!*

I finally said yes to teaching middle schoolers in Sunday school—who knows, I may just learn something myself. —TRICIA GOYER

FAITH STEP: *Is there someone in your life who needs to be taught about Jesus and His ways? Consider how you can serve or help others connect with Jesus by leading them, guiding them, and teaching them.*

FRIDAY, AUGUST 18

By transgression an evil man is snared, But the righteous sings and rejoices. Proverbs 29:6 (NKJV)

MY NEIGHBOR DESCRIBES MY FLOWER beds as an English cottage garden. That's a nice way of saying my flora is out of control. Overgrown mounds of green sprout colorful lilies and irises. Purple phlox crowd the sidewalk. Morning glories creep up the front porch railing. I don't have a green thumb. In fact, my husband nicknamed me the plant assassin since I can't keep a houseplant alive. But we built our home in a former cow pasture, so my outdoor flowers grow in spite of me.

One invasive plant appeared last summer. I call it the Velcro weed. Long and spindly with sticky fingers along its stem, the plant camouflages itself beneath my blooms and multiplies. When it broke through the foliage, I plucked it and tried to toss it to the side. Except the weed wouldn't drop. It stuck like Velcro to my gloves and clothes. A hearty shake wouldn't loosen it. I had to peel it out of the ground with my thumb and forefinger, hold it away from my body, and release it in the trash bucket.

What a perfect reflection of sin that vile intruder is. When I harbor jealousy, pride, unforgiveness, or any other sin, it hides beneath a pleasant facade, growing and multiplying, sprouting more sticky fingers that seem impossible to shake off.

Clingy sin is successfully eradicated with Jesus. Thanks to the Master Gardener's sacrifice, when I pray and intentionally change my behavior, He plucks sin from my heart and removes it permanently, so beauty can better bloom and grow in my heart.
—KAREN SARGENT

FAITH STEP: *Confess a sticky sin you can't seem to shake. Ask Jesus to help you get it out of your life.*

SATURDAY, AUGUST 19

*I no longer call you slaves, for a master doesn't confide in his slaves;
now you are my friends, proved by the fact that I have told you
everything the Father told me. John 15:15 (TLB)*

"WOULD YOU MIND MOVING TO that seat across the table, Jeanette?"
my coauthor, Beth, said. We were the keynote speakers at a women's
retreat. Two of Beth's childhood friends had come to hear her message.

"Oh, sure, no problem," I chirped, and bounded out of my chair
next to Beth. But my heart didn't reflect my bright smile. I was
offended.

*Wow, Beth invites me to speak with her this weekend and then tosses
me aside when her old friends show up. Just like that!*

Before I'd finished pouting, Jesus spoke in my heart with His kind
voice. "Jeanette, think how you'd feel if two of your friends from
third grade stopped by. Wouldn't you want them to sit beside you?"
I didn't have to think about my answer. Of course I'd want to spend
time with longtime friends. I also knew Beth wouldn't be offended
if I'd asked her to change seats.

I love how Jesus calls His followers friends. Although they'd only
known Him for three years, Jesus trusted them with all the Father
had told Him.

I smiled across the table at Beth and her friends and silently
thanked Jesus for being my forever friend. —JEANETTE LEVELLIE

FAITH STEP: *Each day for a week, write down a friend's name on a piece of
paper. Pray for that person and all the blessings he or she brings to your life. Then
thank Jesus for that friend and thank Him for being the best friend of all.*

SUNDAY, AUGUST 20

He replied, "If you have faith as small as a mustard seed, you can say to this mulberry tree, 'Be uprooted and planted in the sea,' and it will obey you." Luke 17:6 (NIV)

I WAITED UNTIL THE LAST minute to send a final reminder to a business colleague. She'd always been prompt in returning assignments; I knew she had the deadline on her calendar. When I finally emailed again, she responded that she'd turned in her submission a couple of weeks earlier. She even sent a follow-up message to me when I didn't respond. Finally, we figured out the problem: She'd gotten one letter wrong in my email address.

A little mistake, like changing one letter or number, can cause big problems when we're entering a credit card number, ID code, or password. But sometimes one little change can be a positive thing. When God made a covenant with Abram in Genesis, He changed Abram and Sarai's names with one or two letters. Those new names marked a world of difference in their relationship with God. In the New Testament, Saul became a transformed man when he met Jesus; from that point on, he was known as Paul.

What a huge difference one little change can make in our spiritual life. Adding prayer or Bible reading to our daily routine will transform our thoughts, our day, and our relationships. Taking a small step of obedience to follow where Jesus leads will guide us to new heights. Reaching out to someone with a simple act of kindness may lighten their darkness.

With Jesus, little changes bring big results. —DIANNE NEAL MATTHEWS

FAITH STEP: *Ask Jesus to help you make a small change in one area of your life, then watch for the results.*

MONDAY, AUGUST 21

Whoever dwells in the shelter of the Most High will rest in the shadow of the Almighty. Psalm 91:1 (NIV)

"I'D HATE TO BE OUT in that!"

The storm hit suddenly on this super-heated summer night. From the comfort of our family room, I'm watching it rage. Trees whip in the wind. The roll of thunder seems unending. Rain pelts our metal roof with the fierceness of hail.

As I sip tea and note an especially strong flash of lightning, gratitude swells. *I'm glad I'm not out in that.*

But I could be…out in life's storms. Unprotected from the harsh words, the biting winds of disappointment, the endless roll of anxiety. Instead, Jesus has invited me inside to take refuge in His shelter. Let the winds blow. I'm safe, secure, aware of what rages outside but undamaged by its fury. I'm living through what threatens because I accepted His invitation to ride it out within the shelter of His love and grace.

Shelter, or Refuge, is one of my favorite attributes of Jesus. Like my taste in favorite songs, my favorite attribute changes depending on the circumstances. Some days it's Jesus as Healer, or as Provider, or as Defender. Tonight, as the storm roars and spits, as it takes trees to their knees and sends anything untethered flying, I rest within the safe shelter of His embrace, grateful that He held the door wide open to welcome me in.

And I'll spend time praying for those who are still out in it, soaked and shivering, cold and lost. Oh, one more thing. I'll turn on the porch light so they can find their way to safety. —CYNTHIA RUCHTI

FAITH STEP: *Is someone within your circle of influence waiting for you to turn on the porch light? Will you?*

TUESDAY, AUGUST 22

In him we have redemption through his blood, the forgiveness of sins, in accordance with the riches of God's grace. Ephesians 1:7 (NIV)

MY SISTER ERICA AND HER husband came to visit us last summer. Erica has an online reselling business that she is constantly curating for. This means hitting thrift shops and secondhand stores on a regular basis. While she was here, we went to a couple of them together.

I lingered in the different aisles looking for cute items that caught my eye, but Erica had a different approach. A woman on a mission, she zoomed through the racks to find specific brands, many I didn't recognize. Some items she chose, such as a worn pair of shoes and a brightly patterned shirt, didn't look like much to me. But Erica knew their true worth at a glance. I was just looking for cute outfits. Erica was looking at the hidden value of each piece she picked up.

My sister isn't the only one who knows the value of something is often below the surface. Jesus sees the true value of each of us. I may not feel like my life is worth much, but Jesus disagreed. He paid the price to redeem me from my sins. Through His costly death, He bought me forgiveness and eternal life. I never have to doubt my worth because I know I'm worthy and valuable—in fact, I'm priceless in His sight. —SUSANNA FOTH AUGHTMON

FAITH STEP: *When you question your true worth, grab your favorite pair of old jeans, hold them close, and remind yourself that no matter how you feel about yourself or what your condition, Jesus thinks you're valuable—valuable enough to die for.*

WEDNESDAY, AUGUST 23

By their fruit you will recognize them. Do people pick grapes from thornbushes, or figs from thistles? Matthew 7:16 (NIV)

IT'S ZUCCHINI SEASON IN MY backyard garden again. Although I plant a big mix of fruits and veggies, it seems that my zucchini is the one plant that the local squirrels and rabbits ignore. The tricky thing about zucchini is that I can check the plant one morning and by the next day discover a fruit the size of a baseball bat hiding beneath the leaves.

Small zucchini can expand suddenly. I've found the same is true of my attitudes. Sometimes, I have tiny seeds of a bad attitude beginning to grow undercover. A bit of sour grapes. A little bitter melon. Or a prickly pear. If I don't expose it and turn to Jesus immediately, overnight those attitudes can stretch and grow through my personality until they can no longer hide.

Jesus said His true followers could be recognized by their fruit. I long for my life to bear fruit that reflects His grace. And I can't do that in my own power. In the same way my backyard garden requires my skills and expertise daily in order to produce healthy plants, I need Jesus to tend my heart and mind.

As Jesus nurtures the good fruit in my soul, the better it grows. The more frequently I spend time with the true Gardener, the more likely my bad attitude will wither away. Jesus sows seeds of unselfish impulses, supernatural peace, and overflowing love. Living through me, He produces a bountiful harvest that glorifies Him.
—SHARON HINCK

FAITH STEP: *Weed a patch of yard, garden, or sidewalk today. Ask Jesus to pull harmful attitudes from your heart before they grow and spread.*

THURSDAY, AUGUST 24

I will remember the works of the LORD: surely I will remember thy wonders of old. Psalm 77:11 (KJV)

"MOM, WHY DON'T YOU THROW that old thing away? It's a hundred years old!" My daughter Brooke glared at the electric can opener as it struggled with a can of pie filling. It stopped and started, spewing lemon filling in my eye, making a scary grinding noise all the while. Just because it's old doesn't mean it's useless. I cherish old things.

I remember the excitement my brothers and I shared when Dad brought this electric can opener home for Mother fifty-five years ago. Dad wasn't one for squandering money on gadgets, but this pristine almond appliance, equipped with a knife sharpener, would surely revolutionize our kitchen!

The sparkling almond has aged and the can opener is beyond cranky. No telling how many cans of cat food, corn, and peaches it has opened. Invented in 1956 by Walter Hess Bodle, my vintage electric can opener has a starting bid of $134.99 on eBay. Or I could buy a sleek black model for $11 at Dollar General. But I'll keep this one. There's a story behind it I don't want to forget.

I also cherish the beautiful stories of old from the Bible. I love reading about the miracles Jesus performed—healing the sick, feeding the multitudes, raising Lazarus from the dead, halting the storm. These ancient stories, retold countless times over the decades of my life, have shaped me and grown my faith.

My mother's can opener will someday quit working and be discarded, but the power of Jesus is eternal. Jesus stands the test of time. His stories never grow old. —PAT BUTLER DYSON

FAITH STEP: *Read your favorite story about Jesus aloud.*

FRIDAY, AUGUST 25

"And when I am lifted up from the earth, I will draw everyone to myself." John 12:32 (NLT)

AFTER MY HUSBAND SURPRISED ME with a new watch, I used a gift card to order some extra bands in various colors. One band quickly became my favorite. It was black mesh with a strong magnetic clasp. I started wearing it daily.

One evening, while eating supper with my family, I was amused to discover that an unused spoon had attached itself to the magnetic clasp and was suddenly dangling from my watch like a charm. My children and I laughed, and we began experimenting with other utensils to see what would stick and what wouldn't.

As the week progressed, it became clear that my watch band attracted more than forks and knives. It also attracted jewelry, key chains, pens, paper clips—even my metal desk. I never knew when the pull from my watch would beckon something else into its magnetic field.

It reminded me of how my friend once described Jesus as *magnetic*. She explained that when Jesus lives in us and through us, others can't help but be drawn to us.

"It's magnetism!" she said.

When I live my life according to my relationship with Jesus and let Him influence my words and actions, others are naturally attracted to the difference they see in me. That difference is Jesus in me. He draws people to Himself—just like a magnet. —EMILY E. RYAN

FAITH STEP: *Find two magnets and pause for a while to play with them. As you observe the force of the magnetic pull, pray that Jesus living in you attracts people and that others are naturally drawn to Him through your life.*

SATURDAY, AUGUST 26

Then he said to the crowd, "If any of you wants to be my follower, you must give up your own way, take up your cross daily, and follow me." Luke 9:23 (NLT)

I RECENTLY READ AN ARTICLE about how common prenuptial agreements have become in recent years. Most are geared toward the protection of individual assets in the event of divorce. Marriage counselors often advise couples to avoid the word *divorce* during heated arguments, since it brings up the possibility, but prenuptial agreements introduce the idea even before the marriage occurs, reminding the couple there is a loophole in case one of them wants out.

Jesus made it clear that following Him was not a temporary gig but an unbreakable covenant. He advises in Scripture to count the cost before choosing to follow Him (John 14:25–33). Jesus doesn't release me from my commitment to Him if I feel like the journey has gotten too inconvenient or demanding. He doesn't dismiss me from the relationship when I mess up. After Jesus's crucifixion, Peter and a few other disciples went fishing. Jesus called to them from the beach, using words familiar to Peter—"Follow Me!" Jesus wanted to reassure Peter of His acceptance and love, despite Peter denying that he knew Jesus during His trials (John 21:4–19).

Jesus departed His heavenly home, then laid down His earthly life. He calls us to follow Him through our lives and then beyond, to join Him in eternity. I'm grateful there are no loopholes in His unbreakable covenant with those who accept Him as Savior.
—DIANNE NEAL MATTHEWS

FAITH STEP: *If you're not familiar with the old hymn "I Have Decided to Follow Jesus," look up the words online or in a songbook. Sing or recite the lyrics as a prayer to honor Jesus.*

SUNDAY, AUGUST 27

And He said to them, "Why are you troubled? And why do doubts arise in your hearts? Behold My hands and My feet..." Luke 24:38–39 (NKJV)

MY OLDEST DAUGHTER, STEPHANIE, LIVES in Washington state. We typically see her and her husband three or four times a year. During the pandemic, the border between Canada and the United States closed, so we were unable to visit in person.

During that time, Stephanie and her husband bought their first home. We'd packed and moved our other three kids' households multiple times, but circumstances made it impossible to help. I felt sad knowing how much Stephanie wished we could share this experience with them. I felt even sadder when she underwent surgery, and I could do nothing to help during her recovery.

Every time my heart grew heavy, I focused on the truth of Jesus's love. He demonstrated it by willingly dying on the cross to forgive our sin and remove our guilt. Since Jesus loved my daughter and son-in-law to that degree, I could trust Him to care for their needs. I placed my faith in His willingness and ability to do so, and He did not disappoint. He provided friends to help them move into their new place, and He restored my daughter's health without her mama's help.

The more I get to know Jesus, the more I realize there's no reason to despair when facing trials. Our human tendency is to question Jesus's love, but one glimpse of His scarred hands and feet erases all doubt about His intent toward us. —GRACE FOX

FAITH STEP: *On a note card, sketch two hands and feet with nail prints. Post it where you will see it often as a reminder of Jesus's love.*

MONDAY, AUGUST 28

"Come to me, all you who are weary and burdened, and I will give you rest." Matthew 11:28 *(NIV)*

THE PANDEMIC WAS TRAUMATIC. MANY people died and many more became sick. Often, people had to find different ways to do their jobs, or some reorganized their households so they could work from home. Not being able to see loved ones and hug them in person was emotionally difficult. The financial security that some families had built up over decades was depleted when there was a job loss, illness, or death. Having to socially distance from each other and limit simple routines, like grocery shopping or beauty appointments, was inconvenient.

The pandemic challenged the whirlwind of activity I was used to. In his loving, yet straightforward way, my husband had been urging me to stop saying yes to every opportunity that came my way for years. He wanted me to take time to relax. I was too stubborn to realize that my husband knew I, like all of us, needed the chance to rest.

In the same way my husband saw I was overwhelmed, I imagine Jesus looked at the masses and empathized with their burdens when He walked the earth. He proposed an unusual offer to those who were tired and overwhelmed. If they would follow Him, Jesus promised He would take on their heavy burdens and make their loads lighter.

When I'm caught in a whirlwind of activity, it can be hard to escape. The only cure is giving it over to Jesus, stopping, and resting in Him. —ERICKA LOYNES

FAITH STEP: *Even if your calendar has already filled up this week, reassess your schedule and create space to rest your mind and body, and refresh your spirit.*

TUESDAY, AUGUST 29

This is the confidence we have in approaching God: that if we ask anything according to his will, he hears us. And if we know that he hears us—whatever we ask—we know that we have what we asked of him. 1 John 5:14–15 (NIV)

MY HUSBAND, JOHN, HAS BEEN in sales for decades. As a new employee, his boss taught him that each customer fell into one of four personality types: Analytic, Aggressive, Amiable, or Expressive. His boss said that a good salesperson provided great customer service by discerning a client's personality type, then tailoring the sales pitch accordingly, thus forming a win/win situation.

As crazy as it might sound, I think I've used the personality sales strategy in my prayer life. I used to have a preconceived notion of who Jesus was and I tailored my requests accordingly. Doing so didn't necessarily draw me closer to Him; it turned my prayer time into a transaction, with me trying to sell Him on why He should give me what I wanted. When He did, I felt as if I'd closed the sale. In His ever-gentle, ever-patient way, Jesus knew I was an Aggressive customer.

As I grew older, I let go of that sales approach. I sincerely yearned for a true and right relationship with Him. By working together, He's made me more Amiable.

These days, I have a new strategy. Instead of making my prayer time about what I desire from Jesus, I try to discern what Jesus desires from me. This way, I'm serving Him instead of Him serving me. And isn't that the best form of customer service—creating win/win situations? —CLAIRE MCGARRY

FAITH STEP: *Lay aside your prayer requests for a day. Focus instead on what Jesus wants from you.*

WEDNESDAY, AUGUST 30

Confess your sins to each other and pray for each other so that you may be healed. The earnest prayer of a righteous person has great power and produces wonderful results. James 5:16 (NLT)

THE MINISTERS' WIVES AT MY church get together once a quarter for an evening of fun, fellowship, and prayer. At our most recent gathering, our girls' minister, Shelby, led us in a prayer exercise that was especially memorable.

First, she told us to think about all the things that were weighing heavily on our hearts. Our questions. Our burdens. Our doubts. Our needs. Then she challenged us to narrow all those thoughts down to a single word that represented the one area of our lives in which we most needed Jesus in that moment, and to write that word on an index card. Some wrote *wisdom*. A few wrote *peace*. Others wrote *reconciliation* or *boldness* or *patience*. I wrote *joy*.

Then, at Shelby's instruction, we spent the next fifteen minutes circling the room in silence, laying hands on each other's index cards and lifting up single-word prayers to Jesus on behalf of our sisters in Christ. Each time we prayed for someone, we initialed that person's index card.

A week later, I found the signed index card in my purse and smiled. I still needed the joy of Jesus in the same ways, but now I had over a dozen signatures happily reminding me that others had prayed over me and were praying for me. That knowledge produced a glimmer of joy that bubbled up in my soul. —EMILY E. RYAN

FAITH STEP: *Write your own one-word prayer on an index card. When you get the chance, lead others in a similar prayer exercise at your next small group gathering.*

THURSDAY, AUGUST 31

"Submit to God, and you will have peace; then things will go well for you." Job 22:21 (NLT)

I'M CRAVING SOMETHING SWEET. THANKFULLY, I remember the delicious handmade chocolate bar that a couple of coworkers had recently given me for my birthday. I'd only eaten part of it and went to retrieve it from the kitchen table where I'd last seen it. Not there. I began to look everywhere for it—the refrigerator, countertops, dining room, bedroom, my office, desk drawers. It's nowhere to be found. Had I already scarfed it down? Although I'm irritated, I stopped searching and worrying and asked Jesus to take care of it.

The next day, while sitting in my home office, I swivel around in my chair and my eyes land on the top of a small file cabinet. *The chocolate!* I thought I'd looked in that spot last night. Had it been there all the time?

From past experiences, I know things that are often lost or misplaced, whether it's keys, a phone, eyeglasses, or even inconsequential things like a chocolate bar, will turn up eventually. And I'm learning that when I surrender a situation to Jesus, no matter how small or worrisome, I save myself a lot of aggravation. I just wish I would give it up to Him sooner, rather than later.

Wouldn't it be sweet if I could hand all my problems over to the Lord as fast as I did the lost chocolate? I took a bite, satisfied to remember His goodness. —BARBRANDA LUMPKINS WALLS

FAITH STEP: *Is there something you need to hand over to Jesus? Write it down and trust Him to take care of it.*

FRIDAY, SEPTEMBER 1

Therefore we do not lose heart. Though outwardly we are wasting away, yet inwardly we are being renewed day by day. 2 Corinthians 4:16 *(NIV)*

I FELT EXHAUSTED AFTER A busy day of numerous appointments with my kids. As I thought about what to make for dinner, a renewed energy sizzled within me. I remembered that my husband, John, and I had planned a date. I'd order pizza for the kids and babysitter, while we enjoyed a meal out.

Dating my spouse has become a beloved activity. Sometimes we go to a restaurant to share the experience of delicious food we don't normally eat in our kid-friendly kitchen. Or we might go on a walk along a nature trail to drink in the beauty of nature while having uninterrupted conversations. Other times, we take in a movie and enjoy popcorn. But the point isn't the food, the entertainment, or a serene setting. The point of our date is to connect with each other—to share my heart and to hear his.

I find the same type of renewed energy when I take time with Jesus. When I sit down with a cup of tea and my Bible, I'm able to forget about the world pressing in and focus on Him. Spending time together, I feel His love for me. Reading His Word, I understand His heart. I feel peace and joy being alone in His presence. Whether a biweekly date night with John or taking time with Jesus, I want to remember to save the date! Time alone always enhances a relationship. —TRICIA GOYER

FAITH STEP: *Plan a date with Jesus. Pick a special place for your time alone with Him or schedule a different time of day. Spice up your relationship with Him as you connect anew.*

SATURDAY, SEPTEMBER 2

. . . He is the One who loves us, who made us free from our sins with the blood of his death. Revelation 1:5 (NCV)

I UNASHAMEDLY SPOIL OUR FOUR cats. I talk baby talk to them, sing them goofy songs, and give them too many treats.

I discovered my penchant for pets the autumn after I turned six. We'd recently moved into a new house. My brother, Danny, and I looked out our kitchen window that first Saturday morning and discovered five black-and-white kittens jumping in a pile of leaves.

Danny beckoned Mom to the window.

"Uh-oh," she said. "Those aren't cats. They're skunks."

Mom called animal control to catch the critters, and we eventually adopted a kitten. I've been a cat lover ever since.

As an adult, I can now easily distinguish a cat from a skunk. But I'm not always as smart with identifying myself. I might base my value on a comment someone makes, whether I prayed that day or not, or how tight my favorite blouse is.

Yet in my heart, I know my true identity lies in my relationship with Jesus. What He thinks of me and what He says about me is God's reality. And because of Jesus's lavish sacrifice, I know He thinks I'm the cat's meow. —JEANETTE LEVELLIE

FAITH STEP: *Do you realize how worthy you are in the eyes of Jesus? Every day for a week, write in your journal or look in the mirror and say, "I am valuable and lovable because Jesus says so." See how your perception changes.*

SUNDAY, SEPTEMBER 3

I have placed my rainbow in the clouds. It is the sign of my covenant with you and with all the earth. Genesis 9:13 (NLT)

HER NAME WAS ALICIA, AND I met her when I was six. She must not have known that a proper houseguest waits for an invitation and then knocks politely on the front door at a respectable hour, because she showed up in the middle of the night and entered by breaking windows and ripping off our roof. Even now, when someone mentions Hurricane Alicia, I still hear the wind screaming, feel the wet carpet squishing through my toes, and smell the moldy aftermath from her intrusion in the walls.

In the South, we pay attention when meteorologists mention named storms building off the coast, but I recently realized that I not only name my weather-related storms, but I also name the storms in my life. I've survived Hurricane Miscarriage, Tropical Storm Unemployment, and many others.

But what if I stopped naming my storms and started naming my rainbows, instead? The Bible says that Jesus created the rainbow to be a reminder of His covenant with us. It's a promise that He will never again send a flood to wash away a corrupt segment of humanity. Within that promise is also a reminder that the storms of life do not have the power to destroy us. They may cause damage, but even in their destruction they leave room for Jesus to step in and provide, teach, comfort, or save. If I stay focused on Him, I will always find rainbows at the end of my storms. —EMILY E. RYAN

FAITH STEP: *Reflect on those times when Jesus has calmed the storms of your life with a rainbow of provision, protection, or peace.*

LABOR DAY, MONDAY, SEPTEMBER 4

And of his fulness have all we received, and grace for grace. John 1:16 (KJV)

THE POWER WALK FROM THE parking lot, eight minutes from our destination, would either get us there in time for our 10:15 appointment…or give us both heart attacks. My friend and I had been blessed to discover two spots had opened up for a modified self-guided tour of the Biltmore "castle" in Asheville, North Carolina.

We'd seen the schedule online. Completely full except for our two spots and a handful at the end of the day when a tour would allow us little more than a wink and nod at the magnificent 250-room edifice. We feared that missing the 10:15 window would either mean we would be relegated to the end-of-day slots or we'd have to forfeit the experience altogether.

We'd done the best we could to get there on time but were surprised that the navigation app's ETA got us only as far as the gate, which was miles from the house itself. Panting and apologetic, we snaked our way through the rope queue to reach the tour volunteer. "So…sorry…we're…late. What do we do now?"

"Step behind that couple," she said, with a smile. "It'll be just a moment and we'll move you through. There's no such thing as late at the Biltmore."

Many other people waited in line. We were shown grace. Our power walk, the fastest we could move, wasn't enough, but she let us in.

Just like the way Jesus receives us. He's well aware that our best effort isn't enough, yet He welcomes us anyway. —CYNTHIA RUCHTI

FAITH STEP: *When you're shown undeserved favor, express your gratitude. If you aren't, make it a point to extend grace to others, and thank Jesus for setting the standard.*

TUESDAY, SEPTEMBER 5

So in Christ Jesus you are all children of God
through faith. Galatians 3:26 (NIV)

MY FAVORITE PLACE TO SPEND mornings with Jesus is on my front porch steps. With a cup of coffee, God's Word, and my favorite devotionals beside me, I feel the warmth of the sun rising over the field, casting a pink glow on the clouds in the sky.

Entangled on the porch railing beside me, morning glories open to welcome the new day. Hummingbirds buzz to the vines and sip sweet syrup from the blossoms. Curious ones zoom inches from my face to inspect my red reading glasses before deciding I'm not a flower.

Across the gravel road, another bird species flies above the wooded tree line. Buzzards circle high, surveying the area for safety before they dive down to partake of their food source.

Hummingbirds and buzzards both feast this morning. The hummingbirds require life-giving nectar. The buzzards prefer a decaying carcass. Both will find what they seek.

So will I. When I seek beauty and joy, I find it. If I search for negativity and nastiness, I'll find that too. With either source, my heart will be nourished.

When others saw a leper, Jesus saw a child of God (Matthew 8:2–3). The Pharisees saw an adulteress (John 8:3–4), but Jesus recognized a loyal follower (Luke 8:1–3). Society despised tax collectors, but Jesus called one to be a disciple (Mark 2:14). And when Jesus looks at me, instead of seeing my sin, He sees my redemption. —KAREN SARGENT

FAITH STEP: *How do you look at others? As you feed your heart and mind today, pay attention to the source of your nourishment.*

WEDNESDAY, SEPTEMBER 6

"For I hold you by your right hand—I, the LORD your God. And I say to you, 'Don't be afraid. I am here to help you.'" Isaiah 41:13 (NLT)

IN LATE AUGUST 2020, RESIDENTS along the Gulf Coast anxiously watched updates on a hurricane rapidly strengthening and heading toward land. Meteorologists indicated that Hurricane Laura would grow into a category 4 or 5 storm with deadly wind speeds and record-breaking storm surges. One afternoon, my friend Towanna's three-year-old great-niece called her to ask if she was okay. Towanna told Lennon that she could help by praying for family members in Louisiana. Lennon bowed her head and asked Jesus to be with each person, calling them by name. She finished by saying, "Jesus, just turn this storm off. Amen!" Then she assured Towanna that things would be okay because "Jesus is holding you."

Whether we're threatened by an impending hurricane or dealing with emotional turbulence caused by our circumstances, it's only natural to want Jesus to turn the storm off. After all, He did it for His twelve disciples on a raging sea. I believe Jesus still intervenes in miraculous ways today, in all sorts of crises. But He did warn that His followers will experience troubles during this earthly life. He also promised that He will walk through them all with us.

Sometimes we can tell when a storm is coming our way so that we have time to prepare; other times a crisis hits with no advance warning. Thankfully, we always have the assurance that even if Jesus doesn't hold back the storm, He will hold *us* as we go through it.
—DIANNE NEAL MATTHEWS

FAITH STEP: *Are you facing a frightening situation? Ask Jesus to hold you more closely and help you remember that He is with you.*

THURSDAY, SEPTEMBER 7

*Everything God made is good. We should not put anything aside
if we can take it and thank God for it.* 1 Timothy 4:4 (NLV)

MY BIRTHDAY IS JUST AROUND the corner, and I dread it. Not just
because of the extra digit added to my age, although I'm not thrilled
about that, but because people will give me gifts. I like giving others
presents—I'm good at giving—but receiving? Not so much. I blush
and mumble. I worry that the giver spent too much. I agonize over
how I will reciprocate.

Recently, my friend Pam sent me a dozen handmade note cards
after I'd admired her handiwork. When the package of lovely all-
occasion cards arrived, I was overwhelmed.

"Thank you so much!" I said. "May I pay you? What can I do for
you?" I wanted to know how I could repay Pam for her thoughtful gift.

"Your thanks are enough," she answered.

Really? How could my thanks be enough?

The greatest gift I've ever received came from God in the form
of His Son Jesus. Yet how often do I remember to thank Him? I'm
good at doing and serving and showing my thanks to Him. I feel
like I should work really hard to prove my gratitude. His priceless
gift is truly the One for which I'm most grateful, but is all my effort
needed? Maybe my thanks is enough for Jesus. After all, I could
never repay Him, no matter what I do.

Thanks to Pam and Jesus, I know that saying thank you is not
only enough, but it's all I can do. —PAT BUTLER DYSON

FAITH STEP: *Write a thank-you note to God for His Son. Tuck it in your Bible
and read it often.*

FRIDAY, SEPTEMBER 8

*Give thanks to the Lord, for he is good; his love
endures forever. 1 Chronicles 16:34 (NIV)*

I'D PUT OFF THE PROJECT for weeks. I'd waited for an open day, when I
had nothing else to do and could proceed in peaceful contemplation.
Moments into my bliss, someone knocked on the front door.

A power company employee stood on my porch. They were
removing ancient and unreliable overhead power lines in favor of
buried cable. "Sorry, ma'am, but it looks like we're going to need to
dig up your driveway."

Because an underground water pipe burst years ago, we had to
replace a strip of the driveway with a concrete patch until we could
afford to replace all the asphalt, which is now also ancient. I pointed
to that unsightly spot, hoping that would be their work site.

"Uh, no. We have to dig it up over there. We'll replace it eventually."

I wondered what his definition of "eventually" was. But it had to
be done. My wide-open day of peace and quiet morphed into the
sound big, truck-powered jackhammers make when breaking up
sections of highway.

But I'm smiling. Why? Because I've learned that when circumstances take a turn and my day seems riddled with hurdles, I'm to
give thanks. Not thankful *for* the noise necessarily, but thankful *in*
the noise. With Jesus by my side, I harnessed peace in my heart and
went back to my project. —CYNTHIA RUCHTI

FAITH STEP: *What project have you been putting off, waiting until circumstances were more favorable? Try plowing ahead in Jesus's strength no matter
what comes up.*

SATURDAY, SEPTEMBER 9

Therefore I urge you, brethren, by the mercies of God, to present your bodies a living and holy sacrifice, acceptable to God, which is your spiritual service of worship. Romans 12:1 (NASB1995)

WHILE WATCHING A MOVIE RECENTLY, I was struck by the powerful message of sacrifice. In an intense moment where the family's plan to fight off an evil creature is starting to fail, the father decides to do something bold and different. He begins making a lot of noise to draw the creature toward him and away from the children. It works. The creature becomes distracted and heads for the father. The children's sense of relief, however, is short-lived when they tearfully watch their dad give up his life to save theirs.

Although I may not be called to give up my physical life, I am still called to a life of sacrifice. Sacrifice means giving up one thing to gain another. In Mark 12:42–44, Jesus called over His disciples to point out a widow who gave two copper coins—all that she had—in the offering plate. Perhaps the widow understood the principle of sacrifice. Maybe she willingly gave up her last coins with the belief she would gain blessings.

As followers of Jesus, we are called to be living sacrifices. By daily laying aside our own desires to follow Him, we will gain so much more in return. —ERICKA LOYNES

FAITH STEP: *What do you value that seems too hard to give up right now? Ask Jesus to help you loosen your grip and let it go, so He can replace it with something that is much more valuable than you can even imagine.*

SUNDAY, SEPTEMBER 10

For by the grace given me I say to every one of you: Do not think of yourself more highly than you ought, but rather think of yourself with sober judgment, in accordance with the faith God has distributed to each of you. Romans 12:3 (NIV)

WHEN MY ATHLETICALLY TALENTED SON, Pierce, was young, he played youth-league sports. Even when the team was totally awful, each child received a trophy. I know that the well-meaning idea was to encourage budding athletes. However, I feared the real result was that the children would get a distorted sense of their true abilities. I worried that their value would be on shaky ground indeed, with all sorts of negative consequences including both false pride and lousy self-esteem.

While some of us, including me, can certainly suffer from paralyzing insecurities, I think many of us have a harder time having the kind of "sober" self-judgment Paul speaks of in this verse. Paul also addresses the key to objective self-assessment: recognizing all we are and have is due solely to the grace of God.

Jesus embodied the opposite of the unearned trophy practice. He didn't assert His equality to God; He made Himself humble (Philippians 2:6–8).

While Pierce is, in fact, an excellent athlete, I've urged him to stay humble and recognize his abilities are gifts to develop and enjoy, but they're not his identity. Healthy self-esteem comes from knowing our true value is imparted from Jesus and to be used for His glory. That's the real trophy! —ISABELLA CAMPOLATTARO

FAITH STEP: *Take twenty minutes right now to list all your qualities, both assets and defects. Reflect on them, thank Jesus for all of them, positive and negative, and pray that He will use them for His glory.*

MONDAY, SEPTEMBER 11

---

*"Now then, stand still and see this great thing the LORD is about
to do before your eyes!" 1 Samuel 12:16 (NIV)*

I ATTACHED THE TOUR DIRECTOR name tag to my shirt, grabbed
my heavy backpack, and headed for the lobby, the hotel room door
slamming behind me. With clipboard in hand, I corralled guests to
an awaiting motor coach, all while answering their many questions.
My busy, wonderful day was off to a great start.

The bus driver maneuvered New York City traffic as I spoke into
the microphone, sharing details about the sites—Times Square, St.
Patrick's Cathedral, Rockefeller Center, the Empire State Building,
and Central Park. We stopped in lower Manhattan.

"New Yorkers call this building the Freedom Tower. Its official
name, however, is One World Trade Center. From the ground to
the tip of its spire, it reaches 1,776 feet, representing the birthday
of our country." I allowed time for reflection at the nearby 9/11
Memorial and then led guests back to the bus.

Rushing to get to our next attraction, I almost missed one of the
most inspiring sights of my life. For some reason, I glanced over my
shoulder. My breath caught. Reflecting from the glass windows of
the Freedom Tower, a giant cross stretched from the bottom floor
to almost the top. "Look!" I said, pointing.

I couldn't explain the image. Maybe lights were on in just the
right offices or shades were pulled down in exactly the right rooms.
The bustle of busyness faded. Our group stood still and silently
praised Jesus. This reminder of His presence in NYC was the best
site of all. —BECKY ALEXANDER

FAITH STEP: *Slow down and look for signs of Jesus as you go through your day.*

TUESDAY, SEPTEMBER 12

I am the vine; you are the branches. Whoever abides in me and I in him, he it is that bears much fruit, for apart from me you can do nothing. John 15:5 (ESV)

RATHER THAN MAKING NEW YEAR'S resolutions, I select a word to focus on. This past year, I selected the word "abide." We've moved frequently and recently settled into a new home. Because abide means to reside, dwell, or remain, it seemed an appropriate choice.

To learn to abide in Jesus, I sought methods to engage Scripture more, such as journaling about sections that jumped out to me, praying Jesus's Word, and learning more about the context and culture of Biblical times. I even pondered significant works of art in light of the Biblical events or truths they portrayed to see if they offered spiritual parallels to my life. All these methods were valuable, but one insight I gained about abiding with Jesus was my need to learn to dwell in the moment.

I heard someone say we spend eighty percent of our mental energy thinking about the past or future and only twenty percent in the present. I battle wandering thoughts that transport me to different times rather than focusing on where I am. Like being in a home, I can't abide in the present if I'm not, well, in the present. This beautiful allegory of a vine and branches is an intimate union between Jesus and us, His followers. Jesus as the vine is the sustenance for everything. As a branch, I'm dependent on Him for everything, every moment of every day of my life. —JEANNIE BLACKMER

FAITH STEP: *Read John 15 and write about what abiding in Jesus means to you. Then list three steps you can take to abide with Him.*

WEDNESDAY, SEPTEMBER 13

Knowing this, that our old man was crucified with Him, that the body of sin might be done away with, that we should no longer be slaves of sin. For he who has died has been freed from sin. Romans 6:6–7 (NKJV)

A PICTURE OF A PUPPY on Facebook made me smile. The photographer caught the canine bounding toward the camera. Its ears were laid back as though windblown, and its tongue flapped from the corner of its mouth. Its facial expression reflected sheer delight. The caption said, "Live like someone left the gate open." I looked at that photo and thought, *This is the way we, as believers, ought to live.*

Before I gave my life to Jesus, the enemy of my soul kept me in chains. He held me captive in his kingdom of darkness. I was a slave to sin and doomed to its consequences. But Jesus purchased my freedom. He broke those chains and opened the gate.

Sometimes I live as though I'm still locked up. I repeat the same sinful behaviors, think the same sinful thoughts, and fall into the same sinful habits time and time again, helpless to change.

When I feel that way, I remind myself of the truth: I was crucified with Jesus when I chose to follow Him. My old self died, sin's chains fell off, and I am free! Learning to live from that truth is difficult, but Scripture says it can be done. I want to live like someone left the gate open because the truth is that Jesus did. —GRACE FOX

FAITH STEP: *Make a small paper chain. When you feel helpless, tear off one of the links and toss it away to remind yourself that with Jesus you are free.*

THURSDAY, SEPTEMBER 14

Be kind to one another, tenderhearted, forgiving one another, as God in Christ forgave you. Ephesians 4:32 (ESV)

IT WASN'T HIM. IT COULDN'T be! But the man sitting in front of me at church resembled my brother from the back—same bald spot, same ears, same slim build. When he turned, I saw it wasn't my brother, but I couldn't ignore the nudge from Jesus. I needed to get in touch with Bob.

A dispute over our mother's care had caused a rift between Bob and me. After Mother died, Bob told me he never wanted to see me again, and that was fine with me.

It had been eleven years since I'd seen my brother. With time, the anger and bitterness had subsided, but pride prevailed. I wasn't going to be the first one to beg for forgiveness.

A few years ago, I began sending Bob Facebook messages wishing him a happy birthday, on his birthdate and on his sobriety birthday. Sometimes, he thanked me. Once, he even wished me a happy birthday. But neither of us apologized.

After seeing that man at church, I went home, sat at my computer, and messaged Bob.

"I'm so sorry for our estrangement, Bob. I miss you!" Within minutes, his response came back. "I'm sorry, too, Sis, and I miss you."

Months later, Bob's daughter called. He was in ICU. I visited once he was released into hospice care. We hugged, cried, and forgave each other. Thanks to Jesus, my brother and I reconciled. Two days later, Bob went to heaven. —PAT BUTLER DYSON

FAITH STEP: *Follow Jesus's example of forgiving another as He has forgiven you. Just don't wait too long.*

FRIDAY, SEPTEMBER 15

Then Jesus cried out, "Whoever believes in me does not believe in me only, but in the one who sent me. The one who looks at me is seeing the one who sent me. I have come into the world as a light, so that no one who believes in me should stay in darkness." John 12:44–46 (NIV)

I'M IN DENIAL THAT I need stronger reading glasses. Instead, I surround myself with more lamps while I read, flooding the space with light to compensate. It's gotten to the point where I pack a book light when I go to my prayer group, just in case the hostess' living room isn't bright enough for me to read my Bible and journal. And God bless the person who thought to build a flashlight into the iPhone! It's helped me read restaurant menus more times than I can count.

We should always be seeking the light of Christ. But when life gets difficult, we need to look for Him more frequently to compensate. He is the light of the world (John 8:12). There is no darkness He can't overcome (John 1:5). His grace becomes my lighthouse in a storm, my spotlight in the cave of despair, and a full moon on a starless night, guiding me to the peace He yearns to give.

Out of His deep compassion and abundant love, Jesus goes a step further and sends His brilliance through other believers. Just as He says seeing Him is seeing His Father (John 14:9), we can see Jesus through those who follow Him, no matter our human eyesight. —CLAIRE MCGARRY

FAITH STEP: *Light just one candle in a darkened room. Then light several more. Notice how much brighter it gets as each candle is added.*

SATURDAY, SEPTEMBER 16

Trust in the LORD with all your heart and lean not on your own understanding; in all your ways submit to him, and he will make your paths straight. Proverbs 3:5–6 (NIV)

MY OLDEST SON, JACK, CAME to Idaho for a visit this summer. While he was here, we headed to the cell phone store to trade in his phone. We hadn't lived in Meridian very long, and I was still finding my way around the downtown area.

Things quickly went awry. I was talking to him and got turned around. I drove onto a one-way street going the wrong way—into oncoming traffic. Luckily for us, it wasn't busy, just a single car stopped in the middle lane at the light. Quick maneuvering got us back on track and to the phone store. For the remainder of his visit, Jack chose to ride with my husband. He wanted to be with the guy who actually knew where he was going.

I often get turned around in life. I head the wrong way with my attitude or get confused about how to navigate the day with grace and hope. This is why I need to trust Jesus with all my plans, hopes, and dreams. Even when I don't understand the direction I'm headed, I can trust Him to know where He is leading me.

Jesus not only knows the way; He is the way. And I want to be with the One who actually knows where He is going. —SUSANNA FOTH AUGHTMON

FAITH STEP: *Take a prayer walk around your neighborhood. As you pray, ask Jesus to guide your steps and make your path straight.*

SUNDAY, SEPTEMBER 17

When the young man heard this, he went away sad, because he had great wealth. Matthew 19:22 (NIV)

THE RICH YOUNG RULER DIDN'T want to give up his wealth to follow Jesus. The typical takeaway of this story is that we shouldn't make wealth our idol. True, but I think there's even more to it.

This man had done the visibly good stuff of keeping the Ten Commandments. But Jesus's truth was uncomfortable to him. Jesus wanted him to come to terms with who he truly was, deep down, behind the facade he presented to appear acceptably "holy."

Maybe the deepest issue tripping him up was his unwillingness to see his hang-ups and strongholds for what they were. Even more than his money, was it his will, his openness to honest self-evaluation, that he was unwilling to let Jesus have and re-create?

When presented with a choice, he chose not to change. In short, the rich young ruler loved his lifestyle more than he loved the Lord.

I don't like change either. I like my stuff. Why do I have to choose? Can't I have it both ways?

The rich young ruler went away sad and for good reason. His story reads tragically instead of victoriously. But I still have a choice. Jesus came to free me and the rest of His followers from every stronghold. But He won't coerce me to accomplish it. He desires my willingness to do things differently and leave things behind so that I follow Him in a new and holy life.

Unlike the rich young ruler, I am spiritually rich but I'm not sad. And that's because I choose Jesus. —ERIN KEELEY MARSHALL

FAITH STEP: *What stronghold might Jesus be prompting you to address? Ask Him to give you a willingness to change.*

MONDAY, SEPTEMBER 18

He always comes alongside us to comfort us in every suffering so that we can come alongside those who are in any painful trial. We can bring them this same comfort that God has poured out upon us. 2 Corinthians 1:4 *(TPT)*

WE BURIED THE HUSBAND OF a dear friend last week. Dawn and Brice would've celebrated thirty years of marriage next month. It was hard to say goodbye, but Brice was very sick.

As I asked Jesus to comfort Dawn the day before the funeral, an idea flashed into my mind. *Make Dawn a care package to take to the funeral along with your sympathy card.* Jesus even showed me what items to tuck inside: chocolate candy, a stress-relieving coloring book, and a box of tissues.

I rushed to the store on my way to work, flying through the aisles. *I hope Dawn likes butterflies.* It was the only coloring book that didn't feature talking sponges wearing pants or flying superheroes. *These pastel markers will be calming.* I tossed the items into my cart.

The Lord instructed me that the only message I should write in Dawn's card was "I love you, I love you, I love you." It didn't seem like enough.

At church a couple of Sundays later, Dawn hugged me tight and thanked me for the gift. Especially the chocolate.

I refused to take credit for Jesus's idea. I felt like I got a gift too, because I listened to and obeyed Him. —JEANETTE LEVELLIE

FAITH STEP: *Ask Jesus to show and tell you a tangible way you can love someone today. Listen for His directions and then obey Him.*

TUESDAY, SEPTEMBER 19

At that time people will see the Son of Man coming in clouds with great power and glory. Mark 13:26 (NIV)

AS I PREPARE TO LEAVE my home, I slip on my favorite watch, an old wind-up style I received at my high school graduation. It's elegant, requires no batteries, and has a feature not often found anymore. The second hand doesn't sweep gracefully around the dial. Instead, it ticks along, sixty times per minute. Every instant that passes is recognized, and that matters to me.

Why is a single, tiny increment of time so important? Because at one particular moment I didn't believe in Jesus and the next I did. In that instant my mind stopped wavering, and I made the decision that would change my life forever. My soul escaped the grip of sin and was set free. All because the Creator of time itself chose to use His years here on Earth for my salvation. It seems things that happen in a flash are intimately connected with the infinite.

One second, Jesus took His first breath as a human. During His crucifixion, one moment He hung on the cross, suffering for my sin. The next, He was gone. Days later, in one magnificent instant, He stepped out from His tomb. And someday He'll return, as fast and bright as lightning, visible to all (Matthew 24:27).

Now He's with me every hour, every minute, every second of every day. I won't take a single one for granted because time—like grace—is precious. I plan to make it count. —HEIDI GAUL

FAITH STEP: *Look back on your most precious moments. How can you make time to create special memories for others?*

WEDNESDAY, SEPTEMBER 20

Whether you turn to the right or to the left, your ears will hear a voice behind you, saying, "This is the way; walk in it." Isaiah 30:21 (NIV)

MY MORNING APPOINTMENT WAS ON an unfamiliar college campus, and I drove through the parking lot, scanning the large letters on the sides of the buildings in search of the administration department. Slowly, I weaved through the rows of parking spaces, keeping my eyes peeled for the correct building. At one point, a gaggle of geese wandered in front of my car. I had to stop, roll down my window, and holler to shoo them out of my way.

That's when a campus police officer appeared in my rear-view mirror. He got out of his patrol car and stomped toward the driver's side of my car, a scowl on his face. "Why are you driving through a restricted area, ma'am?" He pointed to the small signs on the chain-link fence.

I apologized and explained that I had missed the signs because I'd been looking up at the buildings while driving. Even though I remained polite and respectful, the officer berated me for my inability to follow directions. He demanded I turn around immediately. I drove off, ashamed and embarrassed.

Later, I thought about all the times I'd wandered off course in my spiritual life as well, despite a genuine effort to follow Jesus. I'm grateful for His gentleness when I go astray. Jesus never berates me. Instead, He directs my steps and missteps with love and patience. I want to be more like Him, not that campus police officer. —EMILY E. RYAN

FAITH STEP: *Remember a time when Jesus directed you back to Himself after a period of wandering. Thank Him again for His love, gentleness, and patience.*

THURSDAY, SEPTEMBER 21

Jesus replied, "Anyone who loves me will obey my teaching.
My Father will love them, and we will come to them and make
our home with them." John 14:23 (NIV)

WHEN I DRIVE MY SON to school in the morning, I brace myself for the inevitable. Drivers fly down the entrance ramp into my lane, ignoring the yield sign, and dangerously merge in front of me. Day after day, I endure the hardheadedness of stubborn drivers who refuse to pay attention to the merge sign on this busy highway. I could not understand how those drivers could be so defiant, and I often complained to my family.

On my way to pick up my son from school one day, I approached that stretch of highway. It wasn't as busy in the afternoon, and instead of fixating on how drivers disregarded that yield sign, I started thinking about my own disregard for Jesus's "signs." Sometimes, when I sense Jesus telling me to stop and wait, I ignore Him and rush to where I want to go, regardless of the impact my actions have on others. Behind the wheel that day, I realized I wasn't that different from those irritating drivers I complained about.

Unlike me, Jesus isn't annoyed when I fail to follow His directions. He responds to my disobedience with mercy and grace. He continues to keep His signs in view, despite my disregard, waiting patiently for me to yield my will and merge onto the path He has for me. —ERICKA LOYNES

FAITH STEP: *Before racing off to your next destination, take a moment to pause and consider what signs from Jesus you may have ignored. No matter how far you've gone, it's never too late to turn around and get on the right road.*

FRIDAY, SEPTEMBER 22

Cast all your anxiety on him because he cares for you. 1 Peter 5:7 (NIV)

OUR JACK RUSSELL/CHIHUAHUA MIX loves to play fetch. Throw Flash a tennis ball, and he would play for hours if he could. One afternoon, a neighbor threw the ball with Flash for over an hour. Flash could not stop running after and retrieving it. Something innate within him compels him to get that ball and bring it back to the thrower, no matter where it goes or how tired he gets.

The next day, Flash was so sore and exhausted that he couldn't even jump up on the couch to nap. He'd worn himself out the day before chasing after the tennis ball. I had to lift his little body onto his pillow so he could rest and recover.

I'm a whole lot like Flash when it comes to my worries. I just can't stop; I won't let them go. I try to meditate on good thoughts, but I always bring back my worries. I play them over and over in my mind. I map out plans about how to fix them. I talk about them with friends. I wear myself out with them until I make myself dog-tired.

Jesus invites me to cast my anxiety on Him. He catches any worries life throws my way. He is the One with the power to heal my worried mind. He has the strength and the resources to meet my every need, answer my every prayer, and build hope in my heart.

I need not worry—unlike Flash and me, Jesus never grows weary.
—SUSANNA FOTH AUGHTMON

FAITH STEP: *Turn your worry list into your prayer list. Write down everything you are worried about, pray about each one, and ask Jesus to take care of it.*

SATURDAY, SEPTEMBER 23

But each person is tempted when they are dragged away by their own evil desire and enticed. Then, after desire has conceived, it gives birth to sin; and sin, when it is full-grown, gives birth to death. James 1:14–15 (NIV)

WHEN WE FIRST VISITED FLORIDA to figure out where to live, we stayed at a popular upscale hotel chain in West Palm Beach that had an amazingly low room rate. The hotel was a new high rise with a gorgeous resort-style pool. Several blocks from the beach, it was close to plenty of shopping and entertainment. I wondered why the price was so low but shook it off, thrilled with our bargain and the prospect of being surrounded by luxury.

The morning after we arrived, I set out for my early morning run. I stopped at the front desk to ask about a running route. The clerk's eyes grew wide.

"Whatever you do, don't turn left!" he said, explaining the hotel was in a dangerous part of town. The hotel was on the outskirts of a new gentrification effort still underway. Thus, the cheap rates were due to the risky surroundings.

Sin is a lot like that nice hotel in a bad part of town. It's appealing and looks good. It starts out innocently enough, but like an unknowing jog in the wrong direction, it could lead to danger. I think of this whenever temptation strikes, which is mercifully not that often anymore. I know to "turn right" to stay safe and surround myself with Jesus. —ISABELLA CAMPOLATTARO

FAITH STEP: *Be honest with yourself and with Jesus. Are you toying with a wrong turn that could lead to disaster? Ask Jesus for a better route to safety.*

SUNDAY, SEPTEMBER 24

For who sees anything different in you? What do you have that you did not receive? And if you received it, why do you boast as if it were not a gift?
1 *Corinthians* 4:7 *(NRSV)*

TRAVELING AS A SPEAKER ALLOWS me to meet other accomplished speakers. I'm inspired by the passionate, insightful messages I hear. Yet, if I'm truthful, it's easy to compare myself to them.

My comparison struggle is most brutal in exhibit halls where authors and speakers sell their books. I recently looked from their professional banners and displays to my own little book table. Before the next conference, I decided to design a new booth. While the finished product turned out well, deep down I knew I'd done so with the wrong motives. By the time the convention started, I was exhausted from the extra setup. I shook my head, disappointed in myself—all because I wrongly felt like what I had to offer wasn't good enough.

The funny thing about the comparison trap is that I never compare myself with people who have less than I do. I looked at those who had people crowding around their book tables. Perfect hair, suits, heels, and nails as they gestured on stage, giving deep, spiritual insights of how God has been working in their lives.

Jesus didn't call me to be them—He called me to be me, and He called me *because* I'm me. My job isn't striving to make myself, or my book table, look better. Instead, I'm to share the messages Jesus has given me. Everything I have comes from Him—no comparison needed.

And that is enough. —TRICIA GOYER

FAITH STEP: *Do you play the comparison game too? Ask Jesus to show you specific ways that you are enough.*

MONDAY, SEPTEMBER 25

I have given you the power to trample on snakes and scorpions and to defeat the power of your enemy Satan. Nothing can harm you. Luke 10:19 (CEV)

I'D NEVER SEEN A SNAKE in this town until recently. Surprisingly, there was a HUGE garter snake, about five feet long, on the sidewalk downtown. I got a friend to come out of his storefront to see the reptilian visitor slithering out onto the road. We watched as it retreated into a drainage pipe in the gutter.

When I was trying to identify that snake so out of place on the downtown pavement, I learned about brumation. Brumation is a form of hibernation unique to reptiles. A natural science website says reptiles like to hide and burrow in, to stay safe and warm. This causes their breathing, heart rate, and temperature to drop—similar to what happens during hibernation.

After a series of recent upsetting events, I've been in a state of brumation, lying low, trying to stay safe and warm. The real enemy in times like this isn't a formidable garter snake. Rather, it's the enemy of my soul, trying to steal my joy, to make me feel unsafe and defeated. But Jesus says He's given me the power to trample on and defeat the setbacks and heartbreaks of this world caused by the enemy, Satan. Furthermore, Jesus promises that nothing can harm me—not grief, not despair—and certainly not harmless garter snakes. Now when I am feeling unsafe or defeated, I talk to Jesus, thanking Him for His power in me to defeat the enemy. With Him I know that nothing can harm me. —CASSANDRA TIERSMA

FAITH STEP: *Are you feeling defeated by a recent setback or upsetting event? Ask Jesus to wrap you in His Comfort and rest in Him.*

TUESDAY, SEPTEMBER 26

I waited patiently for the LORD; he turned to me and heard my cry.
Psalm 40:1 (NIV)

"MRS. DYSON, YOUR MAMMOGRAM SHOWED a mass…"

The nurse continued talking, but I didn't hear a word. I took a deep breath and asked her to repeat herself. I'd need to come back to MD Anderson for further testing in two weeks. *Jesus, how can I endure the wait?*

My friend Judy, who has suffered more heartbreak than anyone I know, told me she used to try to manage problems by herself, but when she trusted the Lord to handle things, she had peace. I'd tried that, too, but I'm a natural worrier. I always took them back.

Further mammograms revealed the need for a biopsy. My anxiety grew the longer I waited to hear the results. The mass appeared benign, but some atypical cells required the medical committee to decide what to do next. More waiting. I slept little, barely ate. I tried to pray and let go, but I only worried more.

Finally, the committee decided the mass needed to be surgically removed for further study. A segmental mastectomy would be scheduled after I met with the surgeon in a week.

I'd been begging Jesus to help me since the beginning of my ordeal, but finally, I cried out to Him, "Lord, I need You to handle this!" Immediately, I felt a weight lift from my soul. I would trust Him. He would be with me, no matter what.

Thankfully, the mass was benign, but the lesson I learned wasn't: Trust the Lord to handle it and let go. —PAT BUTLER DYSON

FAITH STEP: *What frightening uncertainty do you face? Give it to Jesus and let Him handle it. Feel your body relax.*

WEDNESDAY, SEPTEMBER 27

A good man brings good things out of the good stored up in his heart,
and an evil man brings evil things out of the evil stored up in his heart.
For the mouth speaks what the heart is full of. Luke 6:45 (NIV)

MY SISTER JENNY AND I often talk on the phone. Even though we both live stateside, we greet each other in French. Jenny asks, "Comment ça va?" (How is it going?) I respond, "Comme ci comme ça." (So-so.) This makes Jenny laugh. Jenny spoke French while living abroad for five years. I spoke French for one year in high school. Even though Jenny is more fluent, I like pulling out some good French words like *fatigué* (pronounced fa-tee-gay), which means tired, and *désolé* (pronounced deh-soh-lay), which means sad. I like the way they roll off the tongue.

Whether speaking in English or French, Jenny is always upbeat when we talk. She uses her words to encourage me. Her heart, the wellspring of her words, is full of hope, love, and kindness. Just talking to my sister always makes me feel better.

Jesus wants me to use my words for good too. But what I say echoes the state of my heart. Am I encouraging and honest when I speak? Loyal? Kind? Or anxious and bitter? Jesus is working on my heart, healing me with His grace. I want His words of mercy and love to leave my lips and encourage those around me, no matter what language I speak. —SUSANNA FOTH AUGHTMON

FAITH STEP: *Listen to the words that you say today. Are they kind? Honest? Uplifting? Ask Jesus to work on your heart so that your language encourages those around you.*

THURSDAY, SEPTEMBER 28

And the peace of God, which transcends all understanding, will guard your hearts and your minds in Christ Jesus. Philippians 4:7 (NIV)

I FIRST NOTICED THE SIGNS in a few yards near my home: a thin, unfinished wood cross with three words stenciled in black, *ALL IS WELL.* I assumed a local church had passed them out to members for Easter week. Then the signs began popping up everywhere. An online search revealed that a local family had made the signs to distribute free to residents. Unfortunately, the deadline for picking one up had passed. The next day, a neighbor offered me one of the leftovers she had in her car.

A few months after I stuck that sign in my flower bed, my husband and I left home under evacuation orders. A historic hurricane roared through southwest Louisiana for hours that evening, flattening buildings and uprooting trees. Three days later, my husband drove back to check our house. We had escaped with minor damage: backyard fence gone, some shingles missing, much of the landscaping pulled up or stripped of leaves.

We returned home five weeks later when our power was finally restored. Near my front walkway, I found the cross lying on the ground, broken apart but not blown away. I remembered the strange sense of peace I felt as we fled the storm and later waited for news. We repaired the sign; now I see it as a reminder of Jesus, the One who promises a supernatural peace when I trust Him enough to turn my burdens over to Him in prayer. —DIANNE NEAL MATTHEWS

FAITH STEP: *Think of an area in your life where you need the peace of Christ. Make your own sign as a reminder that since you belong to Him, ALL IS WELL.*

FRIDAY, SEPTEMBER 29

"But you will receive power when the Holy Spirit comes on you; and you will be my witnesses in Jerusalem, and in all Judea and Samaria, and to the ends of the earth." Acts 1:8 (NIV)

AS A YOUNG CHRISTIAN, I learned about Jesus's call to be His witness to the ends of the earth. I assumed I was meant to become a missionary. I read biographies of missionaries to faraway countries. I attended conferences and listened to talks by those serving on the other side of the globe. When Jesus didn't lead me in that direction, I felt as if I'd failed Him.

But Jesus is full of surprises. Through my choreography work, He provided me an opportunity to help a mission group in Hong Kong. In my writing life, He opened doors for my books to be translated into Dutch and Indonesian, and for my devotionals to reach around the world. I'm so grateful for those unexpected experiences to share my faith and the Good News of Jesus.

Serving on short-term mission trips or writing books aren't the only ways to be His witness far from home. In this age of the internet, a post on social media can encourage others to praise Him. A letter can remind a friend far away to keep trusting Jesus. And most powerful of all, my prayers can join with those of missionaries who are serving at the ends of the earth. Just like the disciples, I am part of His kingdom, testifying to His love and grace, whether in my family and neighborhood or the far reaches of the planet.
—SHARON HINCK

FAITH STEP: *Share the love of Jesus with someone from another country today—whether through email, letter, or prayer.*

SATURDAY, SEPTEMBER 30

*Let your conversation be always full of grace, seasoned with salt,
so that you may know how to answer everyone. Colossians 4:6 (NIV)*

IN MY HOUSE, I'M THE chief cook. It's my responsibility to know the unique culinary tastes of each family member in order to adequately prepare cuisine that they will enjoy. For example, I know my son's mashed potatoes will require a few dashes of salt if we are out of beef gravy, and I know that my husband will eat almost any breakfast food that includes cinnamon. Whatever meal I prepare for my family, I ensure it has the right amount of seasoning so they will enjoy the delicious flavor and consume it.

The Apostle Paul compares the Gospel of Jesus to a meal that is made to order. This doesn't mean that the truth should be altered so everyone likes it—quite the contrary. Rather, Paul is referring to the *presentation* of the words we choose. No matter how much sense the message of Jesus makes when I serve it up, it will lose effectiveness if I am unloving or speak harshly or carelessly.

When I share Jesus with others, I can't guarantee they won't be offended, but I can prayerfully consider the words and tone I use to bring the message. Just as my family wouldn't eat their favorite foods without the right seasoning, the more gentleness, kindness, and love I sprinkle into my conversation, the more others will be willing to taste the delicious truth of Jesus and devour His Good News. —ERICKA LOYNES

FAITH STEP: *The next time you are about to share Jesus with someone, ask Him to help you season your words with love and grace so that person can be drawn to Him, just like you once were.*

SUNDAY, OCTOBER 1

Jesus answered: Love the Lord your God with all your heart, soul, and mind. Matthew 22:37 (CEV)

WHETHER SCANNING FRIENDS' POSTS IN my online newsfeed, binge-watching DIY tutorials from my favorite online mentors, or catching up on the latest tweets and videos of my favorite influencers, I'm always being asked to "Like, Share, and Follow." Every time I see or hear those ubiquitous words of online invitation, I can't help but think about how that pertains to the One I'm really meant to be following.

Bombarded with daily social media requests to "Like, Share, and Follow," I often ask myself if I'm doing that with Jesus. In today's scripture, Jesus tells me to not only "like" Him but to love Him with all my heart, soul, and mind. What's more, the Bible instructs me to tell everyone about the amazing things He does (Psalm 96:3). So, I'm meant to "share" the Good News about Jesus. But that's not all. He also wants me to "follow" Him. In fact, He outright said, "Follow Me" (Matthew 9:9). So, there it is. Jesus wants me to "Like, Share, and Follow" Him.

When it comes to my faith life, "Like, Share, and Follow" means more than just a few clicks on a smartphone or electronic keypad. It's all about relationship—my relationship with Jesus, reading His Holy Word, praying consistently as I talk to Him, gathering with others to praise and worship Him. The most powerful international influencer and wisest teacher of all time is also my very best friend. I want to "Like, Share, and Follow" Jesus above everyone else. —CASSANDRA TIERSMA

FAITH STEP: *The next time you see or hear someone ask you to "Like, Share, and Follow," check in with Jesus, and ask Him how you can better "Like, Share, and Follow" Him.*

MONDAY, OCTOBER 2

But he knows the way that I take; when he has tested me, I will come forth as gold. My feet have closely followed his steps; I have kept to his way without turning aside. Job 23:10–11 (NIV)

SEVERAL MONTHS AGO, MY HUSBAND set up slack lines between two trees in our backyard. The lower line served as a tightrope for the kids to walk on while they held on to the upper rope to steady themselves.

Practice has paid off, and they're able to drop their hold on the upper line and walk steadily for longer stretches. Adding another element to the challenge, we had some overgrowth cleared in that area, and the new grass took a while to establish. The ground beneath the line was thick with mud in the early weeks, so falling off the slack line resulted in tugging a lost shoe or sock from the mire—motivation to learn fast how to stay up there.

I'm watching my kids develop focus and muscle memory by making minor adjustments with their feet, legs, hips, arms, and posture. They're becoming more fluid than wobbly. When I watch them, I can't help thinking about my own walk with Jesus.

Sometimes my faith feels more wobbly than steady. I try to do life myself and don't grab hold of Jesus. His grace covers my unsteady effort to go it alone. Practicing my faith walk with Jesus daily, I better develop my focus and spiritual muscle memory. Like my kids, I need to stay balanced to avoid the mucky mire too.
—ERIN KEELEY MARSHALL

FAITH STEP: *Practice stabilizing your faith walk this week as you practice your balance. Stand on one foot to the count of ten as you reach out your arms and concentrate on Jesus.*

TUESDAY, OCTOBER 3

When they landed, they saw a fire of burning coals there with fish on it, and some bread.... Jesus came, took the bread and gave it to them, and did the same with the fish. John 21:9, 13 (NIV)

WHEN MY EIGHTY-EIGHT-YEAR-OLD MOTHER'S HEALTH started spiraling downward, my husband and I made the seven-hundred-mile trip from our home to hers three times in eight weeks. Driving twelve hours each way, stopping only for gas and fast food, was physically exhausting. Sitting vigil at her bedside for a week before she passed away added another layer of weariness. I mourned her deeply.

Upon our return from each of those trips, my husband and I provided childcare for our toddler granddaughter, Lexi. We visited the zoo and the beach, carved pumpkins, fed ducks in our marina, did finger painting, and took lots of walks. It was so much fun!

Jesus knew my weary body and soul needed refreshment, so He brought Lexi. Visiting the zoo and the beach forced me to relax. Seeing Lexi's delight in the simple things of life restored my joy. Her laughter lifted my sorrow. Tiny arms around my neck made me feel loved.

Jesus knew the disciples' physical and emotional state after the trauma of His death, the shock of His resurrection, the confusion of what their lives would look like without His leadership, and the disappointment of fishing all night without results. He remedied it with breakfast on the beach, home-cooked and served with love.

Are you weary? Jesus knows what your body and soul need for renewal. He'll make it happen. Just like He did for me. —GRACE FOX

FAITH STEP: *Ask Jesus to bring refreshment today and look for what He handpicks to meet your needs.*

WEDNESDAY, OCTOBER 4

Early in the morning, as Jesus was on his way back to the city, he was hungry. Seeing a fig tree by the road, he went up to it but found nothing on it except leaves.... Matthew 21:18–19 (NIV)

MY HUSBAND PLANTED A NEW peach tree near the pond behind our house. Unlike apple or pear trees, peach trees self-pollinate. It will produce fruit on its own in a few years when it's mature. Hopefully, it will be more fruitful than the tree it replaced.

Each spring, our original peach tree sprouted a ball of green leaves, but it didn't produce the luscious fruit we hoped for. I gave up on making homemade peach cobbler from its bounty. Then, one summer morning, I spotted a new color mingled with its green leaves. Six round, beautiful peaches. Finally, we had fruit! But the next year the tree was barren, and the following year, it died.

That peach tree reminds me of the leafy fig Jesus encountered. Because a fig tree produces figs first and then leaves, Jesus expected to find breakfast among the foliage, but the tree was fruitless. Jesus cursed the tree, and it withered from the roots up.

This illustration challenges me to inspect my own branches. Do my words and actions make false promises? Am I producing delightful fruit or just a bunch of leaves? Are my roots being nourished in the Word? Am I spending enough time in prayer? I want to make sure my life produces fruit that will last (John 15:16). While I'm waiting for cobbler from homegrown peaches, the fruit I bear in my life is ripe and ready to share now. —KAREN SARGENT

FAITH STEP: *Each time you enjoy your favorite fruit, remind yourself to do a spiritual fruit inspection.*

THURSDAY, OCTOBER 5

Put to death, therefore, whatever belongs to your earthly nature:
sexual immorality, impurity, lust, evil desires and greed,
which is idolatry. Colossians 3:5 (NIV)

I USED TO THINK OF idols as primitive carvings of bizarre figures or the golden calf described in Exodus 32. Raised Catholic, I was accustomed to statues, paintings, and other artistic renderings of Jesus, Mary, biblical figures, and assorted saints as a common expression of faith and worship. Those were never considered idols to me, but that doesn't mean I've lived idol-free.

The dictionary defines idol as both "an image or representation of a god used as an object of worship" and "a person or thing that is greatly admired, loved, or revered." In the language of faith, an idol is anything I put before God. Paul further clarifies sins that are idols—anger, wrath, malice, slander, and abusive language (Colossians 3:8). The reality is, there are much more threatening idols not made of marble, wood, or resin.

I idolized my dear mother, who struggled with mental illness, orbiting around her and trying to help in the unhealthiest ways for the both of us. I idolized professional achievement, chasing desperately after titles and acquisition without regard for God's true call on my life. I've even idolized church, becoming zealously religious, as my heart drifted further and further from Jesus. My idols of codependency, pride, legalism, and the illusion I could do it alone were false idols that needed to be smashed.

That's one of the biggest problems with idols—they break or they break us. But there's a solution. Making Jesus first is the answer to living idol-free. —ISABELLA CAMPOLATTARO

FAITH STEP: *What do you put before Jesus? Ask Him to reveal any idols in your life, then smash them.*

FRIDAY, OCTOBER 6

---

*But the Advocate, the Holy Spirit, whom the Father will
send in my name, will teach you all things and will remind you of
everything I have said to you. John 14:26 (NIV)*

ONE MORNING WHEN I WAS feeling particularly overwhelmed by financial obligations, I turned to Psalm 23, which has always given me great peace and encouragement. But this day, I was moved to do something I hadn't done before. I read the familiar psalm in different versions of the Bible.

I often turn to various Bible translations when I don't quite understand a passage in hopes that one of them will give me clarity. I pulled out the big, heavy parallel Bible that a friend had given me years ago. It had four versions side by side. I focused on the first verse of Psalm 23:

> *The LORD is my shepherd; I shall not want.* (King James Version)
> *The LORD is my shepherd, I lack nothing.* (New International Version)
> *Because the Lord is my Shepherd, I have everything I need!* (The
>   Living Bible)
> *The LORD is my shepherd, I shall not want.* (Revised Standard Version)

I stared at the different words, punctuation, and capitalization and read them out loud. They each spoke to my spirit. Jesus, through the Holy Spirit, was telling me that everything would be all right and that I didn't need to worry about my financial obligations. He was my shepherd, my guide, my provider, my Lord; no matter what the translation, He would take care of it. —BARBRANDA LUMPKINS WALLS

FAITH STEP: *What are some of your favorite scriptures and Bible stories? Read them in different Bible translations or versions and see what new revelations you receive from Jesus.*

SATURDAY, OCTOBER 7

*And I am certain that God, who began the good work within you,
will continue his work until it is finally finished on the day when
Christ Jesus returns. Philippians 1:6 (NLT)*

NEARLY EVERY NIGHT I'M AWAKENED by singing. And not my own.
My ninety-one-year-old grandmother lives with us, and if she awakens in the night, she often sings until she can go back to sleep.

Living with this godly saint has taught me much about how to
live the Christian walk. If my grandma is hurting, she prays aloud.
If she struggles to sleep, she sings praises to Jesus. When she is
concerned about family members, she lifts their names to Jesus in
prayer. Hardships haven't hindered Grandma's close relationship
with Jesus—it's just the opposite. She is close to Jesus because she
turns to Him in the midst of her troubles.

I also have this type of relationship with Jesus because Grandma
has taught me to do the same. Over the years, Grandma's actions
have shown me that Jesus welcomes the hurting and the wounded.
Jesus seeks the lost. Jesus embraces the wayward. Jesus touches
the broken. Jesus cries with the mourners. Jesus gives peace to the
fearful.

Just like Grandma, I wouldn't have a strong relationship with Jesus
if I wasn't wounded, lost, wayward, broken, mourning, or fearful at
times. There are many times in life when the situations can't change
but our souls can.

And that's something to sing about—one song or prayer at a time.
—TRICIA GOYER

FAITH STEP: *Is there a hardship in your life? Do you have trouble sleeping? Are
you worried about a family member? Lift your voice to Jesus in song.*

SUNDAY, OCTOBER 8

I am the door. If anyone enters by Me, he will be saved, and will go in and out and find pasture. John 10:9 (NKJV)

WHENEVER I HAVE A MEDICAL appointment, I know one question I'll probably ask: "How do I get out of here?" One clinic I visit has a front door followed by a door into the orthopedics section. When my name was called, I entered a door into the wing with a group of doctors, then walked through a doorway to find my specific doctor, which led me down several twisting hallways to finally arrive at the designated exam room. I felt like I needed a GPS just to find the exit door.

I like the theme of only one door in the Bible: one door in the ark, one doorway in the tabernacle, and Jesus as *the* Door. In New Testament times, a sheep pen had only one opening. At night, a shepherd guarded the flock by lying across the opening. In the morning, the shepherd led them out to find grass and water, all the while standing watch for danger. As our Good Shepherd, Jesus does far more than that.

Jesus provides all I could ever need, as listed in the twenty-third Psalm: guidance, nourishment, refreshment, comfort, renewed strength, and deep soul rest. Like a shepherd who stretched across the doorway of a sheep pen to protect the flock, Jesus stretched out His body on a cruel cross to save me from sin's power. If I ever feel lost spiritually, I know how to find the right Door, no GPS needed. A simple prayer shows me the way: "Jesus, guide my steps."
—DIANNE NEAL MATTHEWS

FAITH STEP: *Slowly read through Psalm 23, thinking about how Jesus fulfills each of these promises in your life.*

MONDAY, OCTOBER 9

He got up, rebuked the wind and said to the waves, "Quiet! Be still!" Then the wind died down and it was completely calm. Mark 4:39 (NIV)

A TERRIBLE STORM HIT THE area last night. Boards were ripped from fences and branches sheared off trees. As I assessed the damage to our yard, I noticed our old camellia shrub. It had been in full bloom when the gale passed through. Now the ground below it was deep with sodden petals. Only a few flowers remained on the tree, their ragged edges revealing the violence they'd encountered. I stared at those three blooms for a long time. They were beautiful. They were survivors. Just like me.

I'm mourning a loss right now, grappling with a hard lesson—one I'm not yet able to make sense of. Why are some of us plucked from life while others are left broken, struggling just to hang on? Though I don't know the answer to that question, I am learning to accept the situation. Like that trio of flowers remaining on the tree, I'm not alone. Loved ones are riding out this storm with me, talking, listening, praying, and crying. Sometimes even laughing.

That trio of camellia flowers is also a reminder of the trinity that holds firmly onto me. Throughout all the storms in my life, Jesus is the very tree I cling to. He's always with me, protecting me. And just as He settled last night's wind, He'll calm the storm inside of me too. —HEIDI GAUL

FAITH STEP: *Place a damaged flower where you can see it often during the day. Consider your trials and understand that Jesus is there for you always.*

TUESDAY, OCTOBER 10

May the grace of the Lord Jesus Christ, and the love of God, and the fellowship of the Holy Spirit be with you all. 2 Corinthians 13:14 *(NIV)*

A FRIEND ONCE TOLD ME, "How can Jesus fill a wallet that's already full?" I've never forgotten that. It has helped me through many dust-bunnies-in-my-bank-account moments. Jesus is the ultimate provider. He's also the ultimate reminder, through His Holy Spirit.

Yesterday, I had lunch with a new friend and felt moved to pay for her meal too. The week had been especially lean with expenditures, leaving little excess. But the whisper was unmistakable. *Pay for hers too.*

It did not come as a surprise that, almost to the dollar, Jesus restored what I'd spent on lunch before the day was over. He's done that so many times in the past that, although I still marvel at His grace, it no longer shocks me. Is that one of the secrets to living drenched in the grace of Jesus—expecting grace because He is so faithful, but marveling and grateful because He is so faithful?

Jesus encourages me to be generous, then refills the supply when I am. He directs me to love deeply and unconditionally, then offers me a measure of graciousness to do so when it's hard. He places tough assignments in front of me and then provides the tools needed because I came to the task ill-equipped, but He isn't.

It's a marvel, all right—Jesus's boundless grace. —CYNTHIA RUCHTI

FAITH STEP: *Describe the grace of Jesus in a word or two. A marvel? A wonder? Extravagant? Outrageous? Needed? You may wind up with a whole list. Thank Him for it.*

WEDNESDAY, OCTOBER 11

Two are better than one, because they have a good reward for their toil. For if they fall, one will lift up his fellow. But woe to him who is alone when he falls and has not another to lift him up! Ecclesiastes 4:9–10 (ESV)

TWO FRIENDS, CYNDY AND THERESA, and I learned to make sourdough bread together. We gathered in Theresa's kitchen and watched a video of an Irish man, with a lovely accent, demonstrate the process. We imitated everything he did, taking turns doing the different steps. We let the dough rise overnight and met again the next day for the final steps, then we placed the dough in the oven. The loaves turned out wonderfully! The first time I made it on my own, however, my bread was dense rather than airy. I called my friends, and they helped me figure out my mistake of letting the dough "proof," or rise, too long.

Making sourdough bread is more difficult than I imagined. Life is like that, too, especially when challenges arise. Doing it alone can end in discouragement. We all need family and friends to call for help.

We also need Jesus. The last three years of His life, He ate, slept, traveled, fished, performed miracles, and did most everything with others. He even sent the disciples out two by two, not alone, to proclaim repentance and heal the sick (Mark 6:7).

Toiling together makes work lighter. Two are better than one, not just in bread making but in many aspects of life, especially the difficult times. We need others to lift us up—or to simply share a warm slice of bread together. —JEANNIE BLACKMER

FAITH STEP: *Call a friend and plan an activity, such as learning something new or cooking together.*

THURSDAY, OCTOBER 12

Blessed are the pure in heart, for they will see God. Matthew 5:8 (NIV)

WHILE TAKING A WALK, I noticed my shadow on the sidewalk. Its outline was so well-defined. I knew the shape was simply light playing across my body, but it was as if I glimpsed my actual image following behind me. As I turned to head home, the gray silhouette led, silently announcing my imminent arrival. My thoughts turned to the way my reputation can often precede me, just as the impression I leave behind speaks of who I am. How often have I felt excitement at the opportunity to meet someone a friend has told me about? Likewise, I've spent time reflecting on a person long after our interactions have ended. And though I've yet to "meet" Jesus, I believe in Him and all He represents—past, present, and future.

I've never seen God, but His presence is visible in other ways. His shadow spreads across sunsets on the water. His grandeur is sprinkled on the snow-capped mountain ranges. I hear His joy in a baby's coo or the laughter of friends, and I taste His sweetness in a fresh, ripe peach on a summer day. But the best way to see Him is through His Son, who lived every aspect of each of the Beatitudes (Matthew 5:1–12).

Just as Jesus's life was a reflection of God's glory, I want my interactions to shadow the light of Jesus. When I approach others, do they catch a glimpse of Christ? And after I've gone, does the essence of His being remain? —HEIDI GAUL

FAITH STEP: *Take a walk and notice the way your shadow surrounds you, depending on the direction you travel. Does Jesus's light permeate the space around you? Endeavor to make it so.*

FRIDAY, OCTOBER 13

. . . for your promises are backed by all the honor of your name.
Psalm 138:2 (NLT)

I'M BOMBARDED WITH ADVERTISEMENTS PROMISING to make my life better—revolutionary new weight-loss programs, once-in-a-life-time business opportunities, deep discounts on the latest fashions. There's often a built-in element of urgency. Offer expires soon! Hurry, quantities are limited! Our competitors sell items like these for twice the price! How can I resist?

Last comes the guarantee. Their sales pitches are backed by a guarantee based on the company's good name. There's absolutely no risk to me, the customer. I'd be a fool not to take advantage of such fabulous life-improving offers. Right?

In reality, I've everything I need. Today, I'm relaxing in the Truth that there's no expiration date on the Promises of Jesus. Yes, there's an urgency for anyone who hasn't yet received Him as their Lord and Savior. For we won't live in these earthly bodies forever. But there's no built-in scarcity when it comes to the promise of salvation through Jesus Christ. No matter how many people click that figurative "buy" button, Jesus's life-changing products—the forgiveness of sin and everlasting love—are always available.

Over the years, I've made a few mistakes in mail-order purchases. But the one choice I'll never regret is having said yes to Jesus. What He offers—His Promise of eternal life with Him in heaven—is one hundred percent backed by His Good Name. Jesus. The Name I can always trust and rely on. Guaranteed. There's no better deal than that. —CASSANDRA TIERSMA

FAITH STEP: *Tempted to make an online purchase? Why not skip it? Instead, praise Jesus for His Promises that are backed by His Good Name.*

SATURDAY, OCTOBER 14

Do not conform to the pattern of this world, but be transformed by the renewing of your mind. Then you will be able to test and approve what God's will is—his good, pleasing and perfect will. Romans 12:2 (NIV)

I'VE NOTICED IN THE LAST few years, my thoughts tend to stray toward the catastrophic. My overblown worries seem to overflow on those I love most. If my son Jack, who is away in college, doesn't text for a week, I wonder if he's been kidnapped. When my youngest, Addison, goes to the mall with friends, I fret until he's home. My middle son's sarcastic response to my fear-riddled thinking made me realize how frequently fear has wormed its way into my soul.

When Will flew to California last month to visit with friends, I counted the minutes until I could text him. When his plane finally landed, I sent the message, "How was your flight?"

"It crashed. I am dead," came his reply.

Living with anxiety is not how Jesus created me, and it's not how He wants me to live. My life is held in His palm. When I let myself become wrapped in fear, I'm essentially saying I don't trust Him.

Jesus invites me to renew my mind. When I soak in His presence and His Word, I am transformed. The pattern of my thoughts, lately, might have been fearful, but with Jesus, I don't have to be afraid. —SUSANNA FOTH AUGHTMON

FAITH STEP: *What do you need Jesus to transform you from? Fear? Anger? Pride? Envy? Write it down and pray for Jesus to renew your mind.*

SUNDAY, OCTOBER 15

Be thankful in all circumstances, for this is God's will for you
who belong to Christ Jesus. 1 Thessalonians 5:18 (NLT)

ON A RECENT SATURDAY EVENING, as my husband and I returned from dinner, fire trucks blocked our street. We couldn't tell whose house was on fire, but we smelled smoke. Sadness covered me. One of our neighbors would be devastated.

The next day as I rode my bike in the neighborhood, I saw the homeowners standing in the yard, assessing the damage. I introduced myself to Vert and his wife, Mel, told them how terrible I felt for them, and asked how I could help.

Vert responded, "We are blessed."

What? Vert told me he, his wife, and their three boys, one of whom is in a wheelchair, all got out safely, by the Lord's grace. A great blessing indeed. I admired Vert's faith. I contemplated what a close, trusting relationship he must have with Jesus to remain grateful in such dire circumstances.

When I pray, there are so many things I want to ask for, so many people who need prayer, just like Vert and his family. I want to launch into those pleas right away when I come to Jesus each morning. But I've trained myself to thank Jesus first thing—before I start all the petitions and requests.

Expressing my gratitude to Jesus first, for my blessings and the blessings He bestows on others, including my neighbors, allows me to remain close to Him and not feel devastated, even when devastating circumstances arise. —PAT BUTLER DYSON

FAITH STEP: *When your eyes pop open in the morning, train yourself to make your first thought one of gratitude to the One who gave you life.*

MONDAY, OCTOBER 16

Every good and perfect gift is from above . . . James 1:17a (NIV)

FOR THE FIRST FEW YEARS after our move to New Hampshire, I could barely keep my head above water. I had three young kids running me ragged, all while trying to get our family established in the community. I joined the local MOMS Club, volunteered at our church, and hosted a constant rotation of playdates. The incessant *doing* left me operating on caffeine and autopilot to the point that I put the wrong address on the envelope of Mom's birthday card last year, and my mother still lived in my childhood home!

I just wrote my mother a birthday card today. In it, I was effusive about how much I loved and appreciated her. Then, I double- and triple-checked that I wrote the address correctly on the envelope. I wanted to be certain it got to her this year.

Every day is a special occasion. However, when we live on autopilot in the busyness of life, we can sometimes credit circumstances or other people as the source of our good. When we do, our gratitude ends up going in the wrong direction. Of course, it's important to thank the giver when we receive a gift. But it's equally important to thank the True Source of All. Living from a stance of constant thanksgiving to Jesus ensures our gratitude always ends up at the right destination. —CLAIRE McGARRY

FAITH STEP: *Write a thank-you note to Jesus for all the gifts He's blessed you with. Leave it out and visible as a constant reminder to be grateful to Him.*

TUESDAY, OCTOBER 17

And He said to them, "Why are you afraid, O you of little faith?"
Matthew 8:26a (ESV)

WE'D HAD A COLD SNAP in southeast Wyoming. Our pump was deep below the frost line, so we trusted it was good. But the few feet of exposed pipe between the pump and the subsoil froze. My husband, Mike, worked on it for hours, but the water wouldn't flow. I drove to the big-box store for space heaters and heat tape. Nada. Their shelves were bare.

There was nothing else we could do, so we prayed and asked Jesus to unfreeze the pipes for us and went to bed. But I didn't really trust Jesus to take care of the problem. I awoke at 3 a.m. worrying. I was responsible for refreshments after church and couldn't even wash my hands, much less the stack of dishes I'd produce, so I decided to bring store-bought. *And what about a shower?* I tossed and turned, worried about not having water, until sunrise, while Mike slept on peacefully.

The next morning, I started to tell Mike my plans, but he stopped me. "The water came on around two-thirty."

Here I'd spent hours fretting about a problem that no longer even existed. I could have rested easy like Mike. We'd prayed, asking Jesus to thaw the pipes and bring the water back on. Instead of trusting He would, I'd marshaled my own ideas and resources about how to fix what He hadn't. Except He had.

Jesus is rich in mercy, isn't He? Full of grace. All sufficient and trustworthy. *Jesus, help me trust You.* —SUZANNE DAVENPORT TIETJEN

FAITH STEP: *Write down something you can trust Jesus with that is outside of your control. Truly trust Him to take care of it.*

WEDNESDAY, OCTOBER 18

Now may the God of peace ... equip you with everything good for doing his will, and may he work in us what is pleasing to him, through Jesus Christ, to whom be glory for ever and ever. Amen. Hebrews 13:20–21 (NIV)

I HAVE LEARNED THAT SOMETHING can be good, but if it's not God's will for me, it is not good at all. Recently, I accepted a job teaching in a public high school, which I'd considered as a career change post-divorce. While I'd been a volunteer tutor, a mentor, and a Sunday school teacher, I had no formal education or training in the classroom. Still, the opportunity presented itself. The timing was perfect. I enjoyed the students and my fellow teachers, and I could work toward obtaining the proper teaching credentials. With two school-aged children, it seemed like the perfect career for me.

But after the semester started, I had significant misgivings about teaching. I was committed for the school year, and Jesus carried me through it, but it definitely wasn't the career path for me. As difficult as it was to let go of a sure thing, I decided not to renew my contract for another year.

I've learned that God's will trumps even the shiniest sure thing. I'm not going to lie, following God's lead has been scary, but I now know it's the only way I can fulfill His unfolding plan for my life. I'm still on the journey, not entirely sure where it is going, as He's teaching, equipping, and preparing me for the perfect career to glorify Him. —ISABELLA CAMPOLATTARO

FAITH STEP: *Are you at a crossroads with a good option but are sensing hesitation in your spirit? Ask Jesus about it, and then listen carefully for direction before committing.*

THURSDAY, OCTOBER 19

Do nothing from selfish ambition or conceit, but in humility count others more significant than yourselves. Philippians 2:3 (ESV)

IN THE PAST WHEN I received a compliment, I had to fight the urge to put myself down. If I felt that I was getting too much attention, I believed I had to divert praise away from myself and quickly put the spotlight on someone else in order to be humble. *Whew!* Haughtiness averted. Or so I thought. I didn't realize I was actually bringing more attention to myself through a form of false humility.

False humility is self-centered. In his book *The Purpose-Driven Life,* Pastor Rick Warren wrote, "Humility is not thinking less of yourself; it is thinking of yourself less." A sign of true humility is using the talents and abilities Jesus gave me to benefit others. Though Jesus had divine status and authority, the life He lived on earth showed a perfect example of humility. When confronted by critics or praised by followers, He never denied His power or diminished His value to direct attention away from Himself or make others feel worthy.

In the same way, I don't need to downplay the identity I have in Jesus. When people notice my ability, I need not apologize or put down the gifts and talents Jesus has given me or hide from recognition and praise. Instead, I'll proudly praise Him. —ERICKA LOYNES

FAITH STEP: *The next time you are tempted to put yourself down, remember to follow Jesus's example of true humility and accept the compliment.*

Friday, October 20

Good will come to the man who is ready to give much,
and fair in what he does. Psalm 112:5 *(NLV)*

As we cleaned my daughter Melissa's cottage to prepare it for listing, I got teary-eyed. Five years earlier, as a single mother, Melissa moved here with her five-year-old son, Winston. Back then, she was short on cash and in need of some grace.

After her first marriage ended in divorce, Melissa and Winston moved in with us. During those two years, she completed her business degree and started a career. Understanding her desire to be on her own, my husband and I agreed to financially help her buy a house, but the one that seemed perfect was out of our price range.

After much prayer, Melissa tendered her best offer, along with a letter.

Dear Seller, For over a year, I've been searching for the perfect house where my son and I can start over...somewhere we can feel safe and play outside. When I walked through your front door, I had a special feeling...

Melissa's bid was considerably below the asking price. As higher offers poured in, we prayed fervently. *Jesus, Melissa needs grace! Please touch the seller's heart if this is the right house.*

Amazingly, Melissa got the house! Only Jesus could have arranged for a godly seller who placed compassion above financial gain. Jesus's grace provided a wonderful home for Melissa, but that was just the beginning. Now remarried, she and her husband added two new babies. They've outgrown the cottage. We're depending on Jesus's grace, once again, for the perfect buyer. —Pat Butler Dyson

---

Faith Step: *No matter how out of reach your desire may seem, share it with Jesus. Let Him amaze you!*

SATURDAY, OCTOBER 21

For God has not given us a spirit of fear, but of power and of love and of a sound mind. 2 Timothy 1:7 (NKJV)

IN MY FAMILY, I'M THE designated door-checker. I can't imagine drifting off to sleep without going through my nightly routine, making sure the garage door is down, blinds are closed, and doors are locked. Maybe that's because as a child I was so scared from the combination of the dark and my vivid imagination.

After the crucifixion, the disciples were together "with the doors locked for fear of the Jewish leaders" (John 20:19–20, NIV). They had heard that Jesus had risen from the dead but did not know what to think. Suddenly, Jesus appeared, saying, "Peace" and inviting them to see His scars. The disciples were overjoyed when they knew He was with them.

When I allow fear to rule my mind, it locks out many things— opportunities to do His work, to build relationships, to enjoy daily blessings. I have the keys of prayer and the Word to unlock my fear and replace it with faith. Best of all, I have Jesus, the ultimate locksmith. The door the disciples hid behind could not keep Him out. And fear can't keep Him out of my life when I accept His help.

I suppose I'll always have the habit of checking my doors before I go to bed. But I also want to develop the habit of checking my emotions so that fear doesn't lock out the peace and joy that Jesus offers me when I fully trust Him. That's one door I always want to keep open. —DIANNE NEAL MATTHEWS

FAITH STEP: *Ask Jesus to reveal and help you confront any fear in your life that might hinder blessings He wants you to enjoy.*

SUNDAY, OCTOBER 22

Let us keep our eyes fixed on Jesus, on whom our faith depends from beginning to end.... Hebrews 12:2 (GNT)

THE SMALL HALLWAY AT THE school where I taught was congested during the five-minute transition between class periods, so I waited for it to empty before heading to the office. I opened the door and sighed. The hallway was now clear of students but littered with trash. I gathered what I could and was about to throw it away, when a small scrap of paper caught my attention. It was a note, printed neatly on floral stationery, that read, "Fixing your eyes on Jesus will help you stop trying to fix everything yourself. Love, Mom."

I smiled and wondered which of my students had dropped that sweet message of encouragement. What challenging circumstances was the teenager facing, and why was he or she trying to fix them all alone? Who was the loving mother behind the beautiful penmanship, and how did she know that her child needed this reminder? I slipped the note into my pocket and hoped to find the owner.

As the day wore on, however, I found myself rereading the words every time I saw the open note on my desk. *What challenging circumstances was I facing,* I wondered, *and why was I trying to fix them all on my own?* More importantly, how did Jesus know that I needed this reminder too? By the end of the day, my eyes were no longer fixed on the note or on my problems. They were fixed on Jesus.
—EMILY E. RYAN

FAITH STEP: *Think about a problem you are trying to fix yourself and fill in the blank as a prayerful reminder: Fixing my eyes on Jesus will help me stop trying to fix _____ myself.*

MONDAY, OCTOBER 23

... He asked His disciples, saying, "Who do men say that I, the Son of Man, am?" Matthew 16:13 (NKJV)

AS A HIGH SCHOOL ENGLISH teacher, I found that my favorite teaching strategy was questioning. When I had my class analyze literature, rather than lecture as my college professors had, I prepared thoughtful questions to lead my students to discover answers for themselves.

I could have been the "sage on the stage," telling students what I wanted them to know, while watching them doze. Or I could frame a question, write their responses on the board, and let them debate which answer was best. When students had questions, I asked the class if anyone could answer it. This questioning method forced my students to wrestle with the text, with their ideas, and with others' interpretations. As a result, their understanding was much deeper than if I had simply lectured them.

Jesus often taught through parables, but He asked powerful questions as well, forcing people to search inward for answers. His questions were designed to expose issues of the heart, to refine a belief, to reveal an attitude one may not have been aware of or a sin they'd chosen to ignore.

Jesus's inquiries can also comfort. When life has me struggling for answers, I quiz myself with questions Jesus once posed: *Who do you say that I am? Do you believe? Why are you so afraid? Why did you doubt? What does the Scripture say? Do you love Me?*

Like the questioning exercise I used with students, pondering His questions and my answers leads me to understand Jesus deeper—no question about it. —KAREN SARGENT

FAITH STEP: *In a journal, write your answers to Jesus's question: "Who do you say I am?"*

Tuesday, October 24

The Samaritan woman said to him, "You are a Jew and I am a Samaritan woman. How can you ask me for a drink?" (For Jews do not associate with Samaritans.) John 4:9 (NIV)

I KNOW "CHANGE IS THE only constant in life" (according to the Greek philosopher Heraclitus), but I've experienced an unusual amount of change at work recently. In addition to coworkers leaving the company for new opportunities, there's been movement among the management team. This has led to a shift in the way I do my job. I know change often brings opportunity, but it can make me feel unsettled.

Unsettled may also be the way to describe how the disciples felt when they were around Jesus in Samaria. First, Jesus chose to travel through Samaria on His way to Galilee—a route Jews typically avoided. And while in Samaria, Jesus intentionally engaged in conversation with a Samaritan woman. The disciples weren't the only ones surprised by Jesus's behavior. Even the woman questioned why Jesus was talking with her. Samaritans were usually shunned by Jews, and respectable members of the opposite sex who were strangers didn't acknowledge each other, but now the Samaritan woman was communicating directly with the *King* of the Jews. Clearly, Jesus was changing the landscape of the current culture.

Embracing change can be difficult. The more often I get out of my comfort zone, the easier it will be to adjust to the changes around me. Like Jesus walking through Samaria, I might even find opportunities to transform my workplace, or other areas of my life, by following His example. —ERICKA LOYNES

FAITH STEP: *Do you pray that Jesus won't let a situation change? Instead, try praying to be the change in your situations. Ask Jesus to help you get comfortable with being uncomfortable.*

WEDNESDAY, OCTOBER 25

There is therefore now no condemnation to those who are in Christ Jesus, who do not walk according to the flesh, but according to the Spirit. Romans 8:1 *(NKJV)*

As I've GOTTEN OLDER, I've realized the need to eat healthfully. But that's easier said than done. I've identified behavioral patterns that self-sabotage my best intentions. The most flagrant happens when I drive long distances. That's when I tend to binge on potato chips. I justify myself by claiming that the crunch keeps me awake at the wheel. And then there's the red licorice. No crunch there, but I indulge anyway. Guilt floods me when I see the empty junk-food wrappers. *You're a failure. You blew it again,* whispers an accusatory voice in my head.

In past years, I let that little voice heap condemnation on me. The weight of guilt drove me to eating junk food for comfort. I reasoned that gobbling a chocolate bar wouldn't make any difference since I'd already blown it. But now I recognize that voice as belonging to the enemy of my soul. He wants to destroy me, and he uses condemnation as one of his tactics.

Jesus never condemns me or any of His children. He speaks words of truth and life to help us change, grow, and flourish. In His strength, I'm learning to say no to self-sabotaging behaviors more often than not. When I make an unhealthful choice, I listen to Jesus's encouraging voice and not the whispers of disapproval.
—GRACE FOX

FAITH STEP: *Write a prayer asking Jesus to help you recognize the enemy's voice of condemnation in your life. Thank Jesus for His encouragement and for freedom from condemnation.*

THURSDAY, OCTOBER 26

We ask him to strengthen you by his glorious might with all the power you need to patiently endure everything with joy. Colossians 1:11 (GW)

THERE'S A LOT OF "POWER" talk in our household lately. My husband is investigating adding solar power to our home. We're polar opposites in our approach to this subject. While he's studying solar panels, batteries, and inverters, I'm listing the small appliances I'd like to continue using.

Regarding power, I identify with the comedian George Burns' wife, Gracie Allen, who complained about her alarm clock not working. After extensive interrogation, the problem finally became clear when she naively explained, "I only plug it in when I need it."

I have to constantly guard against falling into that trap in my relationship with Jesus. Just as Gracie's alarm clock wasn't working because she only plugged it in when needed, likewise, my connection with Jesus won't be powerful if I'm only plugging in to Him when I need Him.

I know that utilizing the power of the sun is a worthwhile endeavor, but it's more essential to stay plugged in to the power of the Son of God—Jesus. This truth was reinforced when I stumbled upon a website that posted this acknowledgment: "Like the entire universe, this website is powered by Our Lord and Savior, Jesus Christ."

Yes, it would be nice to plug in to the power of the sun. But, more importantly, I aim to stay plugged in to the Son, my spiritual power source, Jesus, whether I think I need Him or not.
—CASSANDRA TIERSMA

FAITH STEP: *Set an alarm on your phone to check in with Jesus twice daily to reflect on the Son's Divine Power. Thank Jesus for the powerful things He's doing in your life.*

FRIDAY, OCTOBER 27

Jesus did many other things as well. If every one of them were written down, I suppose that even the whole world would not have room for the books that would be written. John 21:25 (NIV)

HOW MANY INDIVIDUALS WERE TOUCHED by Jesus during His earth ministry? We may never know the full extent, but we know of a few. The book of John states that if every single thing Jesus did were recorded, every life He touched, every miracle He performed, every grace—large or small—that He demonstrated, all the libraries in all the world couldn't hold all of them. And that was said two millennia ago! Imagine what John would say now.

Not long ago, I had the privilege of visiting the library on the Biltmore estate, George Vanderbilt's collection. An avid reader, Vanderbilt had collected more than 23,000 volumes by the time of his death. That's one massive library, in one building, in one tiny corner of the world.

Impressive as it was to view those magnificent bookcases full of Moroccan leather-bound, gilt-edged books, the sight reminded me that they were mere human words. All of them. Many were fiction and nonfiction from what the world considers masters, but none can match the library of all Jesus has done and continues to do.

Will we catch a glimpse of those pages of "the rest of the story" when we're with Him in glory? Will we pull volume after volume from the shelves of the "more" that He has done? We see only a fraction of the evidence in our own lives. Imagine having access to the entire collection! —CYNTHIA RUCHTI

FAITH STEP: *Someone near you needs to hear one of your stories of what Jesus has done for you. Show them the sacred "pages."*

SATURDAY, OCTOBER 28

Every good and perfect gift is from above, coming down from the Father of the heavenly lights, who does not change like shifting shadows. James 1:17 (NIV)

I'M A GIFT GIVER BY nature. I love finding little treats to give my three boys and my husband, Scott. Even getting their favorite bag of chips lets them know that I love them and I'm thinking of them. I also enjoy finding presents for my sisters and my mom. We have the same taste when it comes to books, magazines, chocolate, and candles. Their looks of delight bring me delight.

Lately, I've been involved in a new kind of gift giving. I joined a community partnership that throws baby showers for expectant and new mothers who are refugees. New moms deserve some treats, and these ladies need a little extra love and care because many are far from extended family.

I remember my days of early motherhood so vividly. Waiting to deliver. The joy of giving birth. The crazy sleepless nights of feeding and caring for an infant.

Even though I'm not a new mom, Jesus likes giving me treats and extra love and care. Not because I deserve them, but because He loves me. He doesn't just throw me a one-time-only shower; He showers me with grace and new mercies every day. He delivers endless forgiveness and restoration of body, mind, and spirit. He delights in delighting me with His goodness. Jesus always gives the perfect gift at just the right time. —SUSANNA FOTH AUGHTMON

FAITH STEP: *Surprise a friend with a favorite treat today. As you find delight in that moment, remember how much Jesus delights in giving you gifts.*

SUNDAY, OCTOBER 29

"The one who is faithful in a very little thing is also faithful in much; and the one who is unrighteous in a very little thing is also unrighteous in much." Luke 16:10 *(NASB)*

ZANE AND I STOPPED AT the grocery store to grab a few items. "Do you mind if I stay in the car?" I asked. Because I've done most of the grocery shopping over the past thirty-four years of our marriage, this has become one of my least favorite errands. It's a necessary task, but it feels insignificant. I'd much rather be doing great things for Jesus than deciding what type of pasta noodles to purchase.

As an empty nester, I expected this stage of my life would be filled with big adventures. But most days, I still need to do the ordinary daily duties: washing dishes, folding laundry, and keeping our pantry supplied. That afternoon, I was reading my Bible and came across the parable where Jesus talked about the dishonest manager. "One who is faithful in very little is also faithful in much..." This spoke to me as I was losing my motivation to be faithful in the little things, like going to the grocery store and buying nourishing food for us. According to Jesus's words, if I persevere in doing what feels meaningless to me—the little things—I will build faithfulness. And faithfulness is a character trait Jesus commends.

Some days are full of adventure and meaningful ministry, but most days are ordinary. Today, I'm more motivated to do the little things, knowing this is building something bigger in my soul.
—JEANNIE BLACKMER

FAITH STEP: *What ordinary task is challenging for you? Read Luke 16:1–13 and ponder Jesus's words. How does doing your ordinary task build your faithfulness?*

Monday, October 30

Let all bitterness, wrath, anger, clamor, and evil speaking be put away from you, with all malice. And be kind to one another, tenderhearted, forgiving one another, even as God in Christ forgave you. Ephesians 4:31–32 (NKJV)

DURING A QUIET AFTERNOON, I visited my social media site. As I scrolled, a friend request and private message popped up. My fingers froze on the mouse pad. My pulse quickened. The name was familiar. One I hadn't heard in decades.

Years ago, my husband and I discontinued contact with a few relatives, moved out of state, and built a new life. Complacent in the comfortable world we now occupied, we forgot the past and the broken relationships we'd left behind. Although we'd forgiven those relatives, we'd never truly resolved our differences.

I braced myself and opened the message. The words held no bitterness or anger. This grown man, whom we hadn't seen since his childhood, had reached out to us in openness and vulnerability. A verse floated through my mind: *Above all, love each other deeply, because love covers over a multitude of sins (1 Peter 4:8, NIV).* This family member had done nothing wrong. He knew nothing of the circumstances surrounding our family's departure, but he'd forgiven us. Healing has taken hold in my heart. My husband and I are planning a visit. I can hardly wait.

As I look forward to our future reunion, I know this story has only begun. I believe the next chapter is ours to write. We can respond in love and forgiveness. Will it have a happy ending? With Jesus guiding us, I believe it will. —HEIDI GAUL

FAITH STEP: *Does part of your story hold heartache or bitterness? Ask Jesus who you need to forgive or reconcile with.*

TUESDAY, OCTOBER 31

Am I now trying to win the approval of human beings, or of God?
Or am I trying to please people? If I were still trying to please people,
I would not be a servant of Christ. Galatians 1:10 (NIV)

MY HUSBAND, JEFF, AND I own a little condominium on the beach in Galveston. We love to vacation there, but it's also our pleasure to offer it to family and friends. My daughter-in-law's parents had planned to use it for the weekend, so Jeff and I drove down and spent hours cleaning furiously to make the place sparkle. One final look told me the condo was perfect and guest-ready.

We'd been on the road, headed for home, for an hour when it dawned on me I didn't buy coffee for them. Jeff reminded me there was a free coffee bar downstairs, or they could walk across the street to Walgreens if they wanted to make their own. My mood soured. Instead of being satisfied with our day of hard cleaning, I couldn't stop thinking about what I didn't do.

It's not easy to live life as a pleaser. As a firstborn child and only daughter, that was the destiny I embraced. That desire to please, to go over-the-top in everything I do for others, has persisted into adulthood.

When I get caught up in people-pleasing mode, I realize I've strayed from Jesus, for it is only Him I need to please and no one else. How much more satisfying would life be if I concentrated on being a servant of Christ? I'm taking a vacation from people-pleasing and plan to find out! —PAT BUTLER DYSON

FAITH STEP: *Make a list of three things you could do that would be pleasing to Jesus. Then do them!*

WEDNESDAY, NOVEMBER 1

. . . he showed them his hands and his side. Then the disciples rejoiced when they saw the Lord. John 20:20 (NRSV)

THE BUMP ON MY JAWLINE was starting to swell. I had problems with it several years ago, but this time was different. The painful protrusion was nearly the size of a golf ball. It started to affect my sleep and movements. I applied hot compresses to help relieve the swelling and sensitivity, but it quickly became apparent that self-treatment would not be enough. I needed to see a dermatologist.

At the appointment, the doctor told me I had an infected cyst. The good news was that it could be treated with antibiotics and later removed. The bad news was that I would always have a scar on my face. My choice was to live with a scar or stay in pain. I wanted to be well and have the cyst gone, so I started antibiotics. The infection subsided within a few days. Several weeks later, the growth was removed and the unsightly scar formed.

Thinking about Jesus's wounds helped me accept my own scar. After the crucifixion, Jesus had scars on His hands, feet, and side—proof of His suffering on the cross that saved humankind from their sins. With Jesus's death and resurrection, those wounds and scars meant healing and wholeness for me and for all who believe in Him (Isaiah 53:5).

I no longer see my scar as a bad thing but as a triumphant sign of healing—proof that I'm now well inside and out.
—BARBRANDA LUMPKINS WALLS

FAITH STEP: *What scars from life do you have? How has Jesus healed your wounds?*

THURSDAY, NOVEMBER 2

But grow in the grace and knowledge of our Lord and Savior Jesus Christ. To him be glory both now and forever! Amen. 2 Peter 3:18 (NIV)

WRITING MATERIALS FOR WOMEN'S BIBLE studies has grown my faith and deepened my understanding of who Jesus is. Before and during the writing process, I immersed myself in research using the Word of God and recommended Bible study tools. Without fail, I discover gems I've overlooked despite reading particular passages numerous times.

Take, for example, the story of Jesus's transfiguration on the mountain. As Jesus engaged in conversation with Moses and Elijah, "His face shone like the sun, and his clothes became as white as the light." Then God spoke from a cloud saying, "This is my Son, whom I love; with him I am well pleased. Listen to him!" (Matthew 17:2–5, NIV).

Peter, James, and John witnessed this and fell facedown on the ground in terror. They'd walked, talked, and lived with Jesus for nearly three years. Perhaps, because of their familiarity with Him, they'd treated Him casually. But this event opened their spiritual eyes to see who He really was (2 Peter 1:16–19).

Like the disciples, I need reminders now and again about who Jesus is. Without them, I begin to regard Him too casually. He's my friend, yes, but He's also God incarnate—absolutely holy, sovereign, wise, and powerful. The more I grow in my knowledge of Him, the more I'm moved to worship. To think that He lavishes His grace on me leaves me in awe. —GRACE FOX

FAITH STEP: *Go out into nature and thank Jesus for the beauty of His creation. Look at the sky today or the stars tonight. Let the wonder of the heavens stir your heart to worship Him.*

FRIDAY, NOVEMBER 3

Moreover the law entered that the offense might abound. But where sin abounded, grace abounded much more. Romans 5:20 (NKJV)

I'M A LIFELONG "GOOD GIRL." I like following the rules and doing sensible things, but recently I've been experimenting with badness. Now, now, don't worry. I'm not doing anything despicable or dangerous. I'm just being mindful of not being so painfully perfectionistic. I'm not being compulsively careful to the point of obsession. Not being pitifully people-pleasing to the point of saccharin. In short, I'm trying to leave my scrupulosity behind.

Scrupulosity is a form of obsessive compulsive disorder (OCD) involving religious or moral obsessions. Somewhere along my Christian journey, I picked up some irritating image of who I was supposed to be. Airbrushed niceness, perfect neatness, conscientiousness that got precariously close to haughtiness. I also apologized for the slightest real or perceived offense.

When God brought my own scrupulosity to light, I started taking it easier on myself. I tried to be kinder about my failings and spoke nicely to myself when I made a mistake. I sometimes let the bed remain unmade, allowed the kids to stay on their iPads all day, ate a Big Mac, and allowed the teensiest edge in my voice.

What I've found is that being more human seems to invite more grace. I'm relying more on Jesus and less on myself, which allows me to enjoy the abounding grace Christ earned for me. I'm getting rid of scrupulosity, and that doesn't seem so bad after all.
—ISABELLA CAMPOLATTARO

FAITH STEP: *Take a "scrupulosity" inventory—things you do in a perfectionistic way. Take a week off from being a good girl. If you feel compelled, ask Jesus for grace instead of acting on the compulsion.*

SATURDAY, NOVEMBER 4

and He died for all, that those who live should no longer live
for themselves, but for Him who died for them and rose again.
2 *Corinthians* 5:15 *(NKJV)*

I SCROLLED THROUGH MY FACEBOOK feed and stopped on an image that took my breath away. My friend Ron stood in front of a stranger. Head bowed, Ron had a stethoscope in his ears. One hand was on the stranger's shoulder. His other hand held the bell of the stethoscope over the man's heart. Instant tears blurred my vision.

Months earlier, Ron had lost his teenage son in a horrific accident. I didn't have to read the text above the photo to understand that Ron was listening to his son's heart giving life to another human being. As I stared at the picture, I wondered what Ron must be thinking at that moment. *Please take care of my son's heart. Remember what I lost so that you could have a new life. Never take this gift for granted.*

Surely conflicting emotions warred inside of my dear friend who had gone through such anguish. Utter grief. Awe and wonder. The bittersweet joy of hearing his son's heartbeat again, despite his tragic and untimely death.

As I stared at Ron's photo, eyes closed, listening so intently, I imagined another Father whose Son gives new life. The cost of Jesus's sacrifice became real to me. Because of His death on the cross, I have a new heart. A new life. Eternal life.

That's a gift I don't want to take for granted either.
—KAREN SARGENT

FAITH STEP: *Give yourself a healthy heart checkup. In what ways are you taking care of your spiritual heart? What action can you do today to make sure you don't take Jesus's sacrifice for granted?*

SUNDAY, NOVEMBER 5

I praise you because I am fearfully and wonderfully made; your works are wonderful, I know that full well. Psalm 139:14 (NIV)

ALL FOUR OF MY GRANDCHILDREN have some variation of brown eyes, but Roman's eyes are the darkest. Around age four, he would gaze in my face each time I visited and say, "Nana, I wish I had blue eyes like you and Mom, 'cause blue eyes are better." I always answered, "Oh no, Roman, you have eyes the color of rich, fine chocolate. And what could be better than that?" He never seemed convinced, and that made my heart a little sad.

Then, on a day trip, I entertained Roman and his older sister in the backseat with a bag of Peanut M&Ms, giving them clues to guess what color I had just poured into my hand before they ate it. On Roman's last turn, I used a fill-in-the-blank rhyme:

Some say blue eyes are the fairest around,
but that is not the case that I've found.
For Roman has eyes that are deep chocolate _____.

I'm not sure if Roman outgrew his dissatisfaction with his eye color or my poetry did the trick, because he never complained again.

God has made His love for diversity obvious through His creation, including humans. King David marveled at how our Creator intricately weaves each one of us in the womb. There's nothing wrong with being the healthiest, most attractive version of ourselves we can be; after all, we are Jesus's representatives. But to honor Him, I want to embrace the choices He made when He created me—blue eyes or brown. —DIANNE NEAL MATTHEWS

FAITH STEP: *Look in the mirror and think about how completely beautiful you are to Jesus.*

MONDAY, NOVEMBER 6

Yet God, in his grace, freely makes us right in his sight.
He did this through Christ Jesus when he freed us from
the penalty for our sins. Romans 3:24 (NLT)

MY FRIEND RAINA, WHO WORKS for a college ministry, told me a simple illustration she uses to explain grace to college students. She described how her daughter, Ellie, had snuck some of her younger brother's candy from trick-or-treating the night before. Raina and her husband decided to take Ellie's iPad away for a week. After discussing it further, they thought this would be a great opportunity to teach Ellie about mercy and not give her the punishment she deserved. Unexpectedly, Ellie provided Raina with a sweet description of grace.

They sat Ellie down and said, "Stealing your brother's candy was wrong, but we want to extend mercy to you this time and not give you the punishment you deserve because Jesus offers us mercy rather than punishment." Ellie, clearly relieved, said, "Okay." Then she asked, "Can I have some candy too?" Raina and her husband laughed and said, "Well, that would be grace."

Jesus is the ultimate grace giver. He frees us from the penalty of our sin and then offers us so much more than we deserve. Jesus hands out the sweet stuff in life such as complete forgiveness, undeserved salvation, unexplainable peace, fullness of joy, unconditional love, and eternal life. Through Jesus, I'm freed from the penalty of my sins and made right in relationship with Him. That's sweeter than candy, any day of the year! —JEANNIE BLACKMER

FAITH STEP: *What's something you've received from Jesus that makes your life a little sweeter? Share that with a friend today and perhaps treat yourself to a little candy.*

TUESDAY, NOVEMBER 7

In their case the god of this world has blinded the minds of the unbelievers, to keep them from seeing the light of the gospel of the glory of Christ, who is the image of God. 2 Corinthians 4:4 (ESV)

TODAY AS I PICKED GREEN beans from our backyard garden, I started to giggle, remembering my first attempt at gardening. After years of apartment living, my husband and I were thrilled to have a big backyard. We'd planted a variety of vegetables, and I waited eagerly for my green beans to appear. Yet as weeks passed, I still didn't see any beans.

One day, I crouched down to pick up something I'd dropped and brushed aside one of the bean plants. I yelped and fell backward because a weird growth was under the leaves. When my heart stopped pounding, I took another look. Beautiful straight beans dangled under the leaves. As a novice gardener, I'd never thought to search under there.

I often walk through life with that same sort of ignorance. Jesus is at work "under the leaves" producing a bountiful harvest. My gaze skims the surface of the situations around me and I don't see growth. The enemy does his best to encourage that sort of blindness, doubt, and hopelessness. I'm so grateful to Jesus for redirecting my gaze and teaching me where to look for His glory: in the lisped lyrics of a five-year-old's Sunday school song, in the gnarled hands of a grandmother clasping her worn Bible, in the boxes of groceries my husband loads into cars during our church's food distribution.

Jesus is growing His people in grace in the most unlikely places. All I have to do is look. —SHARON HINCK

FAITH STEP: *Ask Jesus to open your eyes and see His grace in your circumstances.*

WEDNESDAY, NOVEMBER 8

And without faith it is impossible to please God, because anyone who comes to him must believe that he exists and that he rewards those who earnestly seek him. Hebrews 11:6 (NIV)

IF YOU WERE TO STOP by my house today, you'd notice two things. First, the washing machine is running (with a large family, it always is). Second, I struggle with being compassionate to myself in the middle of the mess. I'm critical of myself when I can't keep up with tending to the household chores, homeschooling kids, and other projects. Even though I added more responsibilities as we grew our family, I still felt the need to keep the same standards. Yet, no one expects me to keep everything in perfect order, especially Jesus.

Compassion for myself has grown as I've understood Jesus's compassionate heart toward me. A few years ago, I was in the laundry room sorting through piles of dirty clothes when I cried out to Jesus, "I can't do this. Help me." Jesus's response to my spirit was compassionate. He let me know He loved me just as much in the middle of those mountains of laundry as He did when it was all folded and put away.

What is Jesus more concerned about: my husband, John, and me opening our home to children who need a place to stay, or making sure the dirty laundry pile is all caught up? I still struggle, but I'm learning to be compassionate toward myself. One load at a time.
—TRICIA GOYER

FAITH STEP: *In what area do you feel you can't keep up? Write it down on a piece of paper. Then write this phrase over the top: "I love you just as much as if you were completely caught up. Love, Jesus."*

THURSDAY, NOVEMBER 9

"Give me your son," Elijah replied. He took him from her arms,
carried him to the upper room where he was staying,
and laid him on his bed. 1 Kings 17:19 (NIV)

ONE OF MY BEST FRIENDS, Jess, has been homeschooling her son
since he was in the first grade. She felt it was God's will to enroll
him in a private high school to make the transition to college easier.
He was recently accepted to several schools for next year, and the
touring process has begun. As much as Jess knows this is what God
wants for him, it's ripping her heart out just thinking about letting
him go. They've shared her son's educational journey every single
day for years.

In 1 Kings 17, the widow of Zarephath has only enough food
for one last meal for her and her son in the midst of a famine.
Regardless, she extends Elijah hospitality, makes a meal, and offers
him the upstairs sleeping quarters. Because of her unwavering trust
in God, He miraculously keeps replenishing her jar of meal and
cruse of oil to feed all three of them.

Later, the widow's son gets ill and dies, but she trusts Elijah
enough to let him take the boy's body to the bedroom where he is
staying. Elijah petitions God. Again, the widow's trust is rewarded
with a miracle: Through the power of God, Elijah brings her son
back to life.

Although Jess is struggling, she trusts Jesus enough to let her son go.
As she relinquishes her educational duties, she eagerly awaits seeing
what miracles Jesus will do in her son's life. —CLAIRE MCGARRY

FAITH STEP: *Search your heart as you read 1 Kings 8—24. What in your life do
you need to let go of and trust Jesus with?*

FRIDAY, NOVEMBER 10

The Spirit himself testifies with our spirit that we are God's children. Now if we are children, then we are heirs—heirs of God and co-heirs with Christ, if indeed we share in his sufferings in order that we may also share in his glory. Romans 8:16–17 (NIV)

MY FATHER EMERGED FROM HIS closet with a jewelry box and set it on the table in front of my siblings and me. "This belonged to your mother," he said. "Go through it and take whatever you want."

We opened the box and peered inside to find an assortment of rings, necklaces, bracelets, and earrings scattered along the plush, velvet lining. My heart swelled. Who would have guessed that a box filled with such treasure had been buried in the back of our father's closet for more than two decades? We spread the contents before us and feasted on the beauty of the glittering gold and sparkling jewels. At the end of the night, we each went home with several pieces of jewelry that our father had safeguarded for us.

Now, when I wear my grandmother's wedding ring or my mother's diamond earrings, they remind me that I'm an heir—both now and in the future. My mother's jewelry may twinkle and shine, but it is nothing compared to the inheritance waiting for me as a co-heir with Jesus. Gold, silver, rubies, and emeralds all pale in comparison to the glory I have as a child of God. The promise of sharing eternity with Jesus is the best treasure of all. —EMILY E. RYAN

FAITH STEP: *As you dress for the day, put on a piece of jewelry with a cross as a reminder of your inheritance as a co-heir with Jesus.*

Veterans Day, Saturday, November 11

*Greater love has no one than this: to lay down one's
life for one's friends. John 15:13 (NIV)*

LIKE MANY OTHERS, TODAY I will visit cemeteries, placing flowers
and flags at the graves of those selfless soldiers who gave their lives
defending our American ideals. They represent the best of the best,
a human almanac of something bigger, something almost holy—
courage, strength, and a depth of love for the United States that few
of us can fathom.

God says in Joshua 1:9 (NIV), "Have I not commanded you? Be
strong and courageous. Do not be afraid; do not be discouraged, for
the LORD your God will be with you wherever you go." I wonder
if these men and women held those words in their hearts as they
entered battle. Did they realize that no matter the outcome, or how
great the sacrifice, they could bravely fight knowing they weren't
alone? Perhaps Jesus meditated on this same verse as He won our
salvation on the cross.

As I go about this day, I'm both grateful and challenged. How can
I stretch my faith to reflect the glory these warriors deserve? I want
to honor them, not just today, but every day.

The answer, I believe, is to approach my personal trials with courage and to understand that whether my wishes prevail or not, Jesus
will be with me. That's what really matters. Because of many soldiers' sacrifices, I can enjoy freedom by being called an American.
Because of Jesus's sacrifice, I can, by His grace, be called a child of
God. I won't forget either. —HEIDI GAUL

FAITH STEP: *Do something today to commemorate those who've died for our
country. As you face life's challenges, reflect that the outcome isn't always the
priority. It's trusting in the company you keep—Jesus.*

SUNDAY, NOVEMBER 12

Love us, GOD, with all you've got—that's what we're depending on. Psalm 33:22 (MSG)

LAST WEEK, WE COVERED A lot of miles. I had a follow-up medical appointment three states away. My husband, Mike, and I drove farther and faster than ever before to complete the trip in four days. Yes, we were road-weary, but otherwise, this trip was a joy!

Through the endless horizons of Wyoming to Colorado's Rockies to the ocher hills of New Mexico and Arizona's high desert, we traveled. Snow, fog, and ice kept us on our toes. We prayed for safety—and even one time for the gas to last until we reached the next service station, which thankfully, it did.

The speed of this journey played so much beauty through our windshield. There were overnight stays with soft linen-lined beds, booked on my phone from the passenger seat while barreling along the interstate. We reminisced about road trips in our early married days when we kept changing drivers because we couldn't afford a hotel. We thanked Jesus for keeping us safe back then when either of us could have easily drifted off to sleep behind the wheel.

Mike and I might think we're better equipped now to take care of our needs, but the truth is we're still at His mercy. The roads were hazardous, but He kept us safe on the icy pavement. Jesus led us to motels with vacancies when we needed to stop for the night. Gas stations appeared when we needed to fill up. Mike and I traveled with confidence knowing who was really in the driver's seat.
—SUZANNE DAVENPORT TIETJEN

FAITH STEP: *Think of a time you didn't depend on Jesus and how He met your needs anyway. Reflect on it or journal your experience.*

MONDAY, NOVEMBER 13

But I am trusting you, O LORD, saying, "You are my God!"
My future is in your hands. Psalm 31:14–15a (NLT)

MY CALENDAR BELONGS TO JESUS. By that, I mean I regularly invite Him to remove any activity or assignment I've planned apart from His approval, add whatever He wishes, and rearrange my schedule to accomplish His purposes.

While living with our youngest daughter to help her through the last trimester of her risky pregnancy, I struggled to keep up with my regular workload. The deadline for this year's assignments for *Mornings with Jesus* was fast approaching. I had no idea how I would make it, and I envisioned working late into the night to finish on time.

One day, I received a phone call from the editor to say she was taking another position. Then she asked how things were going with my assignment. I told her life was crazy and I was struggling to finish on time. She said, "I'll get you a month's extension!"

I expressed my relief and told her Jesus had answered my prayer through her offer of time. The extension lifted the pressure and left me better able to be fully present for my daughter and family. I was able to do my best work with the extra time. I'd never have the nerve to ask for an extension, but Jesus knew what I needed and made it happen. —GRACE FOX

FAITH STEP: *Look at your calendar. Invite Jesus to remove, add, or rearrange anything necessary to accomplish His purposes.*

TUESDAY, NOVEMBER 14

*How good and pleasant it is when God's people
live together in unity! Psalm 133:1 (NIV)*

MY HUSBAND, SCOTT, AND I do things differently. I'm a morning person. He's a night owl. I like my coffee with a little milk and no sugar. His looks like melted ice cream in a coffee cup. I'm a pick-up-everything-in-the-house-straighten-every-room type of cleaner. He is a deep-clean-like-your-life-depends-on-it guy. I come at life's problems from an emotional viewpoint. Scott is a problem-solver. I feel like I'm missing out on life when I take a nap. He loves naps with a passion.

After almost twenty-five years of being married, we know we need to work hard to understand each other for the sake of our relationship. Early on, we argued about our differences, which only pulled us apart.

When Jesus created the world, and us, He gave each of us our own desires, needs, gifts, and strengths. Even with the differences He bestowed on us, by His grace, He calls each of us to live a life of unity. The kind of unity Jesus modeled. Jesus came to earth to live with people who were completely at odds with Him, yet He graciously gave His life, even for His enemies, carving out hope and healing for those who follow Him.

Scott and I still do and see things differently, but we agree on the important things. We put aside petty differences and work together for the sake of our marriage and for the glory of Jesus.
—SUSANNA FOTH AUGHTMON

FAITH STEP: *Is there someone in your life who does things differently? Ask Jesus to show you how to appreciate his or her unique strengths for the sake of your relationship as you strive to live in unity together.*

WEDNESDAY, NOVEMBER 15

"Take my yoke upon you and learn from me, for I am gentle and humble in heart, and you will find rest for your souls." Matthew 11:29 (NIV)

"You need to rest." My friend's emphatic words left little room for argument. "You're still doing too much. It's okay to just *be*."

I liked the idea of sitting and reading or watching TV. Even taking a nap and shutting the world off. But I always felt guilty.

I am a "striver." I keep myself busy—too busy—doing all sorts of things. My husband is the same way, so after tackling one big project after another for years, he and I decided to strive to stop striving, to let things be, to just be. I loved the idea, but doing it was unfamiliar territory.

Just as being constantly busy doesn't always work for me, life doesn't work as well when I overcommit, don't set boundaries, and run my brain and body to the limits. I need physical rest, but I also need to rest in Jesus, in my heart, soul, and mind.

My friend and I moved on in our conversation and had a wonderful visit, but I couldn't stop thinking about her words. And then it dawned on me: Rest is abiding in grace. Grace to listen to Jesus over anyone else. To not get caught up in what I think I need to do for everyone else. To enjoy Him and to please Him first. To rest and be with Him. —Erin Keeley Marshall

FAITH STEP: *From what pressuring influences do you need a break? Take fifteen minutes to rest your body, mind, spirit, and soul.*

THURSDAY, NOVEMBER 16

And walk in the way of love, just as Christ loved us and gave himself up for us as a fragrant offering and sacrifice to God. Ephesians 5:2 (NIV)

I WASN'T BORN WITH THE "love to clean house" gene. So when a friend showed me her robotic vacuum that nearly ran itself, I convinced my husband we needed one.

I love to watch this miracle gadget spin over floors and carpets. It inhales all the dirt in its path, pivots when it hits a wall, and plugs itself back into the charger when it's finished. I also love having a clean floor without lifting a finger.

Nevertheless, our new toy requires more involvement from us than we'd hoped. It needs rescuing if it catches on fringe from a bedspread or hits a carpet snag. We also need to empty the canister after each use.

That vacuum reminds me a bit of me.

I need to grow in many areas. Overcome bad habits. Gain victory over besetting sins, with which I constantly struggle. I'd prefer that Jesus do all the work. I want to come to Him with my worry, gluttony, or envy and have Him make it all disappear like the cat hair that our miracle vacuum sucks up. Without any work on my part. Without having to clean out that pesky dirtbag in my heart. I want to simply watch Jesus do His thing.

Then I remember that He already has. His sacrifice on the cross has made me clean, with no effort required on my part. I needn't even lift a finger—that's the real miracle! —JEANETTE LEVELLIE

FAITH STEP: *Write down a list of your own dirty spots you're struggling with. Pray about them daily and ask Jesus to make you clean.*

FRIDAY, NOVEMBER 17

Now faith is the substance of things hoped for, the evidence of things not seen. Hebrews 11:1 (KJV)

A TREASURED FRIEND, WHO IS now a resident of heaven, used this signature line on all her emails: "Have a happy day. The Son is shining!" So many people connected it with the authenticity of the way she lived her faith that the phrase was part of her memorial service video presentation. I miss her, so I conducted a word search of my archived emails. Hundreds of messages appeared on the screen with that faith-filled signature line, speaking to my heart today, even though she's gone.

What was Jesus's signature line? The last words He said on the cross were, "It is finished" (John 19:30), and the final words He said to His disciples before ascending into heaven were, "But you shall receive power when the Holy Spirit has come upon you; and you shall be witnesses to Me in Jerusalem, and in all Judea and Samaria, and to the end of the earth" (Acts 1:8, NKJV).

But likely, Jesus's sign-off for most of His communications with individuals during His ministry wasn't "See ya" or "Keep it real" or "TTFN" (ta-ta for now), although any of those might actually fit. It's far more possible that Jesus ended His conversations with a repeat of what He consistently said was at the heart of His ministry teaching: "Love one another."

Like my friend's sign-off, I want to keep Jesus's signature line in my heart so that I remember to live His words with everyone I come in contact with—love one another. —CYNTHIA RUCHTI

FAITH STEP: *Have you considered a faith-filled signature line? What words of hope or encouragement would yours be?*

SATURDAY, NOVEMBER 18

We can make our plans, but the LORD determines our steps.
Proverbs 16:9 (NLT)

AFTER HIKING FOR A FEW days with some friends, I stepped up a small stair leading to our front door and my knee painfully popped. I went in for an MRI, convinced I had a piece of cartilage floating around in my kneecap, but I was wrong. I had arthritis in my knee. All I had to do to prevent the pain was to stretch.

Stretching leads to flexibility in our bodies, but isn't being flexible a good characteristic in life too? "Blessed are the flexible for they shall not be broken" is a saying some refer to as the new beatitude. I'm certainly inflexible at times, stubborn with the plans I devise. If I were more pliable, it would be much easier for myself and my loved ones when things don't go according to my wishes. Jesus was certainly flexible. He frequently stretched the disciples' faith. He asked them to feed thousands of people with two fish and five loaves of bread when they were short on resources and may have wanted to rest (Matthew 14:15–21). When He was on His way to heal a ruler's daughter, He stopped to help a woman who desperately needed to be healed (Matthew 9:18–22). Being malleable rather than rigid can result in unimaginable blessings, as it did for those who interacted with Jesus.

Stretching is now part of my daily regimen. It reminds me to stay flexible not just physically but with my plans too. When things suddenly fall apart, I remember "Blessed are the flexible" because Jesus is probably up to something good. —JEANNIE BLACKMER

FAITH STEP: *Watch for an opportunity today to practice being flexible. Write down how Jesus bestowed an unexpected blessing on you.*

SUNDAY, NOVEMBER 19

In all your ways acknowledge Him, And He shall direct your paths. Proverbs 3:6 (NKJV)

I'VE BEEN DRIVING SINCE I was sixteen, and I consider myself a good driver. I'm not aggressive, but I'm cautious and have good reason. The memory of my daughter Melissa's accident when she turned left against the traffic is forever emblazoned in my mind. She was broadsided, resulting in painful injuries and the total loss of her car.

One day when I was leaving the mall, I considered turning left, but traffic was heavy. So I hooked a right into the entrance of an automatic car wash, figuring I could turn around there. Imagine my dismay when I discovered that once I was in the car-wash line, there was no turning back! Stone barriers on both sides of the drive prevented me from changing my mind. I was trapped!

Starting to sweat and feel claustrophobic, I noticed an opening in the double line of traffic. I felt a nudge from Jesus: *Go for it!* I hesitated. I had to admit that lately I'd been ignoring Jesus's nudges. Like last week when I saw a woman standing by her car, obviously in need of help. *Stop*, Jesus urged, but I didn't. And a few days ago, when I saw my neighbor, whose husband was ill, working in her yard, Jesus prodded, *Stop,* but I kept going. This time His nudge advised me to *Go*, so I went!

Safely back on the street, I thanked Jesus and asked Him to forgive me for ignoring his nudges. When I heed His directions, He'll never steer me wrong. —PAT BUTLER DYSON

FAITH STEP: *When you feel a nudge from Jesus, follow His cue. He will never steer you wrong!*

MONDAY, NOVEMBER 20

Once more Jesus put his hands on the man's eyes. Then his eyes were opened, his sight was restored, and he saw everything clearly. Mark 8:25 (NIV)

RECENTLY, MY FAMILY AND I drove to a funeral. Although the 1,540-mile drive was mostly uneventful, it was not without heart-pounding moments. We maneuvered around a ladder in the roadway, swerved around several blown tires, and avoided speedy eighteen-wheeler trucks that sometimes drifted out of their lanes. However, the toughest part of our drive happened when the sunny sky turned dark within seconds and unyielding sheets of rain crashed down onto our windshield, blurring our vision. After a while, the rain thinned out. The visibility was still low, but we could see that the darkness wasn't going to last much longer.

The people of Bethsaida undoubtedly heard that Jesus had the power to heal the blind. They were not timid about bringing a blind beggar to Jesus, and they weren't too proud to beg for His help. Jesus took the man aside, laid His hands on the man's eyes, and restored his sight. Immediately, the man's vision was restored, but he could not make out what was in front of him until after Jesus laid His hands on the man's eyes again.

As a Christian, I'm no longer spiritually blind, but there are times I still may not see clearly. Obstacles, both emotional and physical, may be in my way. Or I might have a tough time navigating unexpected "storms" in my life. No matter where the road leads, though, I have confidence that with Jesus, I can see clearly. —ERICKA LOYNES

FAITH STEP: *When you encounter a "storm," write it down, identifying what's making your visibility to see through it low. Call out to Jesus. Ask Him for clarity.*

TUESDAY, NOVEMBER 21

*I am reminded of your sincere faith, which first lived in
your grandmother Lois and in your mother Eunice and,
I am persuaded, now lives in you also. 2 Timothy 1:5 (NIV)*

MY COUSIN, SAM, TOLD ME he and his daughter were researching the family to learn more about their heritage. Sam and I share maternal grandparents. We know the stories of how Madear and Papa met in Mississippi as children, got married as teenagers, and made their way to Missouri to settle there with their three daughters. With determination and faith, my grandparents made a good life for themselves and their family.

My conversation with Sam made me think about diving into the family genealogy too. Wouldn't it be great to know more about past generations and how they connected to me today? While it would be nice to trace my roots and learn more about my ancestors, I do know the most important thing: My grandparents knew and loved Jesus. They talked about how He often made a way for them and protected them. They loved and served the Lord and taught their children to do the same. My mother, who learned from her parents, passed that legacy of faith down to me and my siblings. We, too, decided to follow Jesus.

I don't have to pore over Ancestry.com or take a DNA test to know that Jesus is a part of my heritage. He's also prominent in my own story and the legacy I'll leave to future generations.
—BARBRANDA LUMPKINS WALLS

FAITH STEP: *Who has influenced your faith journey? How can you pay it forward and show someone in your family the way to Jesus?*

WEDNESDAY, NOVEMBER 22

And we believers also groan, even though we have the Holy Spirit within us as a foretaste of future glory, for we long for our bodies to be released from sin and suffering. We, too, wait with eager hope for the day when God will give us our full rights as his adopted children, including the new bodies he has promised us. Romans 8:23 (NLT)

IT'S LAUGHABLE HOW MY HUSBAND and I keep checking the front porch to see if a package we're expecting has been delivered yet. In anticipation of its arrival, first one of us, then the other, peeks out the front door. Repeatedly. We act like a couple of kids anxiously awaiting presents on Christmas morning. Bordering on silly in our unveiled enthusiastic anticipation of said delivery, we keep an eye out for this expected event.

It's a little embarrassing, because I'm not nearly so vigilant in my watching and waiting for the day of Jesus's return. On that day, I won't get a tracking notification from FedEx or UPS.

We recently sang a song in Sunday school inspired by the story of the ten virgins waiting for the bridegroom (Matthew 25:1–6). The lyrics asked Jesus to hide His Word in our hearts, give us faith, keep us praying, give us joy, keep us singing, and keep us serving.

I want to be in a state of constant readiness for Jesus. That's the lesson I'm taking to heart by staying in His Word, and praying, singing, and serving as I eagerly await His return. Thinking about it makes me feel a little giddy, like waiting for our big package delivery—only better. —CASSANDRA TIERSMA

FAITH STEP: *Write down what you are expectantly waiting for. While waiting, focus on Jesus, who always delivers on His Promises.*

Thanksgiving, Thursday, November 23

. . . But one thing I do: Forgetting what is behind and straining toward what is ahead, I press on toward the goal to win the prize for which God has called me heavenward in Christ Jesus. Philippians 3:13–14 (NIV)

MY SON PIERCE JUST STARTED attending a respected Christian high school, well-known for athletics. He's a solid basketball player and highly motivated, but like me, Pierce can sometimes get in his head and overthink situations. At a recent game, he took an awkward tumble mid-pass. He recovered, but it was obvious he was downcast and distracted the rest of the game.

Debriefing with him on the ride home, he said the coach urged him to let go of errors quickly because they only undermined his game going forward. Coach told Pierce to shake off mistakes and simply keep pressing ahead, focused on the ultimate goal. Great advice for an athlete, and for a believer like me.

I have sometimes gotten bogged down and even paralyzed by the mistakes I've made or simple life detours, even the little ones. I obsess about how I might have done things differently or wonder why something happened the way it did.

While I can learn from my past, I cannot change it. What's done is done, but what I can do is get up, shake off mistakes, and press ahead, focused on my ultimate goal, "to win the prize for which God has called me heavenward in Christ Jesus." Great advice from Pierce's coach taken straight from Jesus's playbook. —ISABELLA CAMPOLATTARO

FAITH STEP: *Are you struggling with something in your unchangeable past? Take time to write what you learned, then conclude with a prayer using Paul's words in Philippians 3:13–14 as you press forward.*

FRIDAY, NOVEMBER 24

Because the Lord disciplines the one he loves . . . Hebrews 12:6 (NIV)

MY PANDEMIC YEAR AS A non-career high school teacher vividly reminded me: Boundaries are loving, not punitive, selfish, or mean.

I was hired to teach English during the historic 2020–2021 school year. After months of isolation, a string of teachers, COVID-19 stress, and related drama, the students were confused, scared, and acting out *a lot*. Many were facing problems at home too.

An enthusiastic novice teacher, I resolved to be firm, patient, and loving. I did really well being loving and patient. I want to say firm, too, but that's not true. With misguided compassion, I gave the kids too much latitude. I was endlessly patient with disruptive behavior. I didn't strictly enforce homework deadlines. I gave out candy just because. Halfway through the term, I had a bunch of failing students and my most challenging classes were extremely unruly. Plus, I was burned out and resentful. I had no one to blame but myself.

As I prayed to Jesus each day, it became clear I needed tougher boundaries. I intuitively knew this, but my people-pleaser self resisted. Still, it had to be done. I got stricter, dispensing consequences promptly. I dropped rewards unless they were merited. I raised the bar. Almost overnight, the kids fell in line. Their grades improved. The classroom was more peaceful and orderly. The kids were more respectful with each other and with me. I was happier too.

Indeed, clear boundaries and wise discipline were needed not just for my students but for me too. With Jesus's help, we all made it through the COVID-19 school year. —ISABELLA CAMPOLATTARO

FAITH STEP: *Are you feeling resentful, frustrated, or abused? Ask Jesus if a boundary is needed.*

SATURDAY, NOVEMBER 25

I will be glad and rejoice in your love, for you saw my affliction and knew the anguish of my soul. Psalm 31:7 (NIV)

HAGAR WAS A TEENAGE EGYPTIAN slave who served a rich man's wife named Sarai. Sarai was desperate for a child in her old age, so she did something that was culturally acceptable—she arranged for her husband, Abram, to sleep with Hagar. If that union conceived a child, Sarai would legally become his mother. Her ploy worked but drove a wedge between the two women.

Hagar fled to escape abuse. As she sat alone in the wilderness, the angel of the Lord appeared, addressed her by name, and spoke with her about her situation. When the divine encounter ended, Hagar called God by the name El Roi, "the God who sees me" (Genesis 16:13).

My heart goes out to Hagar when I read her story. At the same time, I find it offers hope. Life really hurts sometimes, and reminders like this help to ease my pain. I've discovered that knowing Jesus sees me gives me perseverance when contending with a friend's mental health issues. It gives me peace when my adult kids hurt. It gives me courage when uncertainty looms large.

My friend, hang on to the truth that Jesus is with us when we're afflicted and feeling alone. He sees us when we cry, and He knows our deepest disappointments and sorrow. But because He loves us with an everlasting love, He never leaves us alone to languish in our pain. —GRACE FOX

FAITH STEP: *Read Hagar's story in Genesis 16:1–13. Thank Jesus for seeing you just as He saw Hagar in her anguish.*

SUNDAY, NOVEMBER 26

My dear brothers and sisters, take note of this: Everyone should be quick to listen, slow to speak and slow to become angry. James 1:19 (NIV)

I TOSSED AND TURNED AT night, mentally writing an email to a family member with whom I'd had a conflict. My words would explain my position, ease the tension, and all would be well. At least that was what I told myself.

The next morning, I opened my laptop to compose the email, and I felt Jesus whisper, "Wait." *Argh!* But I was ready to make her understand me.

"Why?" I asked.

Gradually, Jesus helped me see my true motives. I wanted to be liked by everyone. I wanted to make myself look reasonable—be the bigger person. I wasn't truly focused on understanding my family member or resolving the conflict at all. I wanted her to understand me.

I needed more time in the Word, more time at Jesus's feet, before I was ready to write a humble note from a heart filled with compassion, my only motive being love.

James 1:19 is about being quick to listen, not only listening to a person I have a conflict with but also listening to Jesus. I needed to take time to hear His perspective, His insights, His love.

Later I wrote a very different email than I'd first mentally drafted. Less defensive and passive aggressive, more compassionate and understanding. I was blessed by a response of forgiveness. Pausing to listen to Jesus made all the difference in her understanding and mine. —SHARON HINCK

FAITH STEP: *Next time you feel upset at someone, stop to listen to their thoughts and feelings, but also listen to Jesus's perspective on the situation. Wait for His guidance before you respond.*

MONDAY, NOVEMBER 27

But if we look forward to something we don't yet have, we must wait patiently and confidently. Romans 8:25 (NLT)

WHEN WE MOVED, SEVERAL FRIENDS brought orchids as house-warming gifts. These stunning flowers adorned our kitchen windowsill for a couple of months until the blooms dropped off, leaving decaying twigs. Knowing nothing about orchids, I assumed they were dead. Then I read that if you are patient and wait long enough, the flowers will bloom again.

This caused me to wonder, *What else in my life am I waiting for?* I hope my adult sons marry and give me grandbabies. I'm anticipating several loved ones will become believers. And, like all Christians, I'm awaiting Jesus's return. *Am I waiting patiently and confidently?* Not really. I tend to expect immediate results, even from these orchids. And as time goes on, my confidence fades. But this is not the attitude Jesus desires. We're encouraged to run this race of life with patient endurance (Hebrews 12:1). And one fruit of the Spirit is patience (Galatians 5:22–23). It seems patience is a Christ-like virtue, one I need to cultivate.

So, I decided to practice patience and nurture the orchids with the expectation they would bloom again. I watered them, kept them in the sunshine, and watched for the tight green buds to appear on the twigs. As time passed, nothing changed. I doubted they would produce flowers. Finally, after nine months, buds appeared and they bloomed again. My patience and confident waiting were rewarded! How wonderful the assurance that other things I'm waiting on, if they align with God's will, are possible too. —JEANNIE BLACKMER

FAITH STEP: *Write a letter to Jesus describing something you're waiting on and entrust it to Him to hold while you wait.*

TUESDAY, NOVEMBER 28

*. . . all things have been created through him and for him. He is before all
things, and in him all things hold together. Colossians 1:16–17 (NIV)*

"IT'S NOT ALL ABOUT YOU!" I've seen that phrase used a lot lately:
the title of an article in a psychology magazine, a piece in a business
periodical, editorial and opinion articles in more than one major
newspaper, and also a pop song. In our age of self-absorption, perhaps it's good to hear that reminder from time to time.

I recently read the first chapter of Colossians and found a
reminder of Whom it *is* all about. I listed everything the passage
teaches about Jesus. Here are a few points: He is the Creator, the
head of the body (church), the firstborn from the dead, and pre-
eminent in everything. Through His blood, He made peace and
reconciliation between God and humans possible. I wrote in my
journal: *This passage is all about Jesus. The Bible is all about Jesus. My
life is all about Jesus, including my identity—He created me; my character—He's shaping it to make me more like Him; my purpose—He's
already determined it and guides me toward my destiny.*

Since I believe that the Colossians passage and what I wrote in my
journal are true, that leads me to only one conclusion: I want my
day to be all about Jesus. My goals and plans focused on His agenda,
not my own. My thoughts fixed on Him. Every conversation hon-
oring Him. Before I close my eyes tonight, I look forward to saying
to Jesus, "This day was all about You." —DIANNE NEAL MATTHEWS

FAITH STEP: *Read through Colossians 1 and choose a few phrases to personalize
as a prayer to Jesus.*

WEDNESDAY, NOVEMBER 29

So faith comes from hearing, that is, hearing the
Good News about Christ. Romans 10:17 (NLT)

THIS PAST WEEK, I'VE BINGE-PLAYED my old vinyl records, dancing as I prepare meals, enjoying the reminders of younger years. My favorite band is the Beach Boys. I belt out their lyrics and ace the harmonies. Why? Because no matter how many years pass or where we choose to live, I'm still a California girl. Their songs speak to me of summer sun, sand between my toes, and tall waves booming along the beach. The scenes conjured up by those tunes are dear to me, as natural as watching a surfer ride a wave. These experiences are part of who I am.

Like those California roots, my faith is planted deep inside. It's the most important characteristic of my identity, a component that can't be erased or altered by time or space. It's my core—who God created me to be.

Just as those oldies drew my attention long ago, Jesus also pulled at my heart. After I'd turned my life over to Him, certain verses and parables became as familiar as the scent of suntan lotion or the smack of flip-flops against my heels. Other passages stretched my soul far and wide like the endless surfside view of the Pacific Ocean.

The Beach Boys may be my favorite band, but these days Someone else sings softly to my soul. I enjoy listening for Jesus's voice and moving to the unique song He's composed for my life. As I rise to follow His lead in this sublime melody, I can't help but dance.
—HEIDI GAUL

FAITH STEP: *Write a list of verses that make your heart sing and commit them to memory like beloved song lyrics. Add to your "dance card" daily.*

THURSDAY, NOVEMBER 30

When I consider your heavens, the work of your fingers, the moon and the stars, which you have set in place . . . Psalm 8:3 (NIV)

WE'D JUST SPENT MANY LONG hours traveling from New Hampshire to Wyoming with the goal of enjoying the magnificent scenery of the Cowboy State. Yet, my husband's eyes were glued to the road as he drove around the windy curves of the Teton mountain range, and my eyes were fixated on our GPS, trying to direct him to our hotel. We were so focused on getting to our destination, we forgot to look at the landscapes.

As I pulled back the drapes in our hotel room the next morning, we both gasped at the spectacular view: puffy white clouds suspended in a deep, cerulean-blue sky, with a spectrum of greens and grays smattered across the majestic mountains. How could we have missed this the day before?

It made me wonder how much of my life is spent with my eyes down, trying to find my path and focused on the destination. Like almost missing that breathtaking panorama, do I notice the blessings Jesus shows me each day—the cornflower blue of my kids' eyes, the glistening-white snowfall blanketing the trees, the vibrant-red cardinal visiting my bird feeder?

Jesus paints our world beautiful every day. When I pray to see with His eyes and trust Him to guide my path, I get a new vision. Like our road trip to Wyoming, life is as much about the journey as it is the destination. And I don't want to miss either. —CLAIRE MCGARRY

FAITH STEP: *Pray and ask Jesus to help you view your surroundings as if you were seeing them for the first time. What beauty have you overlooked while focusing on the tasks at hand?*

FRIDAY, DECEMBER 1

And they were all filled with the Holy Spirit . . . Acts 2:4 (NKJV)

I WAS PRESENTING A WORKSHOP at a small facility without technology, so I packed my laptop and portable projector. In a moment of brilliance, I grabbed an extension cord. Good thing, because the electrical outlet was several feet from the presentation area.

I unpacked my equipment, placed it on the table, and connected the laptop and projector so they could communicate for the presentation. Next, I plugged the extension cord into the electrical outlet and stretched the other end to the table to plug in my electronics.

But there was a problem. In one hand, I held the three-prong plug on my laptop cord. In the other, a two-prong plug-in. I checked the projector cord. Three prongs. Without the ability to tap into the electrical source that I literally held in my hand, my technology was useless. I couldn't power up.

That wasn't the first time I'd failed to tap into a power source. Sometimes I function on a two-prong faith. I know Jesus can do anything, more than I can imagine or request (Ephesians 3:20). And, through Christ who strengthens me, I can do all things (Philippians 4:13). But how often do I connect to the power of the Holy Spirit, the mighty third prong?

After His resurrection, Jesus breathed on the disciples and said, "Receive ye the Holy Spirit" (John 20:22, KJV). But it wasn't until Jesus ascended into heaven that the Holy Spirit empowered them. Unlike that useless extension cord I brought to the workshop, the ultimate power source, the Holy Spirit, is always on hand.
—KAREN SARGENT

FAITH STEP: *What stops you from plugging in? Ask Jesus to reveal what being empowered by the Holy Spirit would look like in your life.*

SATURDAY, DECEMBER 2

For unto us a child is born, unto us a son is given: and the government shall be upon his shoulder: and his name shall be called Wonderful, Counsellor, The mighty God, The everlasting Father, The Prince of Peace. Isaiah 9:6 (KJV)

I HAVE A LONG-RUNNING OBSESSION with Handel's *Messiah*. Each year after Thanksgiving, I find out where I can catch a performance of the Christmas classic. I usually gather some friends for a free *Messiah* sing-along at a local church. Sometimes, we get tickets for a presentation of the work in the grandeur of the John F. Kennedy Center for the Performing Arts in Washington, D.C.

When I first started going to hear *Messiah* many years ago, the moving music captured my attention more than the lyrics that come from the Bible. But now I pay close attention to the words and how they tell the amazing story of Jesus's coming and what it means to humankind.

One of my favorite parts of the sacred oratorio is from Isaiah 9:6. There's so much joy in the musical prophecy of Jesus's birth and the names by which He will be known. Wonderful. Counselor. The mighty God. The everlasting Father. The Prince of Peace. Hearing those attributes of Jesus floods my soul with joy. Knowing Jesus was born for me, lived for me, crucified for me, and rose for me so I could be with Him in eternity is overwhelming—not just at Christmas but year-round.

I may be obsessed with Handel's *Messiah,* but I thank God that THE Messiah, *my* Jesus, is obsessed with me. —BARBRANDA LUMPKINS WALLS

FAITH STEP: *Think about the holiday music you're listening to. What names are mentioned for Jesus and how do they reflect His glory?*

FIRST SUNDAY OF ADVENT, DECEMBER 3

"... You will be called Repairer of the Breach, Restorer of Streets with Dwellings." Isaiah 58:12 (AMP)

TODAY I CORRECTED A THIRTY-YEAR-OLD error. While sorting my craft room post-move, I found a tatted collar I'd never finished (think Ruth Bader Ginsburg's lace embellishment to her judicial robes). I'd made a join in the wrong place on the third and last row, then failed to notice before closing the ring.

For all you non-tatters, tatting is a series of half hitches on a core thread, which is straight or looped. A wise tatter checks carefully for errors before closing a loop. Pulling the core thread slides it through the knots, turning the loop into a ring. This act is irreversible. The loop can't be enlarged again, nor can the stitches be pulled out.

Since the only way to save it was surgery—carefully cutting out the errant ring—I stuffed it away and planned to think about what to do later. I saw it occasionally, but I knew attempting the repair would take a lot of work.

Yesterday, I finally snipped the ring, unraveled its knots, tied on new thread, and hid the ends. It took some time, but the collar is now restored.

Long before Jesus was born on earth, the prophet Isaiah called Him the Restorer, the Repairer of the Breach. A breach is a gap where enemies break in or livestock get out. Jesus's death bridged that gap between heaven and earth. He mended the brokenness of humanity. Like my tatted collar, the Restorer and Repairer's perfect fix makes us beautiful too. —SUZANNE DAVENPORT TIETJEN

FAITH STEP: *Listen to, maybe even sing, the old spiritual, "Fix Me, Jesus." (You can find it on YouTube.) Ask Jesus what areas need restoration in you and sing it to Him.*

MONDAY, DECEMBER 4

*All you need to say is simply 'Yes' or 'No'; anything beyond
this comes from the evil one. Matthew 5:37 (NIV)*

RECENTLY OUR CHURCH MUSIC DIRECTOR invited me to help with the
Christmas program. My pulse quickened. It was a project I would have
loved to be involved with. But before saying yes, I took time to pray.

As I laid this opportunity before Jesus, He reminded me of all
the commitments on my time. Images of my other responsibilities
whirled through my mind. I had said yes to many projects recently.
It became clear that I needed to decline.

As I prayed, I told Jesus about my disappointment, maybe hoping He would supernaturally add a few extra days to my calendar.
Couldn't I help with the Christmas program anyway? After all, it
was a worthy endeavor.

Instead, He reminded me that by stepping back, I would allow
someone else an opportunity.

This verse in Matthew is part of Jesus's Sermon on the Mount and
deals with the problem of swearing by various things to emphasize
truth telling. But as I grappled with my yes/no dilemma, Jesus's
words in the passage struck me in a different way.

As I follow His priorities for my life, there are times I should say
no. I don't need to construct lengthy explanations and justifications
for those decisions. Jesus may have purposes for others that I can't
yet see or that I may never know about. He may be protecting me
from heading in the wrong direction.

After all, no is a good answer too. —SHARON HINCK

FAITH STEP: *When you face a decision today, bring it to Jesus and accept His
answer, whether yes or no.*

TUESDAY, DECEMBER 5

Why, my soul, are you downcast? Why so disturbed within me?
Put your hope in God, for I will yet praise him,
my Savior and my God. Psalm 42:5 (NIV)

"OUR HOPE SIGN IS GONE!" my husband exclaimed with a furrowed brow. "It was there when I left for work this morning, and now it's not. You didn't move it, did you?"

"That can't be," I muttered and went outside. Sure enough, our Christmas decorations were missing. I stood with my mouth agape, remembering how the red, glittery letters had sparkled in the spotlight, proclaiming HOPE to the entire neighborhood. Now the spotlight merely illuminated the emptiness, mocking our Christmas cheer with Grinch-like pleasure. "Who would steal our hope?" I cried.

Even as the words spilled out of my mouth, the irony of the situation fell on me like a suffocating layer of fresh snow. Our barren yard mirrored my soul, once so full of optimism. Over the last several months, the enemy had indeed tried to steal bits of my inner hope. Now, as if to kick me when I was down, even my superficial hope, once festive and shiny in the hard winter ground, had been taken by thieves in the night.

Later, we returned to the store where we had bought our outdoor Christmas decorations and came home with a white wooden nativity that we placed in the yard where HOPE once stood. I smiled. Someone may have stolen my hope, but now I saw clearly what Christmas was all about. Our spotlight illuminated Jesus.
—EMILY E. RYAN

FAITH STEP: *What can you do in your home or yard to focus on Jesus? Use your Christmas decorations to draw attention to Him.*

WEDNESDAY, DECEMBER 6

"... *For you give a tenth (tithe) of your mint and dill and cumin [focusing on minor matters], and have neglected the weightier [more important moral and spiritual] provisions of the Law: justice and mercy and faithfulness...*" Matthew 23:23 (AMP)

I'M A DETAIL PERSON. I enjoy the feeling of satisfaction when every little thing is done with precision. Oftentimes, I focus my attention on the trivial instead of on what's important, and I tend to miss the big picture. I pour my time and energy into small touches, making them priorities. Like the Christmas I spent a significant amount of time wrapping gifts and making the packages look spectacular. The presents were unwrapped in nanoseconds. All my hard work lay discarded in a heap on the floor.

In Jesus's day, the religious leaders were more concerned with touting spiritual pieties than practicing godly virtues. When Jesus healed people on the Sabbath, the religious leaders were appalled and showed no compassion toward those who came to Jesus for healing. They were sticklers for keeping the law and questioned those who didn't follow it as closely as they did (John 5:6–16). All of their energy was focused on appearing righteous.

Just like I found out with my pretty packages, it's what's inside that matters most. I don't want to become so easily distracted by doing good deeds or following religious rituals that I miss out on the big picture—having an authentic relationship with Jesus. Jesus doesn't care about fancy wrappings; He only wants what's inside of me— my heart. That's the perfect gift to give Him. —ERICKA LOYNES

FAITH STEP: *This week, take note of what you're spending your time and energy on most. Determine whether or not those things are most important and should truly be given your attention.*

THURSDAY, DECEMBER 7

. . . Every moment you know where I am. You know what I am going to say before I even say it. You both precede and follow me and place your hand of blessing on my head. This is too glorious, too wonderful to believe! Psalm 139:3–6 (TLB)

QUESTION: WHAT DO ZACCHAEUS AND the woman with the bleeding disorder have in common? They both got more of Jesus than they bargained for. Curious Zacchaeus climbed a sycamore tree just to get a glimpse of Jesus as He passed by. Jesus called to him and announced that He would be Zacchaeus' houseguest. That visit transformed the tax collector (Luke 19:1–10).

The desperate woman who had bled for twelve years simply wanted to touch Jesus's robe to be physically healed. But Jesus had more in mind. After she got what she thought she wanted most, Jesus drew her out of the crowd for a face-to-face conversation. She left that personal encounter spiritually healed as well (Luke 8:42–48).

Sometimes, I act like I only want a little bit of Jesus in my day too. Maybe a glimpse of Him in the background so I know He's got my back. Or I touch base with a quick prayer to start my day before running off to pursue my own agenda. Thankfully, Jesus gives me, too, more than I bargained for.

He knows what I truly need—not a chance encounter but an intentional relationship. I want Him to be in my thoughts every moment of every day, present in every conversation, decision, and interaction. That kind of closeness transforms my life. Since Jesus knows me intimately, I want to get to know Him better every day.
—DIANNE NEAL MATTHEWS

FAITH STEP: *Read through Psalm 139 slowly and prayerfully, thinking about how intimately Jesus knows and loves you.*

FRIDAY, DECEMBER 8

Then you will call upon Me and go and pray to Me, and I will listen to you. And you will seek Me and find Me, when you search for Me with all your heart. Jeremiah 29:12–13 (NKJV)

I CAREFULLY ARRANGED THE TOY nativity set on my hearth—stable, angel, donkey, camel, wise men, cow, sheep, Mary, Joseph…"Baby Jesus is missing!" I exclaimed.

Yes, the piece that depicted Baby Jesus in a manger was glaringly absent from my display. My granddaughter played with the set year-round, so I felt fortunate to have located seventeen pieces. But we just couldn't have a nativity scene without the centerpiece. My husband and I searched in toy boxes, in buckets of bath toys, under furniture, everywhere. In the end, we found Baby Jesus in the sandbox.

God told the people of Judah to search for Him with all their heart. They must have felt far from Him. They had ignored His multiple warnings to turn from their evil ways. Now, they were exiled in the foreign land of Babylon, and Jeremiah said it was going to last for seventy years. Even in the midst of those dark times, God offered grace to the people of Judah. He told them if they would pray, He would listen; if they would search for Him with all their heart, they would find Him.

Sometimes, I get in a dark place from my own doing. Other times, circumstances beyond my control put me there. Either way, Jesus extends His amazing grace, lifting me out of the darkness and into a place of hope. Like the Baby Jesus we found in our sandbox, neither can I hide from His love. —BECKY ALEXANDER

FAITH STEP: *Write down the six actions suggested for God's people in today's Bible verses. Meditate on them.*

SATURDAY, DECEMBER 9

Suddenly a great company of the heavenly host appeared with the angel, praising God and saying, "Glory to God in the highest heaven, and on earth peace to those on whom his favor rests." Luke 2:13–14 (NIV)

FOR MY BIRTHDAY IN NOVEMBER, my husband bought me a vinyl copy of Nat King Cole's Christmas album, *The Christmas Song*. My mom loved that record. She used to play it on our console record player each Christmas when I was a kid.

The music brought back such good memories. Christmas carols are, hands down, one of my favorite parts of the holiday season. When I was growing up, our family sang them together, both in church and at home. We even went caroling with Mom's side of the family around my grandparents' neighborhood each Christmas. The world feels a little more full of wonder when I sing along to Christmas music.

I can only imagine what it must have been like for the shepherds in the field the night Jesus was born. They witnessed the first-ever Christmas carol. In the dark of that crisp night, a dazzling display of angels lit up the sky with their glory and the beauty of their song. They were heralding the greatest event in human history. The Son of God was coming to earth. He was bringing peace and salvation. Their voices rang out pure and strong. How could they not sing? Hope was cracking the sky!

That song is still ringing out thousands of years later. And this Christmas, Nat King Cole and I are joining in. Glory to God in the Highest. Peace on Earth. Good will toward men.
—SUSANNA FOTH AUGHTMON

FAITH STEP: *Play your favorite Christmas carol and sing along, giving Jesus all of the glory for bringing hope and light into your life.*

SECOND SUNDAY OF ADVENT, DECEMBER 10

We know that our real life is in the true one, and in his Son Jesus Christ.
This is the real God and this is real, eternal life. 1 John 5:20 *(PHILLIPS)*

WE LIVE ON THE HIGH Plains of Wyoming, but I can see the faded outline of Nebraska's bluffs from my kitchen window. I'm not sure how far away they are, but one rainy day I passed by the window and my breath caught. Those bluffs that had always been in the distance looked close enough to hike to today.

I've lived in places with far horizons—the west coast of Florida with its fiery sunsets and the south shore of Lake Superior with its dark skies and northern lights, but here in Wyoming it's three hundred sixty degrees of big sky. I know immovable objects don't move, despite their appearance. What I seem to see is a trick of the light. My brain estimated distance by clarity. The recent rainstorm washed the air of dust. Since clearly seen objects generally appear closer, my brain underestimated the distance between my house and the Nebraskan bluffs.

Knowing the truth is important. The world and current culture often go by what can be seen or felt. But what looks to be true may not be. Seeing isn't *always* believing. And knowing what is really true goes beyond what my lying eyes might tell my brain.

Jesus proclaims He is the Truth (John 14:6). Because we're in Christ, Jesus is where we live and move and exist (Acts 17:28). If we know Jesus, we know the truth, because He is the Truth. And that never changes. —SUZANNE DAVENPORT TIETJEN

FAITH STEP: *Talk with Jesus while resting your eyes on a far horizon. Pray to know His Truth in all matters.*

MONDAY, DECEMBER 11

... This grace was given us in Christ Jesus before the beginning of time, but it has now been revealed through the appearing of our Savior, Christ Jesus... 2 Timothy 1:9–10 (NIV)

DURING THIS CHRISTMAS SEASON, ONE word has landed on my heart and become the theme of my preparation and celebrating. It's not what you'd expect. I've never seen it on ornaments, Christmas napkins, or wreath banners. It's not joy, hope, noel, or peace, which are all good words, but not the one I'm focused on this year.

It's grace. The Bible states that grace was given, promised to us, before the beginning of time. Imagine! When Jesus stepped into the world as a babe in Bethlehem to live among us and ultimately prepare for His earth ministry, His sacrificial death, and His miraculous resurrection, the promise was finally realized. Jesus equals grace revealed.

The world hadn't merely been waiting for hundreds or thousands of years. It had been waiting *before* the beginning of time. How long had God the Father been planning for Christ's birth? Since before the concept of time existed! And not just for the birth of a holy Child, a Messiah, but the revelation of grace itself.

Doesn't that put an awe-inspiring spin on a season that is already utterly resplendent with joy, peace, and hope? What we celebrate with bells and lights and candlelight services and songs and gifts is a long-awaited, unmatched grace named Jesus. His grace saves us, keeps us, and changes everything.

Christmas, for a Jesus follower, is even more thanksgiving-y than the holiday we call Thanksgiving. After all, what could warrant more gratitude and thanksgiving than grace? —CYNTHIA RUCHTI

FAITH STEP: *Among your Christmas decorations this year, find a spot for this truth: Christmas = Grace Revealed.*

TUESDAY, DECEMBER 12

But the angel said to them, "Do not be afraid. I bring you good news that will cause great joy for all the people. Luke 2:10 (NIV)

WITHIN THE SPACE OF TWO weeks, one of my family members was diagnosed with cancer and three friends died suddenly. The barrage of bad news filled me with grief, but it also reawakened my awareness of, and appreciation for, the good news of Jesus Christ.

On the night of Jesus's birth, an angel heralded long-awaited news to a group of shepherds: the promised Messiah and Savior had come. This news, the angel said, was good and would bring great joy to all people. The apostle Paul later dedicated his life to spreading the same message to Jews and Gentiles alike. Like the angel, he also called it good news and described it as "the power of God at work, saving everyone who believes" (Romans 1:16, NLT).

Believing and embracing the good news about Jesus alters our lives. He is God's grace embodied in human form. As our Savior, Jesus pays our penalty for sin. He breaks sin's power over us, removes guilt and shame, and gives us a fresh start. He restores our strength and prays for us. Jesus gives wisdom and guidance. And He gifts us with peace and hope when bad news strikes.

The best news in history broke more than two thousand years ago, and it's still relevant today. Jesus has come to save us and to meet us at our deepest points of need. Let's rejoice in its truth this season. —GRACE FOX

FAITH STEP: *List the ways in which the good news of Jesus has impacted your life. Invite a friend to do the same, and then share your lists with each other.*

WEDNESDAY, DECEMBER 13

The true light that gives light to everyone was coming into the world.
John 1:9 (NIV)

EVERY YEAR, I'M ALWAYS AMAZED by the news stories I read and hear about the massive light displays people put up for the holidays. Homes outlined with thousands of colorful, flashing bulbs, sometimes synchronized to music, could easily give the bright lights on the Vegas strip or Times Square a run for their money. I can't help but wonder who has time to do all that? I also wonder how the neighbors feel about the crowds that gather to view such marquee-like exhibitions, not to mention the crush of accompanying traffic on their street.

As a child, I was thoroughly impressed by the holiday light shows I saw as our parents drove my siblings and me around working-class neighborhoods and well-appointed suburbs. The sparkle of various displays drew *oohs* and *aahs* from us kids.

But as I grew older, my taste in holiday displays changed. No Santas with their sleighs, roofs outlined with icicle lights, or glowing nativity displays draw *oohs* or *aahs* from me now. I find myself admiring homes with a single candle stationed in each window, silently shining brightly. Those humble lights in the darkness, glowing much like the true light that the apostle John heralded as Jesus, the One who would come to save the world, yet the world would not recognize Him (John 1:10).

I'll look forward to seeing those stand-alone, glowing lighted candles in neighborhood windows this Christmas. And I will recognize them as a reminder that the light of Jesus is better than any light show here on earth. —BARBRANDA LUMPKINS WALLS

FAITH STEP: *How will you help shine the light of Jesus this holiday season?*

THURSDAY, DECEMBER 14

"Blessed is she who has believed that the Lord would fulfill his promises to her!" And Mary said: "My soul glorifies the Lord and my spirit rejoices in God my Savior, for he has been mindful of the humble state of his servant. From now on all generations will call me blessed." Luke 1:45—48 (NIV)

THIS PAST WEEKEND, MY FRIEND Natalie and I delivered baby presents, diapers, and a stroller to an expectant refugee mom here in Boise through our ministry partnership. One of the great joys of giving those gifts is seeing the looks of wonder and gratitude on these expectant moms' faces. Most are excited about holding their new little one close to their heart, and these practical gifts make that imminent moment seem more real. What could be more exciting than welcoming a new baby into the world? A promise fulfilled.

When Jesus came into the world, He wasn't just the sweet baby Mary was waiting to hold close. For centuries, the nation of Israel had been praying for the arrival of the Messiah, but Jesus wasn't the King they expected. He didn't come wielding a sword to bring swift justice. Jesus came in humility, forgiving sins, offering eternal hope, making a way for humanity to connect with a Holy God.

Jesus is the Christmas promise fulfilled. God's promise of our redemption through a baby born in a manger, the One who holds us close with a love that never fails. For me, there is nothing more exciting than celebrating His arrival and welcoming Him into my heart. —SUSANNA FOTH AUGHTMON

FAITH STEP: *Make a list of all the promises that Jesus has kept and the prayers that He has answered for you this year. Take time to thank Him for blessing you.*

FRIDAY, DECEMBER 15

In him we have redemption through his blood, the forgiveness of sins, in accordance with the riches of God's grace that he lavished on us. With all wisdom and understanding. Ephesians 1:7–8 (NIV)

WHEN MY CHILDREN WERE YOUNG, my mom went all out at Christmas. She arrived at our doorstep with boxes full of gifts for her grandchildren. Sometimes she'd number the presents so the biggest and best one was the last to be opened. Our living room filled with wrapping paper, bows, and exuberant squeals of glee. Since our home was a modest size, I kept reminding Mom that one gift per child would be plenty, but she would have none of that. She epitomized how to "lavish" blessings.

This morning, I prayed for Jesus's help before an online meeting. Everything went better than I'd expected. No technology glitches and a productive discussion. After signing off, I looked at my plans for the rest of the day. I wanted to ask for strength, for direction, for wisdom. But my soul reverted to the "one small gift is enough" mentality. I actually had the thought that I shouldn't ask Jesus for anything else for the day, as if He were stingy with blessings.

Ephesians 1 says Jesus delights in pouring out grace—lavish grace—into my life. He grants forgiveness, He guides and protects, He heals and comforts. Like my mom, Jesus saves the best gift for last. At the end of my life, I'll receive it. My present is celebrating His presence in eternity. —SHARON HINCK

FAITH STEP: *What does Jesus's lavish grace look like in your life? Pray that today Jesus will show you one person whom you can share with in a generous and unexpected way.*

SATURDAY, DECEMBER 16

I thank my God at every memory of you. Philippians 1:3 (TLV)

NOTHING SAYS CHRISTMAS LIKE FRUITCAKE, right? People either love it or hate it. I didn't care much for it when my childhood neighbor Augie offered me a piece. I visited him at his care facility and he cut me a slab. I might have fudged a little when I said it was delicious.

That next week, a fruitcake arrived on my doorstep with the card, "To Blondie, From Augie." I decided I loved fruitcake.

Augie and I went all the way back to my toddlerhood. He and his wife, Merry 'O, and three children lived next door to me and my family. During our visits, we'd reminisce about the old days in Sunset Addition, our neighborhood cookouts, camping at Cow Creek, the friends we missed. My daddy had died years ago, and Augie filled that lonely space for me. His beloved Merry 'O had died on Christmas Day more than thirty years earlier, and Augie often talked about her. Each time I left the care facility, I said a prayer of thanks to Jesus for this kind, godly man.

When Augie died at ninety-five years old, his daughter Lori confided he'd made her promise that as long as he lived, she'd send Blondie a fruitcake. Five Christmases had passed since I'd gotten Augie's fruitcake. Nostalgia prompted me to order one for myself. When it came, I cut a slice and waited to savor the joy. *Hmm.* It tasted bland and sugary. What was missing? I felt Jesus whisper, *Augie.*

Turns out, I'd forgotten. I didn't love Augie's fruitcake gifts. I loved the giver. —PAT BUTLER DYSON

FAITH STEP: *Visit someone who knew you as a child and ask them to share memories.*

Third Sunday of Advent, December 17

. . . You've had a taste of God. Now, like infants at the breast, drink deep of God's pure kindness. Then you'll grow up mature and whole in God. 1 Peter 2:2–3 (MSG)

When I started working in the NICU, I learned that critically ill babies couldn't eat by mouth. Their digestive systems were immature, and, because of the risk of life-threatening complications, they were fed intravenously. Back then, we met most of their needs that way but not all. Their unused digestive tracts and bones atrophied. Some babies fought breastfeedings when they were finally physically able to receive them. Many mothers felt rejected by their little ones when the babies refused to nurse.

Years later, research led to a surprising solution—*early* feeding of the mother's colostrum often within an hour of birth was beneficial, even when the baby was very tiny or ill. A few drops of this first milk were swabbed inside the baby's mouth, causing powerful immune factors to spread through the baby's digestive tract, promoting health, growth, and maturity. Babies tasted the nutritious colostrum soon after birth. Our NICU moms were comforted to be able to help their babies thrive.

Even though I've been born again in Jesus, I need to feed on the Word of God and drink in the teachings of Jesus to grow and mature in my faith. Like babies without nourishment, my spiritual muscles can atrophy when I'm not consistently ingesting His goodness. —Suzanne Davenport Tietjen

Faith Step: *Today consider fasting (or let yourself get a little hungrier than usual). Before satisfying that hunger, pay attention to it. Compare it to your desire for God's Word. Ask Jesus to help you hunger for the Word.*

MONDAY, DECEMBER 18

Then they scoffed, "He's just a carpenter, the son of Mary and the brother of James, Joseph, Judas, and Simon. And his sisters live right here among us." They were deeply offended and refused to believe in him. Mark 6:3 (NLT)

WHEN I WAS A CHILD, my grandfather built a Ferris wheel in his backyard for my cousins and me to enjoy when we visited. Soon after, my father used his carpentry skills to build a swing set for our yard and a toy kitchen for our playroom. Even now, the sound of tools banging and pounding wood into wonder still reminds me of my idyllic childhood.

To me, a man with well-used tools and calloused hands is worthy of respect and admiration, yet every Christmas, I'm reminded that not everyone saw it that way. Though Jesus's earthly father, Joseph, stands as a pillar of strength in the Christmas story, his label as a carpenter made it hard for some to believe that Jesus could ever be worthy of their worship. Wouldn't the Messiah come from a heritage with a little less sawdust?

But when I think of Jesus being born to a carpenter, I can't imagine a more fitting narrative. After all, Jesus was building, crafting, and creating long before His incarnation. The Bible says that the heavens are the work of His fingers (Psalm 8:3), that in the beginning, He laid the foundations of the earth (Psalm 102:25), and that we are His workmanship (Ephesians 2:10).

The hands that learned to create with wood and stone alongside His father, Joseph, are the very hands that formed the universe. Creator, Carpenter, King—a heritage worthy of worship indeed.
—EMILY E. RYAN

FAITH STEP: *Get crafty. Build or make something that honors Jesus this Christmas season.*

TUESDAY, DECEMBER 19

You who bring good news to Zion, go up on a high mountain. You who bring good news to Jerusalem, lift up your voice with a shout, lift it up, do not be afraid; say to the towns of Judah, "Here is your God!" Isaiah 40:9 (NIV)

"HOW MANY CHARACTERS CAN I have on a personalized license plate?" I asked the clerk.

"A maximum of seven," she said. "When you choose a phrase, go to the alabama.gov website, and see if it's available."

I played with combinations of letters, numbers, and spaces to create positive messages—"B LIGHT," "INSPIRE," "HAPPY 1," and "I SMILE." It was December, so I added "JOY2WLD" to the list; it quickly became my favorite. My little red Beetle now proclaims the good news of Christmas all year long and offers encouragement to drivers stuck in traffic behind me.

Isaiah foretold the coming of Jesus seven hundred years before His birth. In Isaiah 1–39, he presented God's warnings to the people of Israel. But in Isaiah 40, he switched to a tone of grace. He wrote of comfort, the payment of debt for sin, preparing the path for the Lord, and good news worth shouting.

We are called to share Jesus with the world. Sometimes, when we talk about Him, people tune us out because they've heard the Gospel before, in more traditional ways. What if we could snag their attention with a fresh, new method, like a joyful message bolted to the back of our car? Perhaps, then, they would pause and listen to the wonderful story of Christmas: "Joy to the world, the Lord is come!" —BECKY ALEXANDER

FAITH STEP: *Think of creative ways to tell the good news of Christmas. Act on one of your ideas this week.*

WEDNESDAY, DECEMBER 20

. . . the desire of all nations shall come: and I will fill this house with glory, saith the LORD of hosts. Haggai 2:7 (KJV)

MY OLDEST SON, MAT, WAS five months old when he commando-crawled for the first time. We'd put up the Christmas tree, hanging breakables on the low branches, laughing to think this would be the last time, for a long time, they'd be out of reach.

Mat was on his tummy, pushing up, surveying the room. I remember the instant he caught sight of a shiny, gold Christmas ball dangling from a branch. Always in motion, he froze when he saw it.

Without losing a beat, he set out to possess it. Arm over arm, knees sliding, he low-crawled with great determination. He wanted that ornament like he'd never wanted anything in his short life. He reached his hand in the air and lost his balance. Rolling onto his back, he wailed.

I moved the ornament higher on the branches, but that didn't distract Mat. Over and over, he reached toward the beautiful ball. I finally had to remove it from the tree and put it out of his sight. It's hard to want what we can't have.

Israel longed for a deliverer. Many people, myself included, thought the phrase, "the desire of all nations" in Haggai referred to Jesus, but recently I read that the word *chemdah,* translated as "desire," actually means the quality of longing we feel for something altogether lovely. The prophet Haggai said after a time of shaking, the nations will want, even long for, the Messiah.

Like my son longed for the shiny Christmas ball, I want that same *chemdah,* or desire for Jesus, desperately wanting, longing, for Him.
—SUZANNE DAVENPORT TIETJEN

FAITH STEP: *What's on your Christmas list? This year, want Jesus most.*

THURSDAY, DECEMBER 21

She lays her hands to the spindle, and her hands hold the distaff. She opens her hand to the poor, yes, she reaches out her filled hands to the needy [whether in body, mind, or spirit]. Proverbs 31:19–20 (AMPC)

HARDLY ANYONE SPINS ANYMORE. IF you look up "spinning" online, exercise bikes and fishing equipment come up in the search.

I'm a hand spinner. I make yarn from fiber, both animal and vegetable. I have a spinning wheel, but most often, I spin using a hand spindle, a wooden tool that people in Bible times would recognize. I like the way it feels.

It's meditative and rhythmic, lending itself to contemplation. Prayer. It also results in an abundance of yarn. The past few years, my yarn turned into thick, warm mittens for the Mitten Christmas Tree at the library in Munising, Michigan, where those who don't have very much can choose whichever pairs they like. The women in the knitting group just keep making more.

Makers often become givers. After fleeing Egypt, the Israelites spent nine months in the desert creating a Tabernacle in the wilderness that God designed. The spinners' hearts "stirred them up in wisdom" to make yarn. People gave their belongings and abilities to obey God by making this place for Him to dwell among them. The people gave so much that Moses had to tell them to stop.

We makers—quilters, knitters, lacemakers, cooks, spinners, painters, and weavers—we can be givers too. That's one way I serve Jesus. —SUZANNE DAVENPORT TIETJEN

FAITH STEP: *Ask Jesus who needs something you could make. Then make it and give it away.*

FRIDAY, DECEMBER 22

. . . Jesus said, "I praise you, Father, Lord of heaven and earth, because you have hidden these things from the wise and learned, and revealed them to little children." Matthew 11:25 (NIV)

I WATCHED A RECENTLY GRADUATED nurse coach a young mother who was learning to breastfeed her newborn. An older colleague criticized the nurse for her newfangled techniques and the young mother who couldn't get the hang of it. That longtime nurse was sure they'd both fail. They didn't. I imagine the mother related better to a younger nurse who was close to her age and learned quickly.

Mary was probably in her teens when an angel announced she would bear Israel's long-expected Messiah. Mary was told who the Baby would be, what He would do, even what to name Him. With all that information, the young woman knew a very important detail had been omitted: How could it be since she was a virgin? The angel explained that the Holy Spirit would overshadow her, and the Child she bore would be called the Son of God.

The angel also announced that Mary's relative Elizabeth, in her old age, was six months pregnant. Mary visited Elizabeth for three months and sang a joyous prophecy when Elizabeth's unborn baby recognized Jesus, in Mary's womb. I imagine, despite their age difference, the two women learned a lot about the wonder of God from each other.

Youth and inexperience don't preclude faith. Wisdom and old age don't mean one naturally has a stronger belief, either. The wonder of Jesus is timeless. —SUZANNE DAVENPORT TIETJEN

FAITH STEP: *Are you set in your ways when it comes to your faith? Try reading a different version of the Bible or listening to another genre of praise music to grow in Jesus.*

SATURDAY, DECEMBER 23

*In peace I will lie down and sleep, for you alone,
LORD, make me dwell in safety. Psalm 4:8 (NIV)*

I'VE ATTENDED THOUSANDS OF BIRTHS in my nursing career. During my time as a neonatal nurse practitioner, I arrived for high-risk deliveries ahead of time to check equipment and discuss plans with the team. Sometimes, we were called to Labor & Delivery following the birth—no problems had been anticipated but, for whatever reason, the infant wasn't transitioning well to life outside the womb.

Birth and transition can be difficult for babies. They've been "practice breathing" with amniotic fluid, but they've never experienced air. Space is at a premium at full term, and the birth canal is tight. The babies turn, extend, and descend, gradually entering the outside world. The squeezing they experience serves a purpose, helping expel the fluid inside their lungs. Some babies sail through the process, while others are left bruised, ill, or exhausted.

On Christmas Eve, more than two thousand years ago, a young virgin labored assisted by her husband. Surely, this would've been difficult for Mary and Joseph, but it was likely difficult for Jesus too. This may have been His earliest experience of pain in His human body.

I would have been afraid in Mary's situation, but I don't believe she was. She'd been prepared, not by a skilled team of nurses and doctors, but by an angel who had told her what would happen. Mary accepted her role and trusted her Father in heaven.

Because of God's plan, Jesus was safely delivered. And because of His birth, so are we. —SUZANNE DAVENPORT TIETJEN

FAITH STEP: *Read the Christmas story in Luke 2:1–20 and meditate on the birth of Jesus.*

FOURTH SUNDAY OF ADVENT, DECEMBER 24

This is the kind of love we are talking about—not that we once upon a time loved God, but that he loved us and sent his Son as a sacrifice to clear away our sins and the damage they've done to our relationship with God. 1 John 4:10 (MSG)

GOD SENT HIS SON TO die for us. *That* is love. It's the last Sunday of Advent and today's fourth candle stands for love. I can't understand the kind of love that would do that.

Myself? I believe I could lay down my life for my child, partly because of my experience caring for mothers of gravely ill newborns in the neonatal intensive care unit. Many of the mothers told me that if they could trade their life for their child's, they wouldn't think twice. They meant it and I believed them. The world doesn't work like that though, no matter how much they wished it could.

Their love gave me a glimpse of God's love. For me. For us. For each precious one of us.

Maybe God loves each of us with a love as fierce, no, even fiercer than that. Each of us, destined to die in our sins without a savior—Jesus too loves us that much.

"Let us fix our eyes on Jesus, the author and perfector of our faith, who for the joy set before Him endured the cross" Hebrews 12:2a (NIV).

Yes, I know this is Advent, not Easter. A time of preparation. For making room. Love, this fourth Sunday of Advent, reminds us that the sending was preparation for the sacrifice.

We are loved. —SUZANNE DAVENPORT TIETJEN

FAITH STEP: *Don't bother trying to comprehend so great a love. Just sit still and let yourself be loved. Beloved.*

CHRISTMAS DAY, MONDAY, DECEMBER 25

. . . May Jesus himself and God our Father, who reached out in love and surprised you with gifts of unending help and confidence, put a fresh heart in you . . . 2 Thessalonians 2:16–17 (MSG)

HAVE YOU EVER BEEN SURPRISED with a Christmas gift when you didn't have one for the giver? When it happens to me, my first impulse is to think fast and try to save face by presenting a gift too. I don't know who I think I'm fooling. I'm sure my facial expression shows the truth. Instead of being honest, my impulse is to prop up a false image of myself, revealing my sinful heart—selfish and proud.

God surprised humanity with the gift of His Son. Those who came to see Baby Jesus humbly worshipped. The shepherds ran to see Him—it never occurred to them to shop. The wise men, told ahead of time they'd be meeting a King, came bearing costly gifts. All were well received.

Jesus has surprised us with the gifts of unending help, love, and salvation, extravagantly and freely given. But what can I offer in return? Christina Rossetti's famous poem speaks of my feeling of inadequacy:

> What can I give Him, Poor as I am?
> If I were a shepherd, I would bring a lamb;
> If I were a Wise Man, I would do my part;
> Yet what can I give Him: Give my heart.

My heart. A fitting gift. Just what Jesus wants.
—SUZANNE DAVENPORT TIETJEN

FAITH STEP: *As you pray, try this: Clasp your hands over your heart. Talk to Jesus, then, as you say your amen, open your hands like a door. Offer Him your heart.*

TUESDAY, DECEMBER 26

"Shout aloud and sing for joy, people of Zion, for great is the Holy One of Israel among you." Isaiah 12:6 (NIV)

ON THE DAY AFTER CHRISTMAS last year, my husband and I caravanned with our daughter and grandkids across several states to spend a week at their house. On the way, my daughter, Holly, announced she planned to listen to all the Christmas music and watch all the Christmas movies she could get in. The holiday planning had been more stressful than ever with her husband deployed and four kids busy with activities. I smiled. Surely she would want our help taking the tree down and getting the house in order. But she was serious.

As dry pine needles dropped, we watched classic Christmas movies, some of which I'd never taken the time to see. Christmas music played in the background while we tackled board games. I baked the Swedish Kringler I used to make before Christmas became a road trip. We spent a day at Sea World, which still had a holiday theme. It was wonderful.

I thought back to our long-ago family celebrations. As much as I loved Christmas, I was always eager to pack away the decorations and get the house back to normal. Now I wonder why I felt that pressure. After all, when God became flesh and came to earth, the world was never the same again. Things never went back to the old normal. Jesus brought unending love, grace, and joy. What better reason to prolong Christmas throughout the whole year? —DIANNE NEAL MATTHEWS

FAITH STEP: *Mark your calendar to tell Jesus "Happy Birthday" on the twenty-fifth of each month this year. Sing a favorite carol, read Scripture passages about His birth, bake a special treat, or simply reminisce about a favorite Christmas memory.*

WEDNESDAY, DECEMBER 27

Therefore, if anyone is in Christ, the new creation has come:
The old has gone, the new is here! 2 Corinthians 5:17 (NIV)

LIKE MOST YOUNG WOMEN, I had an idyllic view of what married life would be like. We'd buy a home with a picket fence, have two or three kids, and immerse ourselves in a stable community that would nurture us for decades. Instead, however, my life has been characterized by new starts. Due to pursuing graduate education and employment opportunities, we've lived in six different cities since we've been married, and our son has attended seven different schools. Each move is like ripping off a Band-Aid as we say goodbye to beloved friends, hoping that our next stop would be our last. I've learned that although starting over is hard, it's sometimes necessary to fulfill the call of Jesus on our lives.

The Apostle Paul did more than start over; he did an about-face. As a well-educated Pharisee, he was so zealous for his beliefs that he began a persecution campaign against those who followed Jesus. He even obtained special permission from the high priest to capture anyone who followed Jesus. And yet, on the road to Damascus, Jesus captured Paul's attention and changed everything Paul thought was true. Jesus did not just call Paul to conversion, but He also gave him the grace to become one of His most devoted followers.

Yes, starting over can be hard. But, whether it's the freshness of a new community or the glorious gift of salvation, Jesus specializes in giving me grace for all the new beginnings I've had and the ones I will have in the future. —ERICKA LOYNES

FAITH STEP: *Read Paul's conversion account in Acts 9:1–30. Pray for those who are experiencing change.*

THURSDAY, DECEMBER 28

"Give, and it will be given to you. A good measure, pressed down, shaken together and running over, will be poured into your lap. For with the measure you use, it will be measured to you." Luke 6:38 (NIV)

I LOOKED AT THE GIFTS I'd unwrapped, and smiled. My loved ones had given me an exquisite piece of jewelry reflecting my faith, a book, a cat puzzle, and a cozy blanket. More than the joy the presents would bring me in the future, I relished how well my family and friends knew me. Every item reflected my passions, from Jesus to my pets to snuggling up with a good book or puzzle. It was obvious they'd spent time considering ways to delight me.

It says in James 1:17a that every good and perfect gift is from above. I believe those people I hold dearest are gifts from the Lord. He knows me inside and out. He provides me with what and who I need, and also delights me, feeding my heart's desires (Psalm 37:4). My life is filled with blessings, each moment and every friend precious and irreplaceable. Jesus has chosen them well. And when I add His gift of salvation to all the other blessings, I am overcome with gratitude.

But what to give Someone who has everything? I can offer Him all of me, my thoughts and my service for others, my prayers, my joys and tears, my hopes and dreams, my life. Will I delight Him? I believe so. Because I am a gift from God to His Son, my Lord (John 17:24a), I will bless my savior Jesus and give thanks, forever.
—HEIDI GAUL

FAITH STEP: *Today, find new ways to delight Jesus. You're a gift!*

FRIDAY, DECEMBER 29

"Everything is permissible," but not everything is beneficial . . . .
1 Corinthians 10:23 (CSB)

OUR NAVIGATION APP DIRECTED MY husband and me through unfamiliar parts of St. Louis.

"Turn left at the light," the automated voice commanded.

The signal was green, traffic was moving, but we weren't in the turning lane. With a few quick maneuvers, Russ put us right where we needed to be. So we thought.

Oncoming headlights blinded us. "Why are cars driving toward us?" he shouted. Russ had turned onto the wrong side of a six-lane boulevard! Swerving through a break in the median, he got the car on the correct side of the street.

How did that happen? The voice said, "Turn." The light indicated it was safe. Did we miss a Do Not Enter sign? Even though we tried our best, we failed to navigate the streets of St. Louis successfully.

Sometimes I don't navigate life successfully, either. I don't see, or maybe I ignore, warning signs and turn down a wrong path. I visit online sales for retail therapy when my budget is tight. I remain in friendships with toxic people because it's easier than confrontation. I RSVP "yes" to a social event when the "right" people, whom I know don't share my values, are invited.

When I start down the wrong path, a voice—Jesus's voice—warns me of danger. Jesus gives me the freedom to choose, but when my choices are not beneficial to me or to others, I can avert potential disaster by listening to Him. And when all else fails, thankfully, He allows U-turns. —KAREN SARGENT

FAITH STEP: *Do you face a choice that is perhaps permissible but not beneficial? Listen for Jesus's voice to guide you.*

SATURDAY, DECEMBER 30

*He brought me to the banquet hall, and he looked on
me with love. Song of Songs 2:4 (CSB)*

THERE IS A DEFINITE HUNGER among ladies for authentic, loving, and encouraging relationships. *That's why I'm so excited for Sister Table to begin this fall…*

It was the last day to sign up, so I decided to read the email one more time before deleting it. The invitation indicated it was a *no-fluff, good old-fashioned, "let's break bread together"* gathering.

We'd lived in Louisiana three years with only two more to go before retirement and another move. I hadn't tried very hard to make friends here. *Seven women will meet in someone's home once a month for six months.* I really didn't need to add another activity to my schedule. Besides, I already attended my church's mid-week ladies' Bible study. *Not a Bible study, there will be deep conversation that brings unity to the body of Christ.* Hmm, I've always loved deep conversation. *With Jesus as our foundation, we will grow not only closer to Him but closer as sisters.* I love my three brothers, but I never had a sister.

I ended up choosing the Tuesday lunch option in a community close to me. That's how I met Mischelle and Lisa, two sweet and generous ladies who love opening their homes to make other women feel loved and special. So many blessings from those Tuesdays—food, laughter, prayer, and yes, deep conversation. Since Jesus compared the kingdom of heaven to a wedding banquet, I'm guessing those luncheons blessed Him too. Belonging to Him means I'm surrounded every day by opportunities to fellowship with other Christ followers, knowing that He will be right there with us. —DIANNE NEAL MATTHEWS

FAITH STEP: *Is Jesus calling you to invite someone to gather around your table?*

New Year's Eve, Sunday, December 31

*"This, then, is how you should pray: 'Our Father in heaven,
hallowed be your name, your kingdom come, your will be done,
on earth as it is in heaven.'" Matthew 6:9–10 (NIV)*

THIS PAST YEAR, I RECONNECTED on the phone with my friend Missy from college. We spent most of our conversation laughing, then Missy began to share all that Jesus was doing in her life. In college, we had both taken multiple mission trips. She wanted to follow Jesus and the path He had for her.

While Scott and I were working in youth ministry, she and her husband, Davis, were on staff with Youth with a Mission. In the last few years, Missy and Davis ended up in North Carolina founding a creative institute that helps anchor young people in Jesus's truth. The way that Missy follows Jesus inspires me. Nothing really prepares us for the twists and turns that life takes. But she is always ready to yield to the next steps Jesus has for her. I want to be like her.

Jesus's journey on earth was full of twists and turns too. Even in the Gethsemane, when He knew the cross was before Him, Jesus yielded His next steps to His Father's will.

Jesus knows I don't always follow Him even though He is leading me on my journey. But I know He will never let me veer too far off the path. He will walk with me through all the twists and turns of life until I follow His steps into eternity. —SUSANNA FOTH AUGHTMON

FAITH STEP: *Pray the Lord's Prayer (Matthew 6:9–13) and take some time pondering each line. How does it apply to your life today? How can you yield your next steps to Him?*

ABOUT THE AUTHORS

BECKY ALEXANDER teaches for the International Guide Academy and leads tours to Washington, D.C., New York, Toronto, Niagara Falls, Charleston, Nashville, and other destinations. She even works on cruise ships from time to time. Before her travel adventures, she taught kids about Jesus for twenty-five years as a children's minister. Now, she invests in kids by volunteering year-round with Operation Christmas Child, a ministry of Samaritan's Purse.

Becky's devotions and stories appear in Guideposts' *Pray a Word a Day*, *Whispers from Above: God's Comforting Ways*, *Whispers from Above: In the Arms of Angels*, and *When God Makes Lemonade*. Becky loves to write about happy things, like the colorful wildflowers and singing warblers on her family's farm in Decatur, Alabama. She collaborated with her biologist brother and teacher sister to create *Clover's Wildflower Field Trip*, a children's book that supports elementary science units on plants and natural habitats. You can meet Clover and say hi to Becky at happychairbooks.com.

SUSANNA FOTH AUGHTMON is an author/speaker who loves to use humor, Scripture, and personal stories to explore how God's grace and truth intersect with our daily lives. Susanna lives in Idaho with her funny, creative husband, marketer/pastor Scott Aughtmon. She is mom to three fantastic young men, Jack, Will, and Addison, who bring her a whole lot of joy. Susanna likes to connect with her readers through her blog, *Confessions of a Tired Supergirl*, and her *Good Things Newsletter*. You can catch up with her on Facebook and her website, sfaughtmon.com.

JEANNIE BLACKMER is an author who lives in Boulder, Colorado. Her most recent books include *Talking to Jesus: A Fresh Perspective on Prayer* and *MomSense: A Common Sense Guide to Confident Mothering*. She's been a freelance writer for more than thirty years and has worked in the publishing industry with a variety of authors on more than twenty-five books. She's also written numerous articles for print and online magazines and blogs. She's passionate about using written words to encourage women in their relationships with Jesus.

She loves chocolate (probably too much), scuba diving, beekeeping, a good inspirational story, and being outside as much as possible. She and her husband, Zane, have three adult sons. Find out more about Jeannie on her website at jeannieblackmer.com.

A longtime Guideposts contributing author, ISABELLA CAMPOLATTARO cherishes the opportunity to transform her mayhem into messages of encouragement. She has been writing for *Mornings with Jesus* since 2018 along with *One-Minute Daily Devotions, Pray a Word a Day, Every Day with Jesus, God's Comforting Ways, Daily Guideposts for Recovery,* and *Witnessing Heaven.* An active blogger and speaker, Isabella is author of *Embracing Life: Letting God Determine Your Destiny,* aimed at helping women navigate challenging life events.

Isabella has an MS in public relations and management and a BA in communications. She and her two boys live on Florida's lush Suncoast, where she enjoys Jesus, travel, cooking, writing, reading, running, arts and culture, random adventures, deep conversation, the beach, and music. Connect with Isabella at isabellacampolattaro.com and on Instagram, Twitter, and Facebook.

PAT BUTLER DYSON is a freelance writer who lives in the Gulf Coast Texas town of Beaumont, best known for hurricanes and crawfish. A former special education and English teacher, Pat shares her life with her husband, Jeff. This year, on their fortieth wedding anniversary, Pat and Jeff built a garage for their daughter Brooke's new house. Some people celebrate milestone anniversaries on cruises to exotic locations, but Pat knew when she married a hardware man, her anniversaries would involve tools.

Pat has written for Guideposts publications for twenty-six years and especially enjoys writing for *Strength and Grace,* Guideposts' magazine for caregivers. She is also a contributor to the website prayerideas.org. Once again, Pat is excited and honored to share devotional thoughts with the faithful readers of *Mornings with Jesus.*

GRACE FOX has been a career missionary for thirty years. Currently, she and her husband, Gene, are codirectors of International Messengers Canada, an evangelical mission serving in twenty-nine countries. She trains church leaders in the Middle East, and she and Gene lead short-term mission teams to Eastern Europe annually.

Grace enjoys speaking at women's events internationally. She has authored twelve books, including *Finding Hope in Crisis: Devotions for Calm in Chaos* (a Selah Award winner). She's also a devotional blogger and member of the writing team for "First 5," the Bible study app produced by Proverbs 31 Ministries. Her passion is to help her audiences develop a love for God's Word and then learn to apply it for personal transformation.

Grace and her hubby live on a forty-eight-foot sailboat moored near Vancouver, British Columbia. They find great joy in spending time with their eleven grandchildren.

Connect with her at gracefox.com and fb.com/gracefox.author. Learn more about her resources at gracefox.com/books.

HEIDI GAUL lives with her husband in Oregon's Willamette Valley, where she gardens, hikes, and seeks new adventures. An ex-Bible Study Fellowship group leader, she has contributed to several Guideposts' devotionals, including *Every Day with Jesus, Mornings with Jesus, One-Minute Daily Devotional,* and *Pray a Word a Day.*

A Cascade Award winner for devotionals, many of her pieces have appeared in *The Upper Room.* Her stories are included in eleven *Chicken Soup for the Soul* anthologies. She has final-judged for major Christian writing competitions and enjoys speaking, leading workshops, and mentoring groups. She'd love to hear from you at heidigaul.com or on Facebook.

TRICIA GOYER is a speaker, podcast host, and *USA Today* bestselling author of over eighty books. She writes in numerous genres, including fiction, parenting, and marriage, as well as books for children and teens. She's a wife, homeschooling mom of ten, and loves to mentor writers through Write that Book with Tricia Goyer: triciagoyer.com/write-that-book/. Tricia lives near Little Rock, Arkansas.

SHARON HINCK is an award-winning novelist whose stories celebrate ordinary women on extraordinary faith journeys. She recently released a new three-book series, *The Dancing Realms.* She continues to work as a part-time writing professor, freelance speaker and teacher, author, and editor. She cherishes her roles as wife, mother, and grandmother. Most of all, she is grateful to be called beloved by Jesus and hopes to encourage others who need reassurance of His grace and faithfulness. Sharon loves interacting with readers and has fun things to explore at her website, sharonhinck.com

A former newspaper columnist, JEANETTE LEVELLIE moved from Los Angeles to southern Illinois in 1999 with her pastor husband, Kevin. Surrounded by corn and soybean fields, Jeanette relishes waking to birdsong and watching squirrels and chipmunks play in her backyard. She loves spring, summer, and fall.

Her relationship with Jesus and her family are the center of Jeanette's heart. She has one husband, two grown kids, three grandchildren, and four spoiled-rotten babies disguised as cats.

Jeanette is the author of six books and hundreds of published articles. She is also an ordained minister and travels near and far to share her (often hilarious) experiences walking with Jesus. Her favorite book of the Bible is Colossians because it resonates with the deity of Jesus.

Her hobbies include watching black-and-white movies, gardening, and reading novels to escape housework.

ERICKA LOYNES first fell in love with words as a child in Chicago, performing speeches under the guidance of her mentor, civil rights activist Mamie Till Mobley, the mother of Emmett Till. Seeing her own mother publish works for a Christian company sparked the idea in Ericka that she, too, could be a writer.

Ericka has written in spaces ranging from college journals to corporate training and also contributed to the book *Blessed Is She: The Transforming Prayer Journeys of 30 African American Women* by Victoria Saunders McAfee. As one of the 2018 Guideposts Writers Workshop winners, Ericka is thrilled to be writing devotions for *Morning with Jesus*.

Currently, Ericka is a senior instructional designer and facilitator. She enjoys encouraging others through career coaching, motivational speaking, and, of course, inspirational writing. Born and raised in Chicago, Ericka currently lives in Memphis with her husband and son.

ERIN KEELEY MARSHALL has been writing and editing for more than twenty-five years. Contributing to *Mornings with Jesus* is near and dear to her heart. She loves spending time with her family, sharing a great talk with a close friend, and exploring new adventures in the Midwest.

DIANNE NEAL MATTHEWS started daydreaming about being a writer at age five when she picked up her first chunky pencil and lined tablet. Her fantasy became reality when she attended a writers' conference in her mid-forties.

Since then she has written, cowritten, or contributed to twenty-three books, including *The One Year Women of the Bible* and *Designed for Devotion: A 365-Day Journey from Genesis to Revelation* (a Selah Award winner). Dianne has also published hundreds of articles, guest blog posts, newspaper features, stories for compilation books, Bible studies, and one poem. One of her favorite writing projects has been sharing her faith journey with the wonderful readers of *Mornings with Jesus*.

Dianne and her husband, Richard, live in southwest Louisiana. When she's not writing, Dianne enjoys volunteering at her church, trying new recipes, reading, soaking up nature, and FaceTiming with her children and grandchildren, who live too far away. She loves to connect with readers through her Facebook author page or website, diannenealmatthews.com.

CLAIRE McGARRY is a maker of lists, mistakes, brownies, and soups. Dirty laundry is her nemesis as she tries to focus more on creating a loving home, rather than cleaning it. She's the author of *Grace in Tension: Discover Peace with Martha and Mary* and the family Lenten devotionals *With Our Savior* and *Abundant Mercy*. A regular contributor to *Living Faith* and catholicmom.com, she has written for *Chicken Soup for the Soul* books and numerous devotionals. A former lay missionary and founder of MOSAIC of Faith, she endeavors to fish for more people to bring to God through her retreats, women's groups, and writing.

Claire lives in New Hampshire with her witty husband and three spunky kids, who always keep her laughing and humble. She'd be thrilled to connect through her Facebook author page and/or her blog shiftingmyperspective.com.

CYNTHIA RUCHTI is the author of more than thirty-five novels, nonfiction, devotional, and other compilation books, drawing from more than three decades as the writer/producer of a daily scripted Christian radio broadcast. She counts writing for *Mornings with Jesus* among her greatest joys and interacting with *Mornings with Jesus* readers pure delight. Cynthia's tagline is, "I can't unravel. I'm hemmed in Hope," and she says those words overarch everything she writes.

She has served a variety of roles within the writing industry and enjoys speaking at women's retreats and events both locally and across the country (and internationally as able). Cynthia married her grade-school sweetheart, and they share life together in the heart of Wisconsin, not far from their three children and six (to date) grandchildren.

EMILY E. RYAN is a minister's wife and mother of four who first dedicated her writing life to Jesus when she was a child. Over the years, she's written books, articles, Bible studies, Christmas pageants, drama scripts, and devotions, and her goal has remained unchanged: to use her words to worship. Emily is the author of *Who Has Your Heart? The Single Woman's Pursuit of Godliness* and *Guilt-Free Quiet Times: Exposing the Top Ten Myths about Your Time with God* and has been speaking at conferences, retreats, and women's events for over fifteen years.

After contributing to two grief-related Guideposts projects, *God's Comforting Ways* and *In the Arms of Angels*, Emily is thrilled to contribute for the first time to *Mornings with Jesus* and is especially tickled to be doing so alongside her literary agent, Cynthia Ruchti. In addition to writing and speaking, Emily is also an English teacher, book lover, and former unicyclist. This year, she hopes to escape the Texas heat with her husband to celebrate their twentieth wedding anniversary. Connect with Emily at emilyeryan.com.

KAREN SARGENT's first submission to Guideposts was published in *Angels on Earth* in 2017. Since then, she has enjoyed writing devotions for *Strength & Grace*, the *Whispers from Above* series, *Pray a Word a Day*, and *Mornings with Jesus*. She is a *Chicken Soup for the Soul* contributor and an award-winning author of *Waiting for Butterflies* and *If She Never Tells*. She and her husband enjoy retirement in beautiful Southeast Missouri.

CASSANDRA TIERSMA is a self-confessed messy-a.n.i.c. (messy, absentminded, normal-ish, imperfect, creative) woman of faith. She's also an author, poet, and reporter/journalist, whose articles, photography, and poetry have been published in multiple newspapers. Her book *Come In, Lord, Please Excuse the Mess!* is a guide for spiritual healing and recovery for messy-a.n.i.c. women who struggle with clutter bondage.

With a colorful history as a performance artist, writer, speaker, workshop presenter, and ministry leader, Cassandra has made it her mission to bless and encourage women in their faith so that they can become the full expression of who God created them to be. Cassandra lives with her husband, John, in a small mountain town in the frontier territory of the mythical fifty-first state of Jefferson, where she serves as women's ministry director at the historic little stone chapel that is their church home. Cassandra loves to hear from her readers. You can connect with her by sending an email to cassandra@cassandratiersma.com.

SUZANNE DAVENPORT TIETJEN is the author of *The Sheep of His Hand* and *40 Days to Your Best Life for Nurses.*

She and her husband, Mike, have lived on his family farm in Illinois, as well as in a cabin deep in the Hiawatha Forest of Michigan and finally (she hopes) on the High Plains of Southeast Wyoming. She has two sons and a daughter who have blessed her with six grandchildren.

Suzanne was a longtime shepherd and currently keeps bees. She loves the feel of wool (especially warm from a newly sheared sheep) and the taste of honey. She knits, crochets, tats, and weaves. Suzanne is currently learning to weave tapestries.

She is a retired neonatal nurse practitioner who cared for sick and tiny newborns for over twenty-five years. Most of all, she loves Jesus, who never seems to tire of showing her more about Himself through His word, the beauty of the natural world, and the events of her everyday life.

BARBRANDA LUMPKINS WALLS is a writer and editor in northern Virginia, where she fights traffic and gets inspiration daily for connecting God's Word to everyday life. Barbranda is the lead essayist for the photography book *Soul Sanctuary: Images of the African American Worship Experience* and serves as the editor for her church's annual Lenten devotional. The former newspaper reporter and magazine editor has written for a number of national publications, including *Guideposts, Cooking Light,* and *Washingtonian.*

Barbranda and her husband, Hal, enjoy spending time with family, especially their adult son and daughter, son-in-law, and beloved grandson. Connect with her on Twitter @Barbrandaw and Instagram at barbl427.

SCRIPTURE REFERENCE INDEX

TOPICAL INDEX

A NOTE FROM THE EDITORS

We hope you enjoyed *Mornings with Jesus 2023,* published by Guideposts. For over 75 years, Guideposts, a nonprofit organization, has been driven by a vision of a world filled with hope. We aspire to be the voice of a trusted friend, a friend who makes you feel more hopeful and connected.

By making a purchase from Guideposts, you join our community in touching millions of lives, inspiring them to believe that all things are possible through faith, hope, and prayer. Your continued support allows us to provide uplifting resources to those in need. Whether through our communities, websites, apps, or publications, we inspire our audiences, bring them together, and comfort, uplift, entertain, and guide them.

To learn more, please go to guideposts.org.

We would love to hear from you:

To make a purchase or view our many publications, please go to shopguideposts.org.

To call us, please dial (800) 932-2145

Or write us at Guideposts, P.O. Box 5815, Harlan, Iowa 51593